A Shout in the Street

A SHOUT IN THE STREET
An Excursion into the Modern City
Written and compiled by
Peter Jukes

Additional photographs by Teresa Watkins

'Wisdom cries out in the streets and no man regards it.'
Shakespeare, Henry IV Part I

Farrar Straus Giroux

New York

First published in 1990 by Faber & Faber Limited, London
First American Edition, 1990

Printed in the United Kingdom

Library of Congress catalog card number: 89-81630

Contents

List of Illustrations   vii
Note on the Text   x
A Window on to the Street   xi
Streetwise   xiii

London: Nostalgia and Poverty
   Back Alleys of Memory   5
   Street as Museum   41

Paris: Commodities and Bodies
   Avenues of Desire   63
   Street as Market   99

Leningrad: Crowds and Monuments and Power
   Crossroads   119
   Street as Forum   159

New York: Mobility and Traffic
   Freeways   181
   Street as Thoroughfare   217

Coda
   The Storm of Progress   235

Author's Note   237
Picture Credits   238
Acknowledgements   239
Index of Names   251
Index of City Sights   257

List of Illustrations

1   Whitehall from Trafalgar Square, 1839 – M. de St Croix   6

2   Trafalgar Square and the Nelson Column, late 1843 –
William Henry Fox Talbot   7

3   Renovation of the Nelson Column, summer 1987 – Teresa
Watkins   8

4   Westminster from Hungerford Market – William Henry
Fox Talbot   11

5   Holborn Viaduct under construction, 11 September 1869   15

6   Farringdon Road from St Andrew's, *c.* 1862   16

7   The Victoria Embankment, looking towards Westminster,
c. 1875   20

8   Chaplin with Coogan and Policeman – still from *The Kid*
(1921)   29

9   The one they left behind, 1987 – Teresa Watkins   32

10   Solitary house in the snow, 1987 – Teresa Watkins   36

11   Outside Les Funambules – still from *Les Enfants du Paradis*
(1944)   67

12   Painting for sale in a Paris gallery window, 1987 –
the author   78

13   Street walker – Eugène Atget   80

14   Dancers on display in front of their booth – André Brassaï   81

15   Wig shop window – Eugène Atget   84

16   Corset shop window – Eugène Atget   85

17   Edward G. Robinson gazes at a portrait – still from Fritz
Lang's *Woman in the Window* (1947)   86

18   Woman appears by her portrait – still from Fritz Lang's
Woman in the Window (1947)   89

19   A mannequin studies its own reflection in a Paris shop
window, summer 1987 – the author   91

20 Capital of Desire: Capital of Fashion, advertisement for
    Galeries Lafayette, Paris, 1987 – the author   92
21 Equestrian statue of Peter the Great, Leningrad   121
22 Nevsky Prospect, Leningrad, today   125
23 Alexander II assassinated by a bomb – engraving   134
24 Petrograd: construction of the Palace Bridge and factory
    smoke from the Vyborg side – engraving,
    Anna Ostroumova-Lebedeva (1919)   135
25 *Meeting* – linocut, Vladimir Kozlinsky (1919)   137
26 Barricade in Moscow, 1905   142
27 Woman at the barricades – still from Kozintzev's *The New
    Babylon* (1929)   143
28 Troops fire into the crowd, Bloody Sunday, St Petersburg,
    1905   145
29 Soldiers on the street – illustration for Blok's 'The Twelve'
    by Yuri Annekov   148
30 The people tear down the statue of Alexander Nevsky – still
    from Sergei Eisenstein's *October* (1927)   153
31 View from the window of the Winter Palace, 1917   154
32 Lenin's statue in the Finland Station, Leningrad   157
33 Manhattan: heaven and hell, steam from buildings, icicles
    on fire escapes, 1987 – Teresa Watkins   182
34 The arches of Brooklyn Bridge, 1987 – Teresa Watkins   187
35 Harold Lloyd hangs from a ledge – still from *Safety Last*
    (1923)   191
36 Ruby Keeler dances among the skyscrapers – still from
    42nd Street (1933)   192
37 *Dies Irae*, 29 October 1929 – James N. Rosenberg   194
38 King Kong on the Empire State – still from *King Kong*
    (1933)   195
39 Cars, cycles and pedestrians reflected in glass wall, 1987 –
    Teresa Watkins   204
40 Robert De Niro in taxi – still from Martin Scorsese's film
    Taxi Driver (1975)   205
41 Shadow of a man, graffiti in New York, 1987 – Teresa
    Watkins   208
42 The Motor Cycle Kid – still from Francis Ford Coppola's
    Rumble Fish (1982)   215

The lights of the city. I go out in the dark, before bed, and look at that glow in the sky ... the pulse of the recognition is unmistakable, and I know I have felt it again and again: the great buildings of civilisation; the meeting places; the libraries and theatres, the towers and domes; and often more moving than these, the houses, the streets, the press and excitement of so many people, with so many purposes, I have stood in many cities and felt this pulse: in the physical differences of Stockholm and Florence, Paris and Milan: this identifiable and moving quality: the centre, the activity, the light.

Like everyone else I have also felt the chaos of the metro and the traffic jam; the monotony of the ranks of houses; the aching press of strange crowds. But this is not an experience at all, not an adult experience, until it has come to include also the dynamic movement in these centres of settled and often magnificent achievement ...

I find I do not say, 'There is your city, your great bourgeois monument, your towering structure of this still precarious civilisation', or I do not only say that; I say also,

'This is what men have built ... and is not everything then possible.'

Raymond Williams, *The Country and the City*

Note on the Text

In the 'montage' sections all excisions are marked with ellipses. Where I have inserted names or dates, these are marked in square brackets. Occasionally paragraphing has been adjusted in the smaller excerpts.

Full acknowledgement of copyright material appears at the back of the book. The title and publication date of works which are easily accessible in the public domain are provided in the text itself. Where no title or date is given in the text, the full source may be found under the author's name in the acknowledgements.

A Window on to the Street

The street . . . the only valid field of experience.

André Breton

Whoever leads a solitary life, and yet now and then wants to attach himself somewhere, whoever, according to changes in the time of day, the weather, the state of business and the like, suddenly wishes to see any arm at all to which he might cling – he will not be able to manage for long without a window looking out onto the street. And if he is in the mood of not desiring anything and only goes to his window-sill a tired man, with eyes turning from his public to heaven and back again, not wanting to look out and having thrown his head up a little, even then the horses below will draw him down into their train of waggons and tumult, and so at last into the human harmony.

Franz Kafka, Meditation

Every phenomenon can be experienced in two ways. These two ways are not arbitrary, but are bound up with the phenomenon – developing out of its nature and characteristics:

Externally – or – inwardly.

The street can be observed through the window pane, which diminishes its sounds so that its movements become phantom-like. The street itself, as seen through the transparent (yet hard and firm) pane seems set apart, existing and pulsating as if 'beyond'.

As soon as we open the door, step out of the seclusion and plunge into the outside reality, we become an active part of this reality and experience its pulsation with all our senses.

Wassily Kandinsky, Point and Line to Plane

To be born on the street means to wander all your life, to be free. It means accident and incident, drama, movement. It means above all dream ... In the street you learn what human beings really are; otherwise, or afterwards, you invent them.

What is not in the open street is false, derived, that is to say, *literature*.

Henry Miller, Tropic of Cancer

Books are not the world, but windows on the world.

The windows of various houses can open a view on one and the same landscape; this landscape is one and the same although it is variously seen. The likeness of the landscapes, at the same time, is not a borrowing from one window or another.

Victor Shklovsky, Pro & Contra

I see through my window: but I can't go out!

W. Eugene Smith

Streetwise

This book is an excursion into an area that most of us know well but probably think little about – the street. In the last 150 years of urbanization, four out of five westerners, and two-fifths of the world's 5 billion population, have come to share a common space, not in the fields, but on the city's thoroughfares. This book explores the impact of that change on our metabolism and our mentality.

A Shout in the Street is composed of four major sections, each concentrating on one great metropolis: London, Paris, St Petersburg/ Leningrad, New York. Thus it can be read either as a kind of travelogue to the street-life of those cities, or as a reader to urbanism in general. More than anything it should act as a map – a topographical map, like those used on undergrounds and metros across the world – which do not pretend to picture the metropolis in its entirety. Like them, it aims less to show *how* things are than to help us find out *where* we are.

The book is designed to have the rhythm and plenitude of the streets it describes. The format – part montage, part essay – can be taken in snatches while waiting for a bus or sitting on a train, read continuously or in sections. Thematically, the guiding principle has been to express the variety of the street, its chance encounters, accidents and incidents. But beside the detail, considerable effort has gone into making sure every excerpt, every essay, every section is also going somewhere. In the end, the book should give some of the flavour of city life, but also has a story to tell.

The Street and the City

Of the traditional ways of looking at the city, most presuppose some kind of distance: the aerial view from a plane or high tower; the silent panorama from an apartment window; blurred images from inside a speeding car. But *A Shout in the Street* approaches urban life from ground level, out on the pavement. Instead of gazing down from above, or looking out from the inside, it takes the involved, complicit point of view of its pedestrians. Such a perspective has important implications. The view from the street is never single or enclosed. It has to admit a variety of other perspectives and is by its nature shifting and contradictory.

When the word 'street' is used in everyday conversation it conjures up this vague plural perspective. Politicians of different persuasions appeal to 'the man and woman in the street', evoking a silent moral majority – as in conservative 'Main Street' America. Activists and historians talk of power 'coming from the streets', of 'street-level' support, appealing to a more radical constituency, the urban equivalent of 'grass roots' popular power. Similarly in the realm of culture the street is often taken as a test of populism. 'Street credibility', for instance, means both being at home with the dereliction of the inner city and sporting the latest chic. To be 'streetwise' celebrates both a kind of urban knowingness, and the capacity to protect yourself against attack. The evocative power of the word 'street' derives precisely from its vagueness. But whether used by fashion magazines or political journals, it always implies a common touch, a feeling of how everyday life is lived by most citizens, appealing to some demotic, sometimes democratic urge.

Though the word summons up a range of connotations, this book sticks to a more limited definition of what is meant by a street – a central metropolitan thoroughfare, an arena where *strangers* encounter one another, come face to face with the size and heterogeneity of urban life. A city is essentially a meeting of minds, a convention of interests, and though we live in the age where these minds can telecommute, the street is still the most visible face of public interaction. On the street, in the strangers we meet there, we confront one of the city's most vital aspects.

Thus streets are means of *communication*; like other media they have their codes and conventions, a language through which different participants perceive and express themselves. Hence the title; for this book is not just about the street, but the 'shout' in the street, the human desires it articulates and channels. And just as 'street' is often short-hand for the urban world, so too somewhere, in the roar of its crowds, in the hum of the city's traffic, is the voice of modernity: the clamour for progress, a howl of protest, a cry for help.

Because the street is a state of mind as much as a particular place, the structure of the book is thematic as well as geographical. Four cities and their main streets serve as models – the London high street, the Parisian boulevard, the St Petersburg prospect, the Manhattan broadway. These are arguments as much as they are locations. Grouped around the four principal concepts of memory, desire, politics and mobility, each respective city street becomes a museum, a market, a forum, a thoroughfare.

My reason for selecting London, Paris, Lenigrad and New York is that to a certain extent they have also universalized themselves. '*Weltstädte*', world cities, their brand of metropolitanism has been imposed throughout the world. This internationalism has two aspects. There is a homogenizing tendency in Western modernism that has made parts of Dallas almost indistinguishable from parts of Frankfurt or Tel Aviv. But there is also a more varied sense of internationalism which preserves differences, so that turning a corner in London, Paris or New York, you could momentarily be transported to Limassol, Algiers or Havana. The text itself shifts beyond its specified cities to, for example, Bloom's Dublin, Kafka's Prague, Calvino's Venice, Mayakovsky's Moscow.

Time, like geography, provides a framework for the narrative, but is not adhered to rigidly. In the city, just as you can encounter another culture around a corner, you can also step into a different time. The one criterion I have stuck to is that the subject is the *modern* metro-politan street, but what is precisely meant by the term 'modern' is part of the book's task to define. A sense of *contemporaneity*, however, is a useful guide. A Parisian *flâneur* in the mid-nineteenth century may have lived simultaneously with a Kalahari bushman, but could not be called his contemporary: half a century later, however, a stroller in Dublin largely could. Modernity, in this respect, is measured not in minutes or years but in cultural shifts, economic development and social change. To that extent, the modern world began in London and Paris in the early nineteenth century when these two cities underwent a phenomenal burst of growth: it spread outwards, through Europe to Russia, across the Atlantic to America, until it reached the cities of the south which today are creating their unique versions of metropolitan life.

As a travel book, then, *A Shout in the Street* is animated by a sense of intellectual as well as physical adventure: it is as much a book of ideas as a book of descriptions. I make no apologies for this. No one text can hope to encompass the particularity of any one of these capitals, let alone four. Besides, my aim has been to give an insight into the urban environment, not provide a literary equivalent to it. In that environment, abstract ideas have been as important as a specific sense of place. One has only to think of Le Corbusier's concept of 'Cities in a Park' (which has had as much impact on the urban landscape as Oppenheimer's concept of the atom bomb) to see that ideas shape the city as much as the city shapes ideas (cf. pp. 201–2). Though a sense of place has been important in what follows, more important has been a sense of relevance.

A View of the Street

In the pages that follow one story is told – but in two ways: through my own essays, and through a parallel montage of quotations. Each half relies on the other, sometimes directly, sometimes obliquely. The essays can be read as a commentary on the montages, the montages as preliminaries to the essays.

Throughout this book I've drawn on the writings of others, and to some it may appear that I've spent more time in libraries than out and about in the city, returning with some recondite findings, and little direct experience. However, nearly every excerpt, source, idea or image has been chosen because it strikes some chord in me, touches some direct experience. If there was any one governing emotion to the book, it would be a sense of recognition – a recognition that others have had a different view of the same thing (cf. Shklovsky, p. xii). The street is, after all, a kind of commonplace, and to ignore its pluralism would be to desiccate its potential.

Among these references, I've drawn on a range of different disciplines. City life can't be confined to one monological expertise; history flows through it, so does politics, so does reportage, pop music, philosophy. However, works of fiction play a large part in both the essays and the montages ahead because, in something as artificial as the modern metropolis, images, fictions, myths are often as formative as bare facts. This does not mean that the city itself is conceived, as it is in a recent study, as a work of art. For a start, the city cannot be said to be a work of art, singular, but many competing works, plural. And even a single work of architecture is distinct from most other art forms in that unlike a symphony, a novel or a landscape painting, people have to live in it. Instead of *a* work of art, the city is best seen as a domain of aesthetic contention. Aesthetics is not just the appreciation of the 'beautiful', but of the ugly, the exciting, the intimidating, the banal as well. As we shall see, the aesthetic perspective is not the end of the argument but the beginning of it.

One of the virtues of an aesthetic approach, however, is that it gives the feel, the grain of city life. Gabriel García Márquez has said that you can discern the entire moral condition of a country from the fragrance of a rotten guava. A sensuous detail, evoking the ethos of a place, yields insights into the city in a way that few other approaches can. Furthermore, as the expression of our patterning activity, aesthetic forms relate to other patterns: political formulas, moral matrices, social networks, economic structures. The essays in this book begin to make such connections between these different disciplines, while the montages leave many more for the reader to make.

Collated from a diverse range of sources, the montage sections should form not only a story, but also a drama – a dialogue between different viewpoints and voices. The idea of making a book of quotations is not entirely new. Walter Benjamin expressed the desire over fifty years ago, and Susan Sontag takes up his suggestion in the appendix of her book *On Photography*. But the form seemed peculiarly appropriate to this subject. The montage, like the collage and bricolage, is one of the obsessions of modernism: not only does it recombine fixed elements in new ways, but breaks the illusion of a single authorial meaning. And the street, by definition, is a place of debate between ambivalent clashing perspectives. Sometimes excerpts may seem torn out of context, but I have been careful not to distort any original meanings in creating a new context for them. Even if I had written a continuous text on the city, these sources would still have been there, in the back of my mind or buried in footnotes. Rather than inter them this way, I've separated my opinions from those of others, and let them speak for themselves.

I have resisted calling the montage sections 'anthologies' because, in one way or another, anthologies are supposed to be representative, to give either a quantitative compendious collection or a qualitative guide. The montages attempt to do neither. For a start, my knowledge is corrigible; and I have tried not to overwhelm with sheer bulk of material, and argue a case by exhaustion. Indeed, the process of compiling this book has been more a process of exclusion, of resisting the wealth of possible sources. And just as it doesn't represent an encyclopaedic collection, this book is not some personal literary manifesto, either. Obviously, some idea of quality has played a part in these selections. But this has not been a judgement of 'good writing', unless that is indistinguishable from sharp perception and clear thinking. Even then, for most excerpts I've had at least one more that could have stood in its place. Often something is included not just for what it says, but where it is said, when and by whom.

A series of voices that invoke, revoke and provoke one another, the montage sections are intended to be a *presentation* on the theme of urban life rather than a *representation* of it. Most of the quotations are kept terse so as not to lose sight of that fact of plurality, that this statement is one among many and that there are others just round the corner, usually on the same page. Working by implication rather than explication, the real significances are to be found in the gaps in the text, its lacunae and silences. They require the reader to be not just a passive consumer of meanings, but a producer of them.

It would, however, be an abnegation of responsibility to pretend that the montage sections selected themselves any more than the essays wrote themselves. So, any error of fact or citation in both is of my own doing and no one else's. This book is, in the end, just a window on to the street. Like any window, it will have flaws which distort the view. But more than that, there is the inevitable limitation – every window has a frame. It shows, however clearly, only part of a view. But if readers are provoked enough to want to go beyond that frame, to go out and construct their own narrative from their own readings and experiences, in that case, this book will have done its job.

Peter Jukes, London, 1989

LONDON
Nostalgia and Poverty

The first photograph ever taken of London, a shot down Whitehall by St Croix, is typical of many views of our urban past (see illustration 1, p. 6). It invites us on an impossible journey, back down a street we cannot now take, into a city we can never revisit. Every day, in most large Western cities, thousands of sightseers also expand their three-dimensional travels to become tourists in the fourth dimension of time. In London, it is not just the odd relic which is given over to such nostalgic pursuits, but whole quarters, from Covent Garden to St Katherine's Dock or Carnaby Street.

This chapter explores the nostalgia for history in modern London, and traces a history to that nostalgia. As such it is less concerned with the past per se *as with the image of the past which has, like any image, a fictional quality. Even St Croix's apparently objective photograph – whose long exposure time eliminated moving objects – has the effect of a neutron bomb, vaporizing the population but leaving the property intact. The city remembers, but it also forgets: and perhaps just as significant, just as telling as the images of buildings and streets that have survived, are the gaps where they did not (cf. Freud, Heller, pp. 8–9).*

Back Alleys of Memory

This was the London of my childhood, of my moods and my awakenings: memories of Lambeth in the spring; of trivial incidents and things: of riding with mother on top of a horse-bus trying to touch lilac trees – of the many coloured bus-tickets, orange, blue, pink and green, that bestrewed the pavement where the trams and buses stopped . . . of melancholy Sundays and pale-faced parents and children escorting toy windmills and coloured balloons over Westminster Bridge: and the maternal penny steamers that softly lowered their funnels as they glided under it.

From such trivia I believe my soul was born.

Charles Chaplin, *My Autobiography*

Men make their own history, but they do not make it just as they please; they do not make it under circumstances chosen by themselves, but under circumstances directly found, given and transmitted from the past.

The tradition of all the dead generations weighs like a nightmare on the brain of the living.

Karl Marx, *The Eighteenth Brumaire of Louis Bonaparte* (1852)

The Urban Unconscious

This London City, with all its houses, palaces, steam-engines, cathedrals, and huge immeasurable traffic and tumult, what is it but a
Thought, but millions of Thoughts made into One – a huge immeasurable Spirit of a THOUGHT, embodied in brick, in iron, smoke,
dust, Palaces, Parliaments, Hackney Coaches, Katherine Docks, and
the rest of it!

Not a brick was made but some man had to *think* of the making of
that brick.

Thomas Carlyle, 'The Hero as a Man of Letters', *On Heroes, Hero-Worship and
the Heroic in History* (1841)

This is one of the very first photographs taken in England . . .

Whitehall is tranquil and empty. The calm beauty of the street is
clear, as are the details of shops and houses. All is recorded with
tantalising precision. All is so real that, Alice like, one is tempted to
enter the picture.

London in 1839 was not empty of traffic or of people. The streets
are empty in early photographs . . . because of the long exposure times
which eliminated moving objects . . .

Gavin Stamp, *The Changing Metropolis*

1 Whitehall from Trafalgar
Square, 1839 – M. de
St Croix.

In vain, great hearted Kublai, shall I attempt to describe Zaira, city of high bastions. I could tell you how many steps make up the arcades rising like stairways, and the degree of the arcades' curves, and what kinds of zinc scales cover the roofs; but I already know that this would be the same as telling you nothing. The city does not consist of this, but of relationships between the measurements of its space and the events of its past ... The city however does not tell its past, but contains it like the lines of a hand, written in the corners of the streets, the gratings of the windows, the banisters of the steps, the antennae of the lightning rods, the poles of the flags ...

Italo Calvino, Invisible Cities

The city carries a story, the city presents a lure into its own version of the past; you could say it tells tales, that it lies.

Marina Warner, Monuments and Maidens

We cannot recollect what is to come, and no purposive action can be directed towards times bygone. Yet ... we cannot be content with these limitations: we want to know our future and we want to change our past.

But the statement that we can't know our future and cannot change our past has only relative validity. Every recollection of what is bygone is an interpretation; we reconstruct our past.

2 Trafalgar Square and the Nelson Column, late 1843 – William Henry Fox Talbot.

3 Renovation of the Nelson
Column, summer 1987 –
Teresa Watkins.

What we construct, how we reconstruct it, what kind of sense we attribute to the reconstructed, all this changes with our experiences; with our interest, with the measure of sincerity and insincerity. In brief, we change the past through selective interpretation ... This is exactly the procedure of psychoanalysis ...

Agnes Heller, A Theory of History

Historians tell us that the oldest Rome was the *Roma Quadrata*, a fenced settlement on the Palatine ... after that came the city bound by the Servian Wall; and later still ... the city which the Emperor Aurelian surrounded with his walls. We will ask ourselves how much a visitor ... may still find left of these early stages in the Rome of today.

Except for a few gaps he will see the Aurelian wall almost unchanged. In some places he will be able to find sections of the Servian Wall where they have been excavated and brought to light. If he knows enough ... he may be able to trace out ... the outline of the *Roma Quadrata*.

Now let us, by flight of imagination, suppose that Rome is not a human habitation but a psychical entity with a similarly long and copious past ... Nothing which has come into existence will have passed away ... Where the Coliseum now stands we could at the same time admire Nero's vanished Golden House. On the Piazza of the Pantheon we should find not only the Pantheon of today, as it was bequeathed to us by Hadrian, but, on the same site, the original edifice erected by Agrippa ...

The question may be raised why we chose precisely the past of a *city* to compare with the past of the mind. The assumption that everything past is preserved holds good even in mental life on condition the organ of the mind has remained intact ... But destructive influences which can be compared to causes of illness like these are never lacking in the history of a city ... even if, like LONDON, it has hardly ever suffered from the visitations of an enemy ...

Sigmund Freud, Civilisation and Its Discontents

In its arbitrary and unplanned way demolition and commercial transformation of nineteenth century London must have involved a greater displacement of population than the rebuilding of Paris under Haussmann ...

By the early years of the Twentieth Century the whole physiognomy of central London had been transformed beyond recognition.

Large and packed residential areas had given way to acres of warehouses, workshops, railway yards, and offices. Wide streets had been cut through the dangerous and semi-criminal slum rookeries of the 1840s.

Gareth Stedman Jones, *Outcast London*

What survives is usually what was made and intended to survive: the edifices and the cultural symbols of the powerful, structures of stone rather than wood, the official rather than the makeshift and the vernacular.

Patrick Wright, *On Living in an Old Country*

Attraction of Repulsion

All those new districts that have sprung up in the last half century, the creation of our commercial and colonial wealth, it is impossible to conceive of anything more tame, more insipid, more uniform. PANCRAS is like MARYLEBONE, MARYLEBONE is like PADDINGTON: all the streets resemble each other; you must read the names of the squares before you venture the knock at a door.

Where London becomes more interesting is Charing Cross. Looking to Northumberland House, and turning your back on Trafalgar Square, the Strand is perhaps the finest street in Europe, blending the architecture of many periods. The fire of London has deprived us of the delight of a real old quarter of the city, but some bits remain, and everywhere there is a stunning multitude, and a great crush and crash of carts and wagons. The Inns of court, and the quarters in the vicinity of the port, Thames Street, Tower Hill and Billingsgate, Wapping, Rotherhithe, are the best parts of London; they are full of character; the buildings bear a nearer relation to what people are doing.

Benjamin Disraeli, quoted in Thomas Burke, *Streets of London*

The London I knew or imaginatively possessed was the London I had got from Dickens. It was Dickens – and his illustrators – who gave me the illusion of knowing the city ... Years later, looking at Dickens during a time when I was writing hard myself, I felt I understood a little more about Dickens's unique power as a describer of London, and his difference from all other writers about London ...

The city of one hundred and thirty years before must have been almost as strange to him as it was to me: and it was his genius to describe it, when he was an adult, as a child might have described it. Not displaying architectural knowledge or taste; not using technical words; using only simple words like 'old fashioned' to describe whole streets . . .

Using, Dickens, only simple words, simple concepts, to create simple volumes and surfaces and lights and shadows; creating thereby a city or fantasy which everyone could reconstruct out of his own materials, using the things he knows to recreate the described things he didn't know.

V. S. Naipaul, *The Enigma of Arrival*

Great Images have both a history and a prehistory; they are a blend of memory and legend . . . Every image has unfathomable oneiric depths to which the personal past adds special colours.

Gaston Bachelard, *The Poetics of Space*

The blacking warehouse was the last house on the left hand side of the way, at old Hungerford Stairs. It was a crazy old tumbledown house, abutting the course of the river, and literally overrun with rats.

4 Westminster from
Hungerford Market –
William Henry Fox Talbot.

I was so young and childish, and so little qualified to undertake the whole change of my own existence that, in going to Hungerford Stairs of a morning, I could not resist the stale pastry put out at half price on trays at the confectioner's doors in Tottenham Court Road: and I often spent in that the money I should have kept for my dinner. When I had no money, I took a turn in Covent Garden Market and stared at the pineapples.

I know that I do not exaggerate, unconsciously and unintentionally, the scantiness of my resource and the difficulties of my life ... I know that I worked, from morning to night, with common men and boys, a shabby child. I know that I have lounged about the streets, insufficiently and unsatisfactorily fed. I know that, but for the mercy of God, I might easily have been, for any care that was taken of me, a little robber or a little vagabond.

Until Hungerford Market was pulled down, until old Hungerford Stairs were destroyed, and the very nature of the ground changed, I never had the courage to go back to the place where my servitude began. I never saw it. I could not endure to go near it ...

In my walks at night I have walked there often, since then, and by degrees I have come to write this. It does not seem a little of what I might have written, or of what I meant to write.

Charles Dickens, 'Fragment of an Autobiography',
John Forster, *Life of Charles Dickens*

THE MYSTERIES OF LONDON
WEALTH AND POVERTY

Unbounded wealth is the neighbour of the most hideous poverty: the most gorgeous pomp is placed in strong relief by the most deplorable squalor; the most seducing luxury is only separated by a narrow wall from the most appalling misery.

G. M. W. Reynolds, *The Mysteries of London* (1838)

There is a period in all languages, when words pass from the mint in which they are coined, their questionable origin is forgotten ... We believe that such is the case with the word ROOKERY ...

We must speak of the dwellings of the poor in crowded cities, where large numbers of men are brought together. We must speak of hideous masses pent up, crowded, crammed into courts and alleys; where, as if by fatal attraction, opposite houses grow together at the top, seem to nod against one another ... We must speak of men and women sleeping in the same apartment, whom, in some cases, not even the tie of relationship unites. We must speak of stories piled on stories in the older part of our towns. Are not these Rookeries, if the description given by the naturalist be correct: 'A Rookery, a village in the air, peopled . . . with numerous inhabitants: it is the nature of birds to associate together, and they build in numbers in the same adjoining trees.'

Thomas Beames, The Rookeries of London (1850)

What involutions can compare to those of Seven Dials? Where is there such another maze of streets, courts, lanes, and alleys? The stranger who finds himself in 'the Dials' for the first time . . . will see enough around him to keep his curiosity and attention awake for no inconsiderable time.

He traverses streets of dirty, straggling houses, with now and then an unexpected court composed of buildings as ill-proportioned and deformed as the half-naked children that wallow in the kennels . . . dirty men, filthy women, squalid children, fluttering shuttlecocks, noisy battledores, reeking pipes, bad fruit, more than doubtful oysters, attenuated cats, depressed dogs . . . are its cheerful accompaniment.

Charles Dickens, Seven Dials (1835)

To be taken out for a walk into the real town, especially if it were anywhere about Covent Garden or the Strand, perfectly entranced him [Dickens as a child] with pleasure. But most of all he had a profound *attraction of repulsion* to St Giles. If only he could induce whomsoever took him out to take him through Seven Dials he was extremely happy; 'Good Heavens!' he would exclaim, 'what wild visions of prodigies of wickedness, want and beggary arose in my mind out of that place!'

John Forster, Life of Charles Dickens

A large class of the genus Rookery are very ancient homes, deserted by those to whose ancestors they once belonged. In the dingiest streets of the metropolis are found homes, the rooms of which are lofty . . . the ceilings beautifully ornamented, the chimney pieces models for the sculptor . . . The names of the courts remind you of decayed glory – Villiers, Dorset, Buckingham, Norfolk, telling of the stately edifices which once stood where you now breathe the impure atmosphere of a thickly peopled court.

Thomas Beames, The Rookeries of London

We have always entertained a particular attachment towards Monmouth Street, as the only true and real emporium for second hand wearing apparel ... Through every alternation and every change, Monmouth Street has still remained the burial-place of fashion ...

We love to walk among these extensive groves of the illustrious dead, and to indulge in the speculations to which they give rise; now fitting a deceased coat, then a dead pair of trousers, and anon the mortal remains of a gaudy waistcoat ... and endeavouring, from the shape and fashion of the garment itself, to bring its former owner before our mind's eye.

We have gone on speculating in this way, until whole rows of coats have started up from their pegs ... lines of trousers have jumped up to meet them; waistcoats have almost burst with anxiety to put themselves on; and half an acre of shoes have suddenly found feet to fit them, and gone stumping down the street with a noise which has fairly awakened us from our pleasant reverie ...

Charles Dickens, Meditations on Monmouth Street (1836)

Dickens became accustomed to wandering these same parts of London at the times when he was either planning a writing project, or actually writing.

Over the course of his writing career, he began to sense the connection between his inspiration and walking these city streets ... In 1844, working on a Christmas Book, he wrote from Geneva: 'Put me down on Waterloo Bridge at 8 o'clock in the evening, with leave to roam about as long as I like, and I would come home, as you know, panting to go on writing.'

In August he complained 'the difficulty of going on at what I call a rapid pace, is prodigious: it is almost an impossibility. I suppose this is partly ... the absence of streets and numbers of people.' ... In Geneva that October he was physically ill, he wrote 'attributable, I have not the least doubt, to an absence of streets'.

F. S. Schwarzbach, Dickens and the City

'Street' has always had a connotation of freedom, even license. It had it even more for the proper Victorian who made a fetish of domesticity and privacy, whose house was a castle in ways never intended by his forefathers, who fortified himself behind closed doors as if to ward off the temptations and provocations lurking outside ...

The street was a place where conventional distinctions of what was legal and illegal, moral and immoral, proper and improper, permissible and impermissible, did not prevail.

Gertrude Himmelfarb, *The Idea of Poverty*

From the entire absence of all wynds, courts and blind alleys, or culs-de-sac, there would be no secret and obscure haunts for the retirement of the filthy and immoral from the public eye.

James Silk Buckingham, 'National Evils and Practical Remedies with the Plan of a Modern Town' (1849)

SEVERAL OBJECTS OF PUBLIC UTILITY, *viz.*
1. The opening and enlarging of communication for the general convenience of public interest. 2. The improvement of certain districts, of which the present state is greatly injurious to the health of the inhabitants. 3. The melioration of the moral conditions of the labouring classes closely congregated in such districts.

Parliamentary Paper, 'First Report on Metropolitan Improvements' (1840)

In the twenty years from 1861 to 1881 the population of the city fell from 113,387 to 51,439 . . .

5 Holborn Viaduct under construction, 11 September 1869.

The vast migration was a consequence, not of workers moving out in pursuit of better opportunities, but of demolition . . .

Between 1836 and 1856 New Oxford Street was cut through St Giles', Victoria Street through the rookeries of Westminster, Commercial Street through Whitechapel, and Farringdon Street, New Cannon Street, and New Victoria Street through the poorest and most densely populated parts of the city.

It was intended that the new streets should remove as much slum housing as possible. The buildings of New Oxford Street displaced over 5,000 persons: it was estimated that the Farringdon Street clearances involved the displacement of up to 40,000 . . .

It is noticeable that the street clearance of the 1840s and 1850s included nearly all quarters embellished with surreal horror by literary imagination . . . Saffron Hill, the alleged home of Fagin, was transformed by the Farringdon Road clearances: Jacob's Island where Bill Sykes met his death was razed to the ground.

Gareth Stedman Jones, *Outcast London*

6 Farringdon Road from
St Andrew's, *c.* 1862.

He walked in darkness under the lamps of Holborn, and was crucified at Charing Cross ... He did not go in for 'observation' – a priggish habit; he did not look at Charing Cross to improve his mind or count the lamp posts in Holborn to practise his arithmetic.

Dickens did not stamp these places on his mind: he stamped his mind on these places.

G. K. Chesterton, Dickens

THE ROOKERY IS NO MORE! A spacious street is in its stead: but can you tell us that any poor man has gained from the clearance? Certainly not: the effect of the late removals are shown in the report of a Committee of the Council of the Statistical Society:

> The council consider that a main cause of this evil is what are falsely called the improvements which have recently taken place in this part in the formation of New Oxford Street. The exported inhabitants cannot, of course, derive any advantage from new erections, and are forced to search out the yet remaining hovels situated to the East.

Thomas Beames, The Rookeries of London (1850)

'We make our new Oxford Streets, and our other new streets, never heeding, never asking, where the wretches we clear out, crowd!'

Charles Dickens, 'On Duty With Inspector Field' (1848)

Who builds? Who builds? Alas ye poor!
  If London day by day "improves"
Where shall ye find a friendly door
    When everyday a home removes?

The Builder, Vol. IX (1851)

THE STREET FOLK

Of the thousand millions of human beings that are said to constitute the population of the entire globe, there are – but two distinct and broadly marked races, viz., the *wanderers* and the *settlers* – the *vagabond* and the *citizen* – the *nomadic* and the *civilised* tribes.

The nomadic tribes of England are of many distinct kinds ... Those who obtain their living in the streets of the metropolis are a very large and varied class; indeed the means resorted to in order to 'pick up a crust' ... in the public thoroughfares are so multifarious that the mind is long baffled in its attempts to reduce them to scientific order or classification.

It would appear, however, that the street people may be all arranged under six distinct genera or kinds

I.   STREET SELLERS
II.   STREET BUYERS
III.   STREET-FINDERS
IV.   STREET-PERFORMERS
V.   STREET ARTISANS, or WORKING PEDLARS
VI.   STREET LABOURERS

The boy crossing-sweeper

I found the lad (who first gave me insight into the proceedings of the associated crossing-sweepers) crouched on the stone steps of a door in Adelaide Street, Strand: and when I spoke to him he was preparing to settle down in a corner and go to sleep. The moment he heard my voice he was upon his feet, asking me to 'give a halfpenny to poor little Jack.'

> I was fifteen the 24th of last May, sir, and I've been sweeping crossings now near upon two years. There's a party of six of us, and we have the crossings from St Martin's Church as far as Pall Mall. I always go along with them as lodging in the same place I do, but if it's wet, we separate, and if I an' another gets a crossing – those who gets on it first, keeps it – and we stand on each side and we take our chance.
>
> We do it this way: if I was to see two gentlemen coming, I should cry out, 'Two toffs!' and then they are mine: and whether they give me anythink or not they are mine and my mate is bound not to follow them; for if he did he would get a hiding from the whole lot of us. If we both cry together, then we share. If it's a lady and gentleman, then we cries 'A toff and a doll!'
>
> Henry Mayhew, *London Labour and the London Poor* (1861)

A city like London, where one can roam about for hours without reaching the beginning of an end, without seeing the slightest indication that open country is nearby, is really something very special … This colossal centralisation, this agglomeration of three and a half million people on a single spot has multiplied the strength of these three and a half million inhabitants a hundredfold … But the price that has been paid is not discovered until later.

Only when one has tramped the pavements of the main streets for a few days does one notice … There is something distasteful about the very bustle of the streets, something that is abhorrent to human nature itself. Hundreds of thousands of people of all classes and ranks of society jostle past one another; are they not all human beings with the same characteristics and potentialities, equally interested in the pursuit of happiness? ... And yet they rush past one another as if they had nothing in common or were in no way associated with one another.

Friedrich Engels, *The Condition of the Working Class in England in 1844* (1887)

LONDON ... Implacable November weather. As much mud on the streets as if the waters had but newly retired from the face of the earth ...

Dogs, indistinguishable in mire. Horses, scarcely better; splashed to their very blinkers. Foot passengers, jostling one another's umbrellas, in a general infection of ill temper, and losing their foothold at street corners, where tens of thousands of other foot passengers have been slipping and sliding since the day broke (if this day ever broke) ...

Fog everywhere.

Charles Dickens, *Bleak House* (1853)

The mud of mid-century London was ... compounded of loose soil to be sure, but also of a great deal more, including soot and ashes and street litter, and the fecal matter of the legion of horses on whom all transport in London depended. In addition, many sewers ... in rainy weather would simply overflow into the streets. The mud must at times have been nothing less than liquid ordure. Millions of people who walked through it daily, it seems, in some important sense were unaware of the fact. Though at every street corner, a waif like Jo might be standing, waiting to sweep a relatively clean path through the mud ... for well-dressed pedestrians, somehow the fact of his existence or that of the mud itself was not 'real'.

F. S. Schwarzbach, *Dickens and the City*

The conversion of the vast and shapeless city which Dickens knew – fog-bound and fever-haunted, brooding over its dark mysterious river – into the Imperial Capital, of Whitehall, of the Thames Embankment and South Kensington, is the still visible symbol of the mid-Victorian transition.

Asa Briggs, *Victorian Cities*

7 The Victoria
Embankment, looking
towards Westminster,
c. 1875.

The Embankment completely changed the Northern aspect of the
Thames which, before the 1860s, had been lined with commercial
wharves and warehouses . . .

While the photographs of the mid-Victorian improvements are of
great interest, perhaps the most valuable photographs . . . are those
which show London just before the transformation wrought by commerce, railways, and the Metropolitan Board of Works . . . Sadly, they
suggest, in meticulous detail and haunting clarity, that almost every
change that has taken place in London since those pioneering days has
been a change for the worse.

Gavin Stamp, *The Earliest Photographs of London*

Let us rid ourselves of Dickensian and Chadwickian images. Whatever its sanitary inadequacies – and the worst had been taken care of by 1869 – whatever the extent of poverty, by contemporary standards London was healthy and technologically advanced, and more remarkable for widely diffused prosperity than for the extremes of riches and distress that existed there as elsewhere.

There is, to be sure, evidence that the poverty that did exist in London was somehow more obtrusive than in continental cities. But we must assume that scenes of squalor did not prevent our visitor from enjoying London in 1869 any more than such scenes seriously interfere with our enjoyment of New York or Lisbon or Mexico City today. A selective blindness is the necessary attribute of the happy tourist.

Donald Olsen, The City as a Work of Art

What surrounds us daily, what is inseparable from us, what is usual, only a deep, great, unusual talent can notice.

Nikolai Gogol, Notebooks

LONDON is a vile place, I sincerely believe. I have never taken kindly to it, since I lived abroad. Whenever I come back from the country now, and see that great heavy canopy lowering over the housetops, I wonder what on earth I do there except on obligation.

Charles Dickens, Letter to Bulmer Lytton

After an unusually long day of writing, on the 8th of June 1870, Dickens began to feel ill. He made light of it, and sat down to dinner with the household. Then, he rose from the table and said he would go to London at once ... Those were the last coherent words he spoke. He died the next day.

John Forster, Life of Charles Dickens

East

London, Hardy wrote, in 1887:

appears not to *see itself*. Each individual is conscious of *himself*, but no one conscious of themselves collectively ...

By the 1880s everyone, it seemed, could see the East End and the West End, and in the contrast between them the shape of a new society that had been quite naturally and generally created.

Conditions in the East End were described as 'unknown' and 'unexplored' ... 'Darkest London' was a conventional epithet.

Raymond Williams, The Country and the City

THE DARK SIDE OF LIFE

I commence, with the first of these chapters, a book of travel ... In this book I propose to record the result of a journey into a region which lies at our own doors – into a dark continent that is within walking distance of the General Post Office. This continent will, I hope, be found as interesting as any of those newly-explored lands which engage the attention of the Royal Geographical Society – the wild races who inhabit it will, I trust, gain public sympathy as easily as those savage tribes for whose benefit the Missionary Societies never cease to appeal for funds.

George Sims, *How the Poor Live* (1883)

Few who will read these pages have any conception of what these pestilential human rookeries are, where tens of thousands are crowded together amidst horrors which call to mind what we have heard of the middle passage of the slave ship. To get into them you have to penetrate courts reeking with poisonous and malodorous gases arising from accumulations of sewage and refuse scattered in all directions and often flowing beneath your feet ...

Andrew Mearns, *The Bitter Cry of Outcast London* (1883)

It is to increased wealth and increased civilisation that we owe the wide gulf which today separates well-to-do citizens from the masses. It is the increased wealth of this mighty city which has driven the poor back inch by inch, until we find them today herding together, packed like herrings in a barrel, neglected and despised, and left to endure wrongs and hardships which, if they were related to a far-off savage tribe, would cause Exeter Hall to shudder till its bricks fell down.

George Sims, *How the Poor Live* (1883)

London's reputation as a world city was not simply a reputation for brilliance. Will Crook's well-known remark about the same sun which never set on the empire never rising on the dark alleys of East London directly linked the preoccupation with poverty and the consciousness of imperial power.

Asa Briggs, *Victorian Cities*

WHY DARKEST ENGLAND?

This summer the attention of the civilised world has been arrested by the story which Mr Stanley has told of 'Darkest Africa' and his journeyings across the heart of the lost continent ... It is a terrible picture, and one that had engraved itself deep on the heart of civilisation. But while brooding over the awful presentation of life as it exists in the vast African Forest, it seemed to me only too vivid a picture of many parts of our own land. As there is a darkest Africa is there not also a darkest England? . . .

The lot of the Negress in the Equatorial Forest is not, perhaps, a very happy one, but is it very much worse than that of many a pretty orphan girl in our Christian capital?

General Booth, *In Darkest London and the Way Out* (1890)

The internationalisation of London was mirrored not only in its trade and its overseas connections but on its populations. Baedeker, in describing the docks, directed attention to 'the large and motley crowd of labourers, to which numerous dusky visages and foreign costumes import a curious and picturesque air'. He also pointed out that there were more Scotsmen in London than in Aberdeen, more Irishmen than in Dublin, more Jews than in Palestine, and more Roman Catholics than in Rome.

Asa Briggs, *Victorian Cities*

As the Red Indian, putting his ear to the ground, could hear murmurs beyond the horizon inaudible to the bystander, so the trained ear could discern the turmoil of the coming flood and the tramp of many footsteps. Our streets have suddenly become congested with a weird and uncanny people. They have poured in as dense black masses from the eastern railways; they have streamed across the bridges from the marshes and desolate places beyond the river; they have been hurried up in an incredible number through tubes sunk into the bowels of the earth, emerging like rats from a drain, blinking in the sunshine . . .

Three times at least during these months the richest city in the world was in the hollow of their hands. They brushed the police away like an elephant dispersing flies. They could have looted and destroyed, plundered and razed it to the ground. We gazed at them in startled amazement. Whence did they all come, these creatures with strange antics and manners, these denizens of another universe of being?

C. F. G. Masterman, *From the Abyss* (1902)

It has been argued that the predominant reaction to the rediscovery of poverty in the early 1880s was not so much guilt as fear . . .

The winter of 1885–6 was exceptionally severe . . . On the morning

23

of 9th February, a dense fog descended upon London. 'Roughs' again gathered in Trafalgar Square, and the West End remained in a state of near panic. Shops were closed and boarded up, and the police went round warning tradesmen to expect new attacks.

But the panic of the 9th February was insignificant beside that of the following day. In the morning the confidence of the West End had been slightly restored and some shops had begun to re-open. But from mid-day the fog thickened, the 'disorderly classes' again began to assemble in Trafalgar Square and the panic grew. All over South London 'the shops closed and people stood at their doors straining their eyes through the fog for the sounds of the 10,000 men who were stated to be marching either to Clapham Common or the City.'

Gareth Stedman Jones, Outcast London

Conan Doyle's London has acquired, with time, a romantic atmosphere which some look back to with a nostalgia as evident and systematic as any rural retrospect: the fog, the gaslight, the hansom cabs, the street urchins . . . London in the Sherlock Holmes stories becomes again the city of 'labyrinthine obscurity and lurid' fascination. Indeed, the urban detective, prefigured in a minor way by Dickens and Wilkie Collins, now begins to emerge as a significant and ratifying figure: the man who can find his way through the fog, who can penetrate the intricacies of the streets.

The opaque complexity of modern city life is represented by crime.

Raymond Williams, The Country and the City

A SOCIAL MAP OF LONDON
Coloured by streets

The inhabitants of every street, and court, and block of buildings in the whole of London have been estimated in proportion to the numbers of children, and arranged in classes according to the known position of the parents of these children.

Streets coloured black (semi-criminal)

Shelton Street: . . . just wide enough for a vehicle to pass . . . Parker Street: . . . as bad as Shelton Street is, Parker Street touches a little lower level.

Dark blue streets (very poor)

Summer Gardens: . . . touches upon Baxter Street. Baxter Street is black, the houses which are interspersed with the business premises having a bad character.

Streets coloured purple (poor)

We find in these streets a very wide range of character ... Lady Street, described among the dark blue streets, changes its colour, becoming first purple, and finally pink before the eastern end is reached.

Charles Booth, *Life and Labour of the People in London* (1889–97)

Within a short distance ... of the heart and centre of the city of London there has existed for the last fifty years, and still exists and flourishes, what is perhaps the foulest and most dangerous street in the whole metropolis.

James Greenwood, *Low Life Deeps* (1876)

The old Flower and Dean Street area was among the last of the London 'Rookeries' ...

For the middle classes who waged a tireless war against the 27 courts, streets and alleys packed into the 'square quarter of a mile' of the Flower and Dean Street neighbourhood, the realities of life in the ranks of Victorian London's reserve army of labour were both un-important and inconvenient.

It was not the reality but the image which provoked Church and State into doing battle with sledge hammers and pick-axes. The real Flower and Dean Street problem revolved around casual or seasonal employment, starvation wages, a heartless system of poor relief and brutalising living conditions ... What concerned the middle classes were street-crime, prostitution, the threat of revolt, expensive pauperism, infectious disease spreading to respectable London – the whole panoply of shame of the 'boldest blotch on the face' of the capital of the civilised world.

Jerry White, *Rothschild Buildings*

Brick Lane was a hotbed of villainy. Women paraded up and down the street, took the men to their 'doubles' and sold themselves for a few pence. Thieves hung round the corner of the street, waiting, like Mr Micawber, for something to turn up. In the back alleys there was garrotting – some of the brides would lumber a seaman while he was drunk and then he would be dropped – 'stringing someone up' was the slang phrase for it. There were some wild characters about ...

The 'brides' were mostly down the other end of Brick Lane, where the lodging houses were in Flowery Dean Street ... The girls who stayed in Spitalfields were very poor. That was what you called a 'fourpenny touch' or a 'knee trembler' – they wouldn't stay with you all night. Jack the Ripper's victims were all fourpenny touches.

Arthur Harding, *East End Underworld*

Within six years ... Jack the Ripper had done more to destroy the Flower and Dean Street Rookery than fifty years of roadbuilding, slum clearance and unabated pressure from Police, Poor Law Guardians, vestries and sanitary officers. Yet the response he had provoked varied from those less successful efforts only in its rapidity. It, too, pretended to offer a cure for prostitution and crime by destroying the homes where the 'fallen' and 'vicious' lived.

Jerry White, *Rothschild Buildings*

The result is everywhere the same: the most scandalous alleys and lanes disappear, to the accompaniment of lavish self-glorification by the bourgeoisie on account of this tremendous success – but they appear at once somewhere else, and often in the immediate area.

Friedrich Engels, 'The Housing Question' (1892)

A STREET

This street is in the East End. There is no need to say in the East End of what. The East End is a vast city, as famous in its way as any the hand of man has made ... Foul slums there are in the East End, of course, as there are in the West; want and misery there are, as wherever a host is gathered to fight for food. But they are not often spectacular in kind.

There is no house without children in this street, and the number of them grows ever and ever greater. One after another the little strangers come, to live through lives as flat and colourless as the day's life on the street ...

Where in the East End lies this street? Everywhere. The hundred and fifty yards is only a link in a long and mightily tangled chain – it is only a turn in a tortuous maze. This street of the square holes is hundreds of miles long. That it is planned in short lengths is true, but there is no way in the world that it can properly be called a single street, because of its dismal lack of accent, its sordid uniformity, its utter remoteness from delight.

Arthur Morrison, *Tales of the Mean Streets* (1894)

In the last quarter of the nineteenth century there were some 6,000 people – men, women and children – who lived in the Nichol ...

Arthur Morrison in his novel called it 'the Jago'. The whole district bore an evil reputation ... Some people would have liked to build a wall right round it, so as we wouldn't have to come out.

The Nichol was something like a ghetto. A stranger wouldn't chance his arm there, but to anyone brought up in it every alley was familiar ... Everybody knew the children belonged to the Nichol and everybody was kind to the children.

Arthur Harding, East End Underworld

Here in the East End, the obscenities and brute vulgarities are rampant. There is no privacy. The bad corrupts the good, and all fester together. Innocent childhood is sweet and beautiful; but in East London, innocence is a fleeting thing, and you must catch them before they fall out of the cradle, or you will find the very babes as unholily wise as you.

Jack London, People of the Abyss (1903)

When Dickens described Oliver Twist, he didn't describe him properly. Oliver Twist could never have existed because he wasn't able to help himself. The children of the Nichol were far superior to a normal child coming from a respectable family. The poverty had sharpened their wits.

Some children went busking at the theatre. Any song that was popular ... The kids used to do their little acrobatic tricks there. Somersault and jumping over each other, leap frog – anything to attract attention. Some of them done nothing, they just simply went and started cadging along the queue – telling tales with a cap in hand: 'I ain't had nothing to eat.' 'Mummy and Daddy's in the prison or the workhouse and we're all on our own, and my little sister's over there, she's crying.' This was part of everyday life, in some cases it was true ...

If you saw a child begging in Liverpool Street it was something you'd have to admire for its dexterity – it was clever the way they played on a human being. If they say, 'Go away,' he'd say, 'You wouldn't say that, Madam, to a starving child would you' ... Some children are born actors, they can cry at will.

Arthur Harding, East End Underworld

Mother had taken a room in one of the backstreets behind Kennington Green ...

An incident stands out at that period. At the end of our street was a slaughterhouse, and sheep would pass by our home on their way to be butchered. I remember one escaped and ran down the street to the amusement of onlookers. Some tried to grab it and others tripped over themselves. I had giggled with delight at its lambent capering and panic, it seemed so comic. But when it was caught and carried back to the slaughterhouse, the reality of the tragedy came over me and I ran indoors, screaming and weeping to mother: 'They're going to kill it! They're going to kill it!' That stark spring afternoon and that comedy chase stayed with me for days; and I wonder if that episode did not establish the premise of my future films – the combination of the tragic and the comic.

Charles Chaplin, *My Autobiography*

DESCRIPTION OF 'THE KID'

At first appearance the tramp looks grim-faced. Someone throws garbage at him. We see a close-up of his hands wearing torn gloves: in genteel fashion, the hands open a tin containing cigarette butts. The lighting is harsh. Most of the objects are cast-offs: a worn out pair of boots, ancient chairs, dilapidated prams, dustbins, rubbish. The tramp's lodgings, the street corner, the church mission and the doss-house are all oppressive: and the brick walls spread everywhere as though the district were a prison. Inventions subsist on threadbare surroundings, and their energy consists of an economy of means. The kid breaks windows, the tramp follows in his footsteps as a glazier. Chaplin's wit transforms the world without changing it. When the tramp dreams, his dream resembles a Victorian oleograph. Bewinged children, dressed in gauze, fly about like pantomime angels: yet they remain trapped within brick walls.

The experience of poverty gave Chaplin an unusual insight into states of extreme wealth, and a number of his ideas depend on a comparison between his childhood past and his equally unbelievable present . . . He appears to have taken pleasure in recalling details of his miserable past. As a child, he had hungered after fame and recognition: as a rich and famous man, he looks back almost yearningly to the deprivation of his Kennington days.

Eric Rhode, *A History of the Cinema*

8 Chaplin with Coogan and Policeman – still from *The Kid* (1921).

One headline stated:

HOMECOMING OF COMEDIAN TO RIVAL ARMISTICE DAY

Another:

ALL LONDON TALKS OF CHAPLIN'S VISIT

Another:

CHAPLIN GOING TO LONDON ASSURED MIGHTY WELCOME

And another in bold type:

BEHOLD OUR SON

Charles Chaplin, *My Autobiography*

29

So we wandered along through South London by Kennington Cross and Kennington Gate, Newington Butts, Lambeth Walk, and the Clapham Road, and all through the neighbourhood.

Almost every step brought back memories, most of them of a tender sort. I was right here in the midst of my youth, but somehow I seemed apart from it. I felt as though I was viewing it under glass. It could be seen all too plainly, but when I reached out to touch it it was not there – only the glass could be felt, thick glass that had been glazed by the years since I left . . . If only I could get through the glass and touch the real live thing that called me back to London. But I couldn't . . .

A man cannot go back. He thinks he can, but other things have happened in his life. He has new ideas, new friends, new attachments. He doesn't belong to his past, except that the past has, perhaps, made some marks on him.

Charles Chaplin, My Wonderful Visit

Charlie Chaplin does not give the impression of a happy man. I have the notion he suffers from the *nostalgia of the slums*.

To him the streets of Southern London are the scene of frolic, gaiety and extravagant adventure. I suspect that the only home he can ever look upon as such is the second-floor flat back in Kennington Road.

One night I walked with him in Los Angeles and presently our steps took us through the poorest quarters of the city. There were sordid tenement houses and the shabby, gaudy shops in which were sold the various goods that the poor can buy from day to day. His face lit up and a buoyant tone came over his voice as he exclaimed:

'Say, this is the real life, isn't it? All the rest is just a sham.'

Somerset Maugham

I have yet to find a poor man who has nostalgia for poverty or who finds freedom in it. I found poverty neither attractive nor edifying. It taught me nothing but a distortion of values, an over-rating of the virtues and graces of the rich and the so-called better classes.

In spite of Maugham's assumption, like everyone else I am what I am: an individual, unique and different, with a linear history of ancestral promptings and urgings; a history of dreams, desires, and of special experiences, of all of which I am the sum total.

Charles Chaplin, My Autobiography

HOME AND STREET

Most people meet their acquaintances on the street ... Quite often
people have themselves lived there for a long time ...

'They're all related on this street,' said Mr Lamb. 'It's awful, you
can't talk to anyone on the street about any of the others, but you find
it's a relation. You have to be very careful.' But if he is careful ... he
only has to stand at his front door to find someone out of his past who
is also his present:

I suppose people who come here from outside think it's an awful
place, but us established ones like it. Here you can just open your
door and say hello to everybody.

The streets are known as 'turnings', and adjoining ones as
'back-doubles'. Surrounded by their human associations, the words
had a glow to them. 'In our turning *we*', they would say 'do this, that, or
the other.' 'I've lived in this turning for fifty years', said one old man
proudly, 'and here I intend to stay.'

Some turnings have little war memorials built on to walls of houses
with inscriptions like the following:

R.I.P.

IN LOVING MEMORY OF THE MEN OF CYPRUS
STREET WHO MADE THE GREAT SACRIFICE

1914–1918

J. AMOS, E. AGOMBAR, A. BOARDMAN, A. H. COLE

– there follow the names of twenty-two soldiers from Cyprus Street.
Above it is a smaller plaque to the men killed in 1939–45: 'They are
marching with their comrades somewhere on the road ahead.'

Michael Young and Peter Wilmott, *Family and Kinship in East London*

The old, poisonous, crumbling houses of old London are doomed.
And we must boldly face the necessity of rebuilding London some day
for the masses in blocks.

Frederic Harrison, *The Meaning of History* (1887)

West Ham, towards the middle of the war, was a borough of ghosts.
Part of it had been so completely devastated that the infantry used it as
a training ground for street fighting. Fifteen Wren churches in the City
of London were gutted or destroyed. There was havoc in the Inns of
Court and among the historic halls of the City Companies ... It would
be idle for any observer of modern Britain to pretend that the

Luftwaffe added much to the ignoble efforts of peacetime demolition firms. Private enterprise, over the centuries, had accounted for nineteen of Wren's City churches, irreparably ...

By June 19th, 1941, over two million houses had been damaged or destroyed, sixty per cent of them in London. Over the remaining years of the war, this increased to an estimated three and three-quarter million, or two houses out of every seven, of which a quarter of a million were beyond repair. In the central London area, only one house out of ten would have escaped damage of some kind.

This was not sheer loss. Even before the war, the slums of the city centres, including the East End's, had been losing population as local councils completed housing estates on the verges of the conurbations. The Luftwaffe effected a much overdue programme of slum clearance.

Angus Calder, *The People's War*

9 The one they left behind,
1987 – Teresa Watkins.

We are saddened by the sight of an individual suffering amnesia, but we are often less concerned when an entire community is subjected to what amounts to social amnesia as a result of massive clearance or alteration of the physical setting.

The demolition of dwellings and factory buildings wipes out a significant chapter of the history of the place. Even if it does not erase them from local memory, it tends to reduce or eliminate the recall of that memory, rendering less meaningful the communication of that heritage to a new generation.

Such destruction deprives people of tangible manifestations of their identity . . . the condemnation and clearance of physical structures can be read as a condemnation of the way of life which had been lived there.

Tamara Hareven and Rudolph Langenbach, Our Past Before Us

Now the world when I was a child when I lived in the East End of London was a much happier world than it is today, do you know that? The people who come here, they all say the same thing. I say to them, 'But you're better off today than you were. No fear of starvation.' They say, 'We miss the friendship of the East End, of streets where everybody was neighbourly.' There was always someone knocking at your door to help you. Now your neighbours don't want to know you.

The people round here are just ordinary working class people who have got on. But they act as if they were lords of the land. They'll never let on they came from Bethnal Green or Hoxton. Next door from here are some people who have bought a house. I asked the man, 'What part of the world do you come from?' He said 'Walthamstow.' I looked at him and I thought, 'You don't sound like Walthamstow to me.' His wife told me the other day he comes from Hoxton. Now why's he afraid to say he comes from Hoxton . . . ? He would have possibly been like I was once, with one room for the family to sleep in. But now he's made a step up in the world he doesn't want to know.

Arthur Harding, East End Underworld

Back Down Memory Lane

DELUSION WHICH LEADS MEN TO OVERRATE THE
HAPPINESS OF PRECEDING GENERATIONS

It may at first sight seem strange that society, while constantly moving forward with eager speed, should be constantly looking back with tender regret. But these two propensities, inconsistent as they may appear, can be easily resolved into the same principle. Both spring from our impatience of the state in which we actually are. That impatience, while it stimulates us to surpass preceding generations, disposes us to overrate their happiness.

It may well be, in the twentieth century . . . the mode . . . to talk of the reign of Queen Victoria as the time when England was truly Merry England, when the rich did not grind the faces of the poor, and when the poor did not envy the splendour of the rich.

Thomas Babington Macaulay, The History of England (1848)

One way to picture the past is through images of the rise and fall of a prized way of life. These images naturally produce a sense of regret, and regret is a dangerous sentiment. While it produces empathy for the past, and so a certain insight, regret induces resignation about the present, and so a certain acceptance of its evils.

Richard Sennett, The Fall of Public Man

Winston got up and dressed himself. The indefatigable voice sang on:

> They sye tha time 'eals all things,
> They sye you can always forget;
> But the smiles an' the tears acrorss the years
> They twist my 'eart strings yet!

As he fastened the belt of his overalls he strolled across to the window. The sun must have gone down behind the houses; it was not shining in the yard any longer. The flagstones were wet as though they had just been washed, and he had the feeling that the sky had been washed too, so fresh and pale was the blue between the chimney pots. Tirelessly, the woman marched to and fro, corking and uncorking herself, singing and falling silent, and pegging out more diapers, and more and yet more.

'She's beautiful,' he murmured.

George Orwell, Nineteen Eighty-Four

The Prole Quarter [in *Nineteen Eighty-Four*] is approximately situated in 'the vague, brown coloured slums to the north and east of what had once been St Pancras Station' . . . There is a place some miles to the 'north and east' of a still existing St Pancras Station called Stoke Newington.

Stoke Newington is fairly typical of many inner-city areas . . . an increasingly *preservational* emphasis has established itself in the area over recent years … closely connected with what is often called 'gentrification' …

Patrick Wright, On Living in an Old Country

Perhaps Orwell himself was the first of these people when he moved to Islington in the 1940s. The movement really started … with the colonisation of the western side of Camden Town … Then they went steadily eastwards; across Camden, into Islington, Lower Holloway and Barnsbury: now they are working in a pincer movement south of the Thames, through New Cross, Camberwell, Clapham and Battersea.

Jonathan Raban, Soft City

The houses which the planners of the nineteen sixties so loudly decried as slums are being refitted in more ways than one … There may indeed be reggae and funk in the air, but these days there is also the quiet purring associated with consumer durables – along with the bangs and crashes of middle class self sufficiency and house renovation. The middle classes, in short, have been moving in since the late sixties, and the signs are everywhere to be seen.

Patrick Wright, On Living in an Old Country

The Victorian public lavatory, the horseshoe pub bar, the railed verandah, the Edwardian gilt shop sign, the heavy portico, even sheet-metal advertisements for cocoa and cigarettes, turn into prized antiques at the same time they are being torn down as vulgar objects in other quarters of the city … The frontiersmen want to conserve the working class past at the very moment when the working class themselves are trying to escape it.

Jonathan Raban, Soft City

The texture of poverty used to be called 'patina'. It is the appearance of old age, a kind of spurious spirituality endowed upon the art work by the passage of time … Patina is that warm, worn, safe feeling worshipped by immature materialist societies shell-shocked from progress. Post-modern collectors buy new art covered in patina for the same reason that post-modern architects build Neo-Georgian buildings, to gain a respite from the decision making processes of the present. They are literally buying second-hand time.

Waldemar Januszczak, 'Shine of Steel'

Back Alleys of Memory

10 Solitary house in the
snow, 1987 – Teresa
Watkins.

Under Troy lay seven cities
Someone dug the whole lot up again.
Are seven cities buried under London?
Is this where they sell off the bottommost remains?

Bertolt Brecht, Caledonian Market

London is essentially a modern city, in the sense it was the first great metropolis of the modern age ... The 'historic' Roman, medieval or Elizabethan periods have attracted more attention, and the tourist visiting London for the first time is often confronted with a peculiar sense of unease. He or she has been led to believe that this is an ancient city, which of course it is, and that much of its venerable past is still observable, which it isn't.

Gavin Weightman and Stephen Humphries, The Making of Modern London

The tourist trade – whose aim is to attract crowds to a particular site – historic city, beautiful view, museums, etc. – ruins the site insofar as it achieves its aims: the city, the view, the exhibits are invisible behind the tourists, who can only see one another.

Henri Lefebvre, Everyday Life in the Modern World

For those who want it, this imagined past will keep looming into view ... What looks like nothing more than a Spar supermarket redeclares itself as an eighteenth century hostelry. And underneath the green-grocers next door there are apparently cellars where the horse used to be stabled. Meanwhile those run-down and densely tenanted houses further to the east are actually four-storey town houses ... The past doesn't just endure: it displays itself against a present it actively indicts.

But at other times the connections seem more strained. Thus on the Street there is a Turkish Mosque and community centre. This is housed in a building which until recently was being used as a cinema and which was originally built as an entertainment palace with exotic domes thrown in for orientalist effect ... The point should be clear enough. People live in different worlds though they share the same locality: there is no single community or quarter.

Patrick Wright, On Living in an Old Country

There is perhaps only one place within Hackney's boundaries where all its diverse elements can be seen in combination: Ridley Road Market ... On Fridays and Saturdays, stalls line the street between the permanent booths, and between the stalls is a crush of people.

Behind those faces lie reaches of space and time, the wheat and rice fields of South Asia, the hills and olive groves of the Mediterranean, the plantations of the Caribbean, the ghettos of Poland, Russia and Germany, underemployment and poverty in shanty towns and villages; and behind the history of each individual the history of parents and grandparents and ancestors, of Atlantic crossings and slave-masters, of Turks and Greeks, Islam and Christianity and Judaism, wars of imperial conquest, wars of independence, civil wars, pogroms and persecutions, and of oppression in the British Isles, of colonialism in Ireland, of clearances and enclosures in Scotland and England.

If you pursued the chain of causes that led these people to this place, you would encapsulate much of the history of humanity and of inhumanity. If you investigated the present circumstances of their lives, you would discover much of the reality of deprivation and injustice in Britain today.

Paul Harrison, Inside the Inner City

All the world's a museum and men and women are its students.

Robert Kerr, The Gentleman's House (1864)

13 JANUARY 1987

Seven in the morning and freezing cold. Streets covered with snow. Behind me I can hear tubes rattling along the back of the house . . .

These West London streets by the railway line have gone wrong. In 1978 most of the five-storey houses near the railway line with their crumbling pillars, peeling façades and broken windows were derelict, inhabited by itinerants, immigrants, drug-heads and people not ashamed of being seen drunk in the street. On the balcony opposite a man regularly practised the bagpipes at midnight. Now the street is crammed with people who work for a living. Young men wear striped shirts and striped ties; the women wear blue jumpers with white shirts, turned up collars and noses, and pearls. They drive Renault 5s and late at night as you walk along the street, you can see them in their clean shameless basements having dinner parties and playing Trivial Pursuits on white tablecloths. Now the centre of the city is inhabited by the young rich and serviced by everyone else . . .

Hanif Kureishi, Sammy and Rosie Get Laid: The Diary

Anyone seeking refuge in a genuine, but purchased, period style house, embalms himself alive.

Theodor Adorno, Minima Moralia

One should totally and absolutely suspect anything that claims to be a return. One reason is a logical one: there is in fact no such thing as a return.

Michel Foucault, 'Space, Knowledge and Power'

How can we condemn something that is ephemeral, in transit? In the sunset of dissolution, everything is illuminated by the aura of nostalgia, even the guillotine. This ... reveals the profound moral perversity of a world that rests essentially on the nonexistence of return, for in this world everything is permitted in advance and therefore everything cynically permitted.

Milan Kundera, *The Unbearable Lightness of Being*

Behind the colour, clamour and energy of the Third World City, effaced and half-forgotten landscapes spring into life: the city grows and its people survive in ways familiar in Britain in the nineteenth century.

Bombay distracts with its grandiose fantasy architecture of the Raj, its slabs of skyscrapers, but its air is sulphurous, its waters polluted ...

Survival means having something to sell; no object however insignificant doesn't find its purchaser; no service, however demeaning, is refused. The headloaders of fruit and vegetables recall Mayhew's costers or Hogarth's shrimp-girl. In the rich areas, the beggar children cling to the clothes of passers-by, selling their poverty ...

The city sleeps early, the sleep of total exhaustion; an energy spent on earning never quite enough money to replace itself – that mirror image of the cities of the West, where the energies of the young lie dormant, unused and unwanted.

The city cries out its unacknowledged relationship with the rich world – our present and our past; its desperate insufficiency against our superfluity, and those landscapes, suppressed within us, that live on only in the pages of Booth and Mayhew and Engels in the West, but in flesh and blood and bone in the cities of the South.

Jeremy Seabrook, *Bombay*

Street as Museum

City Time

First, a long view: history from above.

Nostalgia is a product of development in the city. In peasant societies, time is predominantly cyclical, the time of the seasons, of growth and decay: the rural past is like a soil which sustains the present through recurrence and ritual. But in the urban world, time appears irreversible: a linear succession of redevelopments and changes, its past more like the rubble of a building site, bulldozed over, lost for ever. On these ruins of no return the feeling of nostalgia flourishes (cf. Foucault, Kundera, p. 39).

Troy is the classic image of this irreversible linear time. The city of Homeric legend is the prototype for Hamburg, Coventry, Stalingrad, Nagasaki, Hiroshima; a testimony to mankind's phenomenal ingenuity in destroying the things it has made. The eleven layered Troys discovered by modern archaeology also show how, in its course, the city consumes itself, each new era built on the compacted ashes of its predecessor. City development, in the Trojan model, proceeds by a series of catastrophes.

A subtle change happens to the Trojan model of development in the other great classical city of the West: Rome. The historiography Rome has inspired – renascences and reformations, declines and falls – brings cyclical time back into the time of the city. Since the Renaissance, even the relics of Empire – the broken ring of the Colosseum, the Forum's shattered walls – have been traditionally depicted covered by vegetation and in the golden light of sunset. It is as though, accompanied by the images of natural decay, the ruins of Rome contained the possibility of natural rebirth. Where Troy shows that history is catastrophic, Rome still holds up – like the seasons – the promise of return.

41

Modern London has, in many ways, taken on the mantle of Renaissance Rome, capital of a now vanished empire, living on borrowed time. It persists. It survives. But though billed as an historic capital, little remains of London's Elizabethan or medieval quarters (cf. Weightman and Humphries, p. 37): few cities can have obliterated their pasts so completely, and then gone on to idealize them so thoroughly. And, unlike either Troy or Rome, it effected this destruction with little help from invaders. Instead modern London's catastrophe arises internally, from the dynamics of its own success (cf. Stedman Jones, pp. 15–16).

History from Below

From above a repository for the collective memory of a nation, at street level, the city contains histories of a more personal, everyday kind. Individuals have a habit of spatializing time, giving their thoughts a location, a place. A walk down a street you haven't passed through for a while will prove this: a café may recall some failure at work, a line of railings a friend's secret, a corner a romantic rendezvous. We construct imaginary geographies for our lives, and in the crowded, contested space of the city, every brick is a mnemonic for someone (cf. Carlyle, p. 6).

One of the peculiarities of reminiscence in the city as distinct from the country is that its symbols are so clearly artificial and planned. What makes Fox Talbot's photograph of the construction of Nelson's Column (see illustration 2, p. 7) intriguing is that it shows how this commonplace of London life was actually manufactured, its ordinariness ordained. For most Londoners, Trafalgar Square probably evokes more memories of drunken celebrations on New Year's Eve than the famous naval victory. But although we may remain ignorant of its origin, the past still determines our horizons.

Through the titles of avenues and institutions, the vistas leading to some military cenotaph or statue, a city, especially in its official centre, is a kind of monumental propaganda – an attempt to engineer our memories (cf. Leningrad, pp. 159–62). When people talk of the 'establishment' (meaning the rigid apparatus of state), one of these urban spaces comes to mind: the Mall or Whitehall in London, the Piazza Venezia in Rome, the Brandenburg Gate in Berlin, Washington's Capitol Hill. Beside them, you can feel an anxiety of influence: the weight of all that history pressing, as Marx expressed it, like a nightmare on the brain (see p. 5). And that's exactly what its builders wanted us to feel; for whatever we project back into the past is just a dream compared

42

to what it projects forward on to us (cf. Mandelstam, pp. 123–4).

Away from the planned city centres, in deregulated commercial quarters, neon signs and shop displays also vie to be memorable. As a young child, one of my clearest recollections of the London Underground was an advertisement for Start-rite shoes, which depicted a boy and girl wearing clogs starting hand in hand down an endless path of white palings and dark conifers. The poster became for me a melancholy and (I thought) entirely private symbol for the corridor of schooldays, school terms, school years ahead. When, nearly two decades later, I discovered the image had similar resonances for others my age I was struck how, through the platforms of the London Underground, our separate childhood fears had secretly linked up. The city had provided a shared 'background', both physically and emotionally: its landmarks personal milestones. Many nursery rhymes instil these lessons of geography ('Oranges and lemons say the bells of Saint Clement's'); several sentimental songs ('Maybe it's because I'm a Londoner, that I love London Town') exploit the commonplaces of commemoration.

The past determines our horizons – the skyline is proof of that. For a Londoner of my age, the image of Big Ben, the GPO Tower, St Paul's, Tower Bridge silhouetted against the evening skies of the sixties is as poetic as any blue remembered hills. The real difference between the urban and rural idylls is the speed of desecration. Already the GPO Tower has been privatized into Telecom Tower, and for a decade now has been overshadowed by the monolith of the NatWest Tower, soon itself to be dwarfed by Canary Wharf. The city may be inhabited from below, but changed from above. As it is refashioned, our memories are restructured, and thereby our identity as citizens.

Memories of Underdevelopment

Despite the fact that London is now known as a mecca for nostalgia, just over a century ago it was nominated 'The Rome of Today', 'City of the Present'. Pre-eminent in its industrial and imperial power, the first city in the world to expand to such a size, what London manufactured (and manufactured in abundance) was modernity.

London is essentially a modern capital, a nineteenth-century construction, its main legacy an infrastructure of railways, sewers, banks, new suburbs and broad straight streets. Yet these innovations were overshadowed even in their heyday by something more archaic – back alleys, crooked buildings and culs-de-sac – in short by the labyrinthine city of Dickensian myth. Dickens was not alone in his obsession with the grotesque face of the capital: other novelists, such as Reynolds (see p. 12), were part of a widespread vogue for 'Gothic' accounts of London's underworld. But a comparison of the riverside of Dickens's youth with how it appeared after the Embankment was built (see illustrations 4 and 7, pp. 11 and 20) shows that the capital was in fact being straightened out during the Victorian era. Convoluted Gothic forms were replaced by rectilinear constructions; broad thoroughfares driven through the maze of back streets (see illustrations 5 and 6, pp. 15 and 16). Perversely, the making of modern London seems to be accompanied by a fixation with the unmaking of old London. It is as though writers, artists and their audience came out to celebrate the pre-modern city on the occasion of its funeral.

In his obsessive walks around the alleys of Seven Dials and St Giles' to Hungerford Market (see pp. 11–13), Dickens was in many ways the last to make these journeys into old London low-life. The paths he described were also paths back to his own (temporarily) impoverished boyhood, when he felt out 'on the streets' what many children still experience now in other developing cities: hunger sharpened by being so close to its relief, a lack of direction among so many people who seem to know where they are going. This is a central experience of poverty in the city. It is not the biological needs that hurt as much as the social wants, the relative deprivation, and a child feels the inequalities with a particular force. Years later, as a rich and successful writer, Dickens would keep on coming back to these scenes of destitution both in his walks and in his work. And as he paced for hours up and down the back alleys of his memory, which exercised his conscience as much as they did his legs, his progress was much like that of the city itself, remorselessly marching forward, guiltily looking back.

Dickens's biography is, in a sense, the biography of Victorian London. Disraeli also dismisses the symbols of Victorian success, the 'Bran New' districts of Marylebone and Paddington in the west, for the old parts of the City, the Inns of Court and the docks, to the east (see p. 10). This middle-class taste for 'slumming it' was, simultaneously, a fascination for poverty (cf. Forster, p. 13), and a trip to the old curiosity shop that is the past. 'Slum', after all, in contemporary usage, evoked an image less of a hotbed of crime than of a 'slumbering' suburb, a dormitory backwater left out of the mainstream of development. Thomas Beames, in the notorious 'rookery' of St Giles', notes how the unrefurbished buildings are relics of a bygone age (see p. 13). In the second-hand clothes stalls of Monmouth Street, Dickens uses the recycled rags of the poor to animate his own playful reconstructions. Today, this mixture of whimsy and squalor might be called 'deprivation chic', but the mechanism has not changed; affluence expunges the past, leaving poverty with the glamour of backwardness.

It is this nostalgia for poverty that makes Dickens's view of the city 'modern'. He expresses an attitude not so different from the New York 'retro-chic' artists of the eighties who pasted together pieces of refuse because, they maintain, only rubbish really contains a sense of time. And on Monmouth Street today, where Dickens wandered through the 'burial place of fashion', there is a boutique in which you can purchase old fifties clothing for nearly new prices. It is just one of the thousands of such second-hand clothes shops which, in the seventies and early eighties, began to transform a market catering for the poor and elderly into one for the young and hip. To a generation like mine brought up in the clinics and multi-storey car parks of the sixties, the fashion for 'Granny's Wardrobe' and 'Dead Men's Overcoats' was also an attempt to capture a sense of the past; inasmuch as cloth caps, belts, braces and a lost working-class past were the obscure objects of our nostalgia, we were Dickens's heirs (cf. Raban, Januszczak, p. 33).

Gutter Press

In a modern city, dominated by the lines of rapid transit, our sense of space becomes two-dimensional (see New York, p. 222). As commuters, we think of getting from A to B in terms of linear distances. What we forget is that every mile of the city is actually a mile squared.

A walk round the back streets can open up this extra dimension, and this in part explains their appeal. The Byzantine street patterns of the rookery have a similar attraction as the casbahs, bazaars and medinas to the western tourist of today (cf. New York, Fanon, p. 197). They allow you both to lose yourself and to hide from sight. Encounters and buildings appear suddenly round corners. You don't know quite where you're going, what you'll find. The haphazard dwellings appear to have accreted by an endless series of individual decisions, rather than to have been determined by some official plan. And the activity of the back alleys often appears more open to the visitor. Owing to the housing in such districts, and the urgency of its trade, life is more likely to be lived out on the street. For the domesticated Victorian of the mid-nineteenth century, or the young backpacker of the late twentieth, the abundance of contact in the narrow alleys, the almost promiscuous density of the crowds, can be felt as a kind of relief (cf. Himmelfarb, p. 14).

In mid-Victorian London, the image of the rookeries might have stirred the imagination, but their reality excited repression. With the advent of city planning and the Metropolitan Board of Works, the commercial street became a weapon against the slum, an excuse for surgical attack. The medical metaphor is apt. Reformers often compared the sanitary conditions of the slums with the moral state of their inhabitants. The back alleys were described in contemporary literature as 'Devil's acres', 'dark purlieus', 'sinks of iniquity', 'plague spots', 'poisoned wells'. The labouring and 'dangerous classes' were portrayed as 'deviants', or 'moral filth', the 'scum', the 'slime', the 'dregs' of humanity: the 'residuum'. This equation often led to a facile technical solution for poverty: destroy the buildings and the back alleys, clean out the filth, and the social conditions which produce it will also disappear.

Of course they didn't, and these 'improvements' more often served not to *abolish* poverty but to *remove it from sight* (cf. Beames, Dickens, *The Builder*, p. 17, Engels, p. 26). The aesthetic considerations here are paramount. Haussmann called his demolition of working-class central Paris a 'strategic beautification' (cf. Paris, pp. 104–5). The Indian Premier Indira Gandhi also pursued a policy of 'beautification' during the emergency of the seventies, fulfilling her pledge '*Garibi Hatao*' – to remove poverty – by bulldozing shanty towns and dumping beggars in the remote countryside. In modern city planning, as we shall see again and again, the aesthetic surface often conceals the ethical reality. And because redevelopment is concentrated around notions of ugliness and beauty, aversion and desire, the influence of art and fiction has been strategic.

In the clearance of London, as Gareth Stedman Jones points out, the areas most under attack were precisely those areas mythologized in the writing of Dickens and his contemporaries (p. 16). So, if the street had an impact on literature, literature also had a massive impact on the street. Perhaps this explains the implicit sense of regret in Dickens's work. For like a travel writer who spreads the news of some unspoiled and undiscovered coast, in portraying these places he also betrayed them.

Capital/Capital

Today, on the edge of New Oxford Street, on the site of what used to be the 'rookery' of St Giles', is a massive office block – Centrepoint – which, for a decade after it was built (in the late sixties), stood for the perversity of property speculation, its acres of floor space kept empty while thousands remained homeless in the capital. Even now, Centrepoint is only semi-occupied by offices, one more monument to the mass evacuation of central London which began over 150 years ago. Increasingly, as the Victorian centre became dominated by shops, offices, railroads and warehouses, and the middle classes drew up their drawbridges in the suburbs, those who built, maintained, and pro-visioned the capital – the bricklayers and labourers, the sweeps and stallholders – were exiled from residence in their own city.

The process is like a lesson in *laissez-faire* economics: bricks, property, capital amassed at the expense of labour. And as the housing stock decreased, the street was often the only remaining refuge for outcast Londoners: the place where they would work, play and – often enough – sleep (cf. Mayhew, pp. 17–18). In contrast to the upward mobility of the middle classes, a member of the 'street folk' such as 'Little Jo' (in Dickens's *Bleak House*) was faced with forced mobility, of being constantly 'moved on' by the authorities.

This redevelopment of central London along the lines of social mobility had a drastic effect on how the street, its public aspect, would be perceived. Instead of an identifiable community, Engels can see only a space for traffic and trafficking, for individual pursuits of happiness in an atomized mass (p. 18). Engels's moral vision corres-ponds to Dickens's description of the City outside Lincoln's Inn. Pedestrians are foot passengers struggling in the mud churned up by their manic scramble for success. The veil between them, the lack of cohesion or contact, is expressed by the fog. There are no courts or culs-de-sac for residence on this street. Little trade or play is now conducted on its pavements. No balladeers sing. No piemen cry. The main transactions of society take place behind the closed doors of offices and shops. The street is not to stay in but to pass hurriedly through.

The historic City – to tire of which, according to Dr Johnson, was to tire of life – is becoming a dead business centre populated by fugitive commuters: the shout in the street replaced by the roar of traffic.

Heart of Darkness

Not to abolish poverty, but to remove it from sight. This imperative informs the overall structure of modern London, indeed of any *laissez-faire* metropolis which bifurcates between east and west, centre and suburb, uptown and downtown. But the city's reputation for destitution is in itself a paradox. A metropolis is actually an accumulation of surplus food, labour, materials, a testimony to general riches if it is anything at all. Poverty in a city is not a question of production but *distribution*. To keep itself turning over, the capitalist city seems to require an axis of inequality, surplus wealth at one pole, and thereby surplus poverty at the other.

The recent gentrification of the inner city has often been described as a kind of 'colonization', and this metaphor has a long history. In the 1880s the East End became known as 'Darkest London' (after 'Darkest Africa') (cf. Booth, Sims, Mearns, pp. 22–3), making it simultaneously a source of poverty *and* exoticism, a kind of internal colony. Conrad saw a heart of darkness stretching from the London Pool to the Congo, a connection between the docks and the Empire which was more than fanciful. For, as an entrepôt, the East End was in direct contact with Britain's colonial hinterland, the main disembarkation point for large immigrant communities.

Like the Orient itself, the East End attracted explorers and missionaries. It became the object of research for urban anthropologists. Skirmishes with the natives, like the battle of Sidney Street, began to rival Rourke's Drift. But even after Bloody Sunday (cf. Stedman Jones, pp. 23–4) the West End's fears of being 'swamped', 'overrun', 'invaded' by hordes of the unwashed from the east was an inversion of the reality of conditions. It was the east which was under siege, subject as it was to a slump in employment, a decaying housing stock and rack rents. But as Edward Said shows in his study *Orientalism*, one of the classic responses of the 'West' when faced with its culpability is to blame the victim.

Appropriately, one of the most memorable figures to emerge on the streets in the 1880s was a man of analysis and observation. Picking his way through the fog, Sherlock Holmes is the epitome of the urban detective: the empiricist who makes connections, who links broken chains of cause and effect, and who, symbolically, solves the riddle of the city not in terms of collective responsibility but culpable individuals (p. 24). Holmes's methods are not so different from those of a social scientist like Charles Booth who, using data collected from school registers, took an essentially forensic approach to poverty (pp. 24–5). As it is in the Holmes stories, the key to Booth's Social Map of London is criminality (sanitation was the main metaphor for the back streets in the mid-nineteenth century; now it was replaced by crime): the personalizing of economic and social forces; the turning of conflict into a matter of one man's enterprise and the law.

The schism of London was also echoed in some of its most representative individuals. Dr Jekyll and Dorian Gray possess the same duality as the capital, split between darkness and light, vice and respectability. But the split becomes especially apparent in the legends surrounding Jack the Ripper. Two of the most popular images of the first recorded serial sexual murderer were that, by the precision of his mutilations, he was a doctor, or else a demented reformer trying to draw attention to the appalling conditions in east London. Though Jack the Ripper was essentially a blank space into which people could project anyone they didn't like, it is as if, through his legend, the victimization had been redressed. Now the professional man of the West is seen clearly as the persecutor of the 'fallen' East. Indeed, the catastrophic impact of the Jack the Ripper outrage on the Whitechapel district underscores the irony, repeating the process of demolition that occurred with St Giles' thirty years before (see p. 26).

In both his direct and indirect effect on the East End, Jack the Ripper seems to take the logic of the 'improvements' to its furthest degree. Combining the zeal of a vigilante with maniacal violence, he is the prototype for a series of urban anti-heroes who, like Travis in Martin Scorsese's *Taxi Driver*, also want to clean the 'filth off the street' using any means (see illustration 40, p. 205).

Towards a Poor Theatre

One of the problems with the genre of 'mean streets' literature which was developed in London in the nineteenth century is that it evokes a feeling *for* the underprivileged, instead of feeling *with* them. It is a small step from seeing people as objects of pity to making them the victims of it. Even Arthur Morrison's (cf. p. 26) attempt at an authentic account of childhood in an East End ghetto – *A Child of the Jago* – caused the area around Nichol Street to be demolished with no provision for its inhabitants.

In the reminiscences of Arthur Harding – a real child of the Jago – it is as much the image as the reality of poverty which he has to survive, moved out of his home because the area was, as he says, 'vilified' by

Morrison's book. On the whole, in Harding's childhood the city figures as an adventure playground: cadging a ride on the back of a tram to the exotic distance of Haggeston Banks; a friend's heroic attempt to scale Tower Bridge before a policeman pulls him off. Many of his experiences will be familiar to anyone who has spent their childhood playing in the streets: for as the underdog in the world of adults, the child nearly always feels underprivileged, economically disadvantaged in front of market stalls and shop windows, dodging rival gangs and fast traffic, lacking independence, without rights. But Harding has to come to terms with something else: the middle-class images projected on to him, the stereotype of urchin or street Arab (pp. 26–7). These he often turns around to his own use, adopting a waif-like caricature to extract coinage from the people arriving at Liverpool Street, to gain more relief from the visiting ladies from the Mission. Like the children in Bombay today, Harding had, in effect, to sell his poverty (cf. Seabrook, p. 39).

Chaplin also learnt the hard and soft sell of the streets from his childhood in south London; he used the melodrama of poverty for subversion as well as sympathy (see p. 27–8). Chaplin's is a 'streetwise' style because it implies a capacity for emotional double-takes, constantly looking over your shoulder and switching to another point of view. The Tramp is 'on the move', physically and metaphysically, swinging from sadness to brutality, high tragedy to high farce, changing masks at terrific speed. His identity is patched together from scraps of cliché, snatches of parody and romantic rags. Picked up from the street, for use on the street, the essential elements of Chaplin's 'little man', the bowler hat, the cane, the moustache, the waistcoat, are both pathetic attempts at gentility and ingenious improvisations on limited means. And always there is a sense of the audience, the public: for the Tramp's homelessness is not just a matter of lodgings or cash, but of a deeper-seated class restlessness. Unlike the country hobo, the urban 'down-and-out' is constantly having to define himself, down compared to those above him, out compared to those who are in (cf. Rhode, p. 28).

Upward mobility was the route that Chaplin himself would take, but he never regained the sense of a community, of being 'in'. Like Dickens before, we find him returning to London, rich and successful, but still hypnotized by the background from which he has escaped (pp. 29–30). Albeit more prosperous and successful, the life the self-made man builds for himself always seems more provisional than the one he is born to. The alleys of childhood are more animated and magical; they make an impression on him before he can make an impression on them. And the successful man who returns to these back alleys, alighting at the station where he once dreamt of escape, down past the shops displaying goods he never thought he would be able to afford, into his old neighbourhood, is really trying to find himself – the self he would have been – had he never walked from the back alleys of his childhood, up past the shops, into the station and away.

Down Paradise Way

Chaplin's personal history of moving out and up is an extreme version of the history of millions of Londoners who by eviction or compulsory purchase, cashing in or selling out, have also moved away from their old neighbourhoods, creating a collective compulsion to return.

Within the lifetime of an individual, nostalgia is almost as inevitable as ageing. In the hindsight of the elderly, the streets of childhood are almost bound to appear happier because they, unlike the present, had a future. But if you talk to those who have lived in the East End from the beginning of the century to today, within their regrets is also a record of real loss. Given the restricted housing, the street could become a kind of home ('in those days you could leave your front door open'), a place where children played on the pavements ('today's kids are on bikes or have gone mad'), where the young men and women could promenade ('up monkey's parade', as it was called). When these people mention their fears for today, rumours of muggings in now empty and badly lit streets, newspaper reports of old women dying alone and unnoticed in high-rise tower blocks haunt their imaginations. They testify to the loss of the street as a social space mediating between the public and the private (cf. Young and Wilmott, p. 31).

Before and after the war, it was the planners who did as much to change the face of the East End as the Luftwaffe (cf. Calder, p. 32). In place of the mean streets, the back-to-backs with their alleys and turnings, an alliance of architects, developers, and politicians began to create a futuristic landscape of lift shafts, walkways, towering slab-built blocks, surrounded by windswept swards of grass. The politics of these developments are still controversial: the tower blocks are monoliths of grey municipal socialism and totalitarian 'modernism': they are cost-cutting exercises by property sharks, corrupt contractors and unimaginative architects. But the truth really comes down to money. During the post-war baby boom, and another of London's chronic

Street as Museum

housing shortages, there was a national consensus about this rapid and cheap form of public housing.

The aesthetic impulse behind the 'skyscrapers in the park' is the subject of a later chapter (New York, pp. 223–4, 227–8), but here they appear as a new departure in 'improvements'. Hitherto, the art of architecture had been the province of the rich; the poor had to make do with the buildings vacated by the rich, or devise some shelter of their own. But in the early twentieth century architecture was for the first time *aimed* at the poor. It became, like the street clearances, a technical means of attacking insanitation, crime and social unrest.

Hitler realized the strategic importance of the East End, both in the British economy and the capital's psyche, and paid it the tribute of dropping most of his bombs on it. But if today parts of it still look like bomb-sites – its streets shattered, its communities smashed – it is as likely to be the result of the impact of planning decisions as of V2s. Given the catastrophic violence of London's development, is it any wonder whole populations appear shell-shocked, and turn to some version of their past to escape an unrecognizable present (cf. Hareven and Langenbach, p. 33)? For nostalgia is really a form of home-sickness, when longing is all that's left of belonging.

No Man's Land

The view from my window is typical of much of London: an eclectic jumble of half-finished projects, half-ruined relics, haphazard and makeshift. Looking at this scene I sometimes wonder what holds it all together.

The view is full of contradictions. Divided from an affluent and desirable 'conservation area', my flat is part of a block of two early Victorian houses, sitting over a video shop, squashed between a garage and a pub. My window looks out over the plastic roofs of new indus-trial units, across the arches of London's first suburban railway, to a fifties council tower block faced in brick, and a complex of seventies council flats. Down towards Deptford Creek a neo-Gothic flour mill that's been derelict for years has recently been clad with scaffolding. Northwards, by the river, the scene is dominated by an obsolescent power station, its yellow chimney like its four brothers in Battersea, a lost spirit of industrial optimism. Around it are some of the few cranes that still work this section of the Thames, dropping scrap into barges, but which soon will stop work for ever as the industry is relocated and the area upgraded. For like Battersea too, this power station is to be sold off, converted into a theme park, leisure centre – who knows? And beyond, over the river, is that vast post-modern theme park of the Isle of Dogs, where new cranes go up virtually every month, and skeletal skyscrapers rise to meet them. Even now as I write, they are digging the foundations for Canary Wharf, supposedly the largest redevelopment in London since the great fire, whose towers will, by 1992, cast their shadow on my window.

Given the chaos and inconsistency of this view, one can understand the need to imagine something more coherent, more continuous, to invoke some mythical 'conservation area' of the past. These houses stand in a transitional zone, lost, like erratics left behind in glacial moraine. Their brickwork changes colour where they were rebuilt after the Blitz, and I used to think it was the war that was to blame for the chaos of styles around here, the loss of continuity, until I discovered that on the site of the council flats and industrial units ahead used to be a gas works and a bottle factory, not more streets in the same style. From the beginning, these houses were built this way, speculatively, on a frontier. Old photographs of this bend in the river show a landscape constantly shifting, half-built, half-demolished, by the changing fortunes of the docks and the downwind 'stink' industries. Still older paintings show that 200 years ago this area was a few boggy meadows between the plebeian shipyards of Deptford and the Royal Palace at Greenwich. When I try to work out a past that holds all this together, the only continuous theme I can discover is a history of discontinuity.

Discontinuity may be unsettling, but it is a liberation too. It leaves gaps, inconsistencies, room to manoeuvre and rebuild. And when an old building is being knocked down I'm partly appalled, partly exhilarated. I stand rapt with the other passers-by while the iron ball slowly nudges a wall; I feel the excitement as it collapses and light breaks through the shattered masonry. Demolition changes your perspective. A new horizon opens up. Half-ruined, the buildings appear to be waiting to be finished. A fireplace hangs mid-air: wallpaper from fifty years ago flaps in the wind. In a city, you have to destroy in order to build. Who needs the familiarity of the past? We desire the strangeness of the future too. And only then, when I think about what is likely to be built; then, when I imagine the chrome office block or frictionless glass shopping mall likely to occupy this site, do I begin to feel a sense of regret. For it's not the destruction of the past that makes me nostalgic: it's the future they'll put up in its place.

Period Features

Not so long ago people used to look at the city to get a glimpse of the future. In the first half of this century, projections of what the metropolis *would become* were as much a pastime as what it *has been* is today. But history has played a trick on these Early Modern dystopias and utopias. Whether it's William Morris envisaging a forest in Trafalgar Square, or a London Transport photomontage of an overhead monorail in Regent Street, these predictions of how life would be lived now seem as dated and quaint as any historical record – as intriguing as the fact that the Black Prince used to hunt in Marylebone Forest. For the Early Moderns overestimated the rate of change – and underestimated it. They forgot the law of uneven development. They envisaged the future, like we see the past, as something continuous.

Nowhere in London is the joke of discontinuity made more evident than in the area Orwell designated as the 'Prole Quarter' in *Nineteen Eighty-Four*, the source of working-class tenacity: Islington (cf. Wright, Raban, p. 35). By 1984, Islington was *par excellence* the model of gentrification in London. The Angel, which with the Old Kent Road had once commanded one of the the lowest rents on the Monopoly board, now had the fastest-rising property prices in London; its betting shops were transformed into wine bars; its old Agricultural Hall into the Business Design Centre. Estate agents and building societies began to take over its junk shops and soon the main trade in Islington seemed to be its own desirable Georgian housing stock. The transformation of the area roughly corresponds to the growth of Camden Passage near by which, through the seventies, became one of London's largest ephemera markets. This demand for old buildings and the market for old things reflected a common desire: a whole generation, brought up in the rubble of a post-modern, post-industrial society, started doing the one thing there was left to do – buying and selling the rubble.

The ephemera markets of Islington, the stalls and shops that sell bric-à-brac and memorabilia, are only the most visible example of how much of our cities is given over to the indiscriminate resale of the past. The labours of the dead provide an ideal market equation: limited supply, inexhaustible demand. A pair of Edwardian braces, genuine turn-of-the-century matchboxes, thirties lamp stands – they can all be sold. So quick is the nostalgia business to cannibalize the past (Second World War gas masks, fifties record players, sixties chairs) that it seems to be about to swallow the present. And – whoops – so it has. One stall looks as though a bin has been emptied on it. Gift-wrapped in patina, no real use of themselves, these melancholy objects supply fantasies about their former users (cf. Januszczak, p. 35). After an hour or so of wandering through the detritus of the decades, maudlin memories begin to weigh down your dreams.

One can see a similar process happening on a larger architectural scale to whole sections of the modern metropolis: Beaubourg and La Villette in Paris; the Lower East Side in New York (cf. Paris, p. 111, New York, p. 236). The renovation of Covent Garden is London's central showpiece. What for years, like Les Halles in Paris, was the belly of London, with a dense community around its market for vegetables and fruit, is nowadays populated by sightseers and shoppers: people who have no more commitment to the area than what they carry away in their bags. In the refurbished arcades are a variety of stores, but some version of the past also adds to the sale. Out-of-work actors are hired to play Victorian flower girls. One establishment actually confesses its trade: 'Trivia'. Like the ephemera markets, these shops take the past out of its context. But here they also wall it off from the present with a showcase, then bathe it in a golden nostalgic light. These streets have transformed the vital relationship between the living and the dead into a procession of antiques.

The subject of this essay is the street as a museum, but there is a crucial difference between these streets and a museum: a museum seeks to conserve history, not renovate it; to allow the past to age with dignity. But renovation is a kind of cosmetic surgery, tightening the skin to remove the lines of experience, massaging the countenance of the past into some characterless, inane grimace. All over London, this kind of face-lift is going on. Film directors and top politicians take up residence in converted warehouses. Banks and insurance companies clothe themselves in sweatshop façades. All along the Thames, eastwards from Hays Galleria, St Katherine's Dock, Wapping, Rotherhithe to the Isle of Dogs, a forest of cranes is turning what were once some of the most deprived corners of London into some of the most desirable, making the landscapes of poverty into playgrounds, but only for those who can afford it. In this sense the heritage industry and the memorabilia phenomenon are Modernism come full circle. If the Early Moderns claimed a continuous future, the post-moderns lay claim to a permanently distanced past. In both, time, the last absolute, is made the sole arbiter of value.

More than ever London seems less intent on *making* history than in *consuming* it.

55

The Red Brick Road

If you really want to see the future of London in the making, you would do well to take a road back to the east.

The red brick road round the Isle of Dogs is the long red road of redevelopment. Laid out in the early eighties, it was the inaugural act of the new Development Corporation, and the first sign that the docks, made obsolete by the growth of containerization, were now open for another kind of business. And they soon moved in – the builders, the property speculators, to be followed by the financial headquarters spreading out from the booming square mile of the City. Soon the London marathon was run round this road: and the lean hungry joggers, like the lean hungry businesses, seemed to express not only the renovation of the Docklands, but the revitalization of the British economy. When she visited it during the 1987 election campaign, and rode on its light railway, Prime Minister Margaret Thatcher claimed it as her dream colony, her vision of what the new enterprise culture should be like. And what an urban vision that was – sandblasted brick combined with Big Bang hi-tech. The billboards hiding the marked lots showed corporate towers shimmering over the dock-water, with this legend beneath: 'Canary Wharf – It will look like Venice, but work like New York'.

The past – Venice; the future – New York. It was Docklands and its red brick road that really started me thinking that there was an intrinsic link between rapid redevelopment and the glamour of backwardness.

Like the Yellow Brick Road in *The Wizard of Oz*, the red brick road promises a future, a new start. But unlike that imaginary highway, built on a greenfields site, the red brick road is constructed on the rubble of what preceded it. So the newcomers moving in (like the ousted locals) dwell imaginatively in that past which they no longer have to live with. In the dock, a windsurfer slides past a refurbished Thames barge. Behind, derricks are kept as relics, to mourn their haggard shadows in the water, reflected in the tinted glass of software packagers, micro-vision industries and cybernetic manufacturers. Even the 'Docklands' style of post-modern architecture, with its stick-on Dayglo pediments, cornices and flutes, alludes to an antique style. About the only past that isn't parodied is the post-war council tower blocks that the remaining local population still have to live with; that, and the old black dock walls which are retained around the rich compounds for their original purpose: to keep marauding natives out.

Whatever your opinion of this vast urban 'renewal' scheme, no one can help being impressed by its phenomenal energy and shattering force. Come back in a month or so and you'll scarcely recognize the landscape: bricks, girders and glass seem to be spewed out of the ground. Beneath the whirr of the Docklands model trains, the chatter of props from the Docklands model planes, signs say DANGER: DEEP EXCAVATION or THIS IS A HARD HAT ZONE. And that's what it is, a place for hard hats, hard heads, hard cash. It's not just new building you can smell here, but the new designs, new industries, new lifestyles of a global culture. Indeed this *could* be a business district in New York, or it could be Venice. It could be Hong Kong or Bogotá. The only thing making it recognizable is its nostalgia for a vanished identity: the relics it smashes into manageable fragments, pawns and parodies and makes interchangeable with any other past.

A few miles away in the City, the foundations of a new office block have revealed a Roman amphitheatre: over the river, protesters fight to stop pilings being driven through the remains of The Rose. The deeper the impact of change, the more of the past is momentarily exposed. Compared to that upheaval, the Isle of Dogs is like an earthquake, its tremors lifting up blocks of the city's sedimentary strata. In those strata can be seen memories of previous developments, from St Giles' to Flower and Dean Street to the Blitz. In it can be traced the fault lines and fractures of so many 'improvements' of London's past which didn't succeed in *abolishing* poverty but *removing it from sight*, buried under layers of forgetfulness.

Meanwhile, the long red road of redevelopment goes on. It pretends to make progress, but it does not. Instead, it goes round and round in circles, repeating the lessons it has not learnt. As it goes on into the future, as it doubles back into the past, all of us, in some way or other, are also running this road.

PARIS
Commodities and Bodies

In this chapter the street becomes a market, not the old open market, but the advanced consumption of those commercial streets that in London, and most particularly Haussmann's Paris, began to replace the residential back alleys of the centre. The theme of this chapter is romance, both the romance of commodities and the commodity of romance as it was developed in Paris – named Capital of the Nineteenth Century by Walter Benjamin, because it led the way in developing the new language of retail, fashion and advertising. Unlike the chapter on London, 'Avenues of Desire' focuses on the richer quarters: on Paris de luxe, *that vast emporium for the* gourmand *and the connoisseur, for the* flâneur *and the* bohème, *which eventually led to the enclosure of the street in shopping malls and arcades. And behind these changes in commerce is a shift in the conventions of self-presentation on the street: fashion and self-fashioning, image and self, increasingly become a spectacle in which identities are targeted, marketed and mass produced. Finally, 'Avenues of Desire' pursues sex and consumerism to its logical conclusion – to the red-light districts where men go shopping for love.*

Avenues of Desire

Something seemed to emanate from this crowded mass of lives that made her dizzy. Her heart swelled as though the one hundred and twenty thousand palpitations beating down there had all at once discharged a vapour containing the passions she had imagined of them. Her love grew in the presence of the vast spaces spread out before her, absorbed the vague tumult which arose from the valley. She poured it out again, onto the squares, the promenades, the streets, the old Norman city looking to her eyes like some incredible metropolis, a Babylon which she was about to enter.

Gustave Flaubert, Madame Bovary (1856)

Civilisation is not merely an imitation of nature, but a process of making a total human form out of nature, and is impelled by a force . . . called *desire*.

The desire for food and shelter is not content with roots and caves: it produced the human forms of nature that we call farming and architecture. Desire is thus not a simple response to need, for an animal may need food without planting a garden to get it, nor is it a simple response to want, or desire *for* something in particular. It is neither limited to nor satisfied by objects, but is the energy that leads human society to develop its own form.

Desire in this sense is the social aspect of . . . emotion.

Northrop Frye, Anatomy of Criticism

I'm beginning to feel the drunkenness that this agitated, tumultuous life plunges you into. With such a multitude of objects passing before my eyes, I'm getting dizzy. Of all the things that strike me, there is none that holds my heart, yet all of them together disturb my feelings, so that I forget what I am and who I belong to.

Avenues of Desire

I don't know what I'm going to love from one moment to the next.

Jean-Jacques Rousseau, Julie, ou La Nouvelle Héloïse, Part II (1761)

Stage and Street

The smallest social unit is not one person, but two.

Bertolt Brecht, Brecht on Theatre

The direct, natural, and necessary relation of person to person is the *relation of man to woman* . . . From this relationship one can therefore judge man's whole level of development.

Karl Marx, Economic and Philosophic Manuscripts of 1844

Outside it is daytime. Long shot of the Boulevard du Temple . . .

The whole life of the Boulevard straggles in front of the camera . . . the throng of people, the carnival music, the cafés and theatres, the street entertainers and pretty girls, the elegant carriages, the dandies, the itinerant pedlars, the cheap open-air cookshops, the cheerful fraternity of thieves, the children's merry-go-rounds . . .

Marcel Carné and Jacques Prévert, Les Enfants du Paradis

Everything in (a village) community lends itself naturally to the indispensable preliminaries of love-making and courtship, which, however much they may be laughed at, contribute more than most things to the happiness of life. But in a great city all this is destroyed.

The street is no doubt the city substitute for the village green, and what a substitute it is!

General Booth, On Darkest London and the Way Out

FRÉDÉRICK: Oh look . . . sheep's head . . . look!

(*General shot, slightly high angle of the street from their point of view: a pretty young woman, recognizable as 'Truth', crosses the street and, smiling gaily, approaches a flower-seller whose flowers, laid out on a little cart, make a cheerful display.*)

(*Tight close shot of the* STAGE DOORKEEPER *and* FRÉDÉRICK.)

STAGE DOORKEEPER: (*Allowing himself to be convinced*) It's true, she's not bad at all! . . . a fine looking girl . . . Do you know her?

FRÉDÉRICK: (*Still staring after the* YOUNG WOMAN) No . . . Not yet . . .

(*He leaves the* STAGE DOORKEEPER *and dashes off . . . The* YOUNG WOMAN (GARANCE) *pointed out by* FRÉDÉRICK *carries on*

her way, calm and indifferent among the crowd . . . FRÉDÉRICK
appears in the background, walking fast. When he catches up with the
YOUNG WOMAN, *he passes very haughtily, without looking at her, and*
passes out of shot. The YOUNG WOMAN *walks on, without noticing . . .*
FRÉDÉRICK *turns round abruptly and retraces his steps, very much at*
his ease, to meet the YOUNG WOMAN *he has just passed. As he passes*
her again, he leans towards her, smiling broadly, and salutes her as if
they know each other. The YOUNG WOMAN *smiles and carries on*
walking through the crowd. Backwards tracking shot of the two of them
as they walk towards the camera – FRÉDÉRICK *has once again turned*
round to catch up with the YOUNG WOMAN.)

FRÉDÉRICK: (*Out of breath*) Oh, you smiled at me! Don't deny it. You
   smiled at me. Oh! It's wonderful! Life is beautiful! . . . and you
   are beautiful too . . . Oh! You are so beautiful! . . .
   (*The* YOUNG WOMAN *looks at him, smiling, but does not stop . . . He*
   gently takes her arm and tries to continue walking. She pulls away
   abruptly.)

FRÉDÉRICK: (*Taking her by the arm again*) And now, I shall never leave
   your side. (*She pulls away again.*) Where are you going?

YOUNG WOMAN: It's perfectly simple. (*Looking him straight in the eye*)
   You go in your direction, and I will go in mine.
   (*She starts to take a step forward, but* FRÉDÉRICK *leaps in front of her*
   and bars her way.)

FRÉDÉRICK: Perhaps we're going in the same direction.

YOUNG WOMAN: No . . .
   (*She tries to pass on the right.* FRÉDÉRICK *prevents her by taking a*
   step to the left.)

FRÉDÉRICK: Why not?

YOUNG WOMAN: Because I have an appointment . . .

FRÉDÉRICK: (*Playing a big tragic scene*) An appointment! Oh, tragic
   destiny . . . we've only been together for two minutes and already
   you want to leave me, and why? . . . for 'another', of course! . . .
   And, of course, you love him, don't you, this 'other man'?

YOUNG WOMAN: (*Smiling and shrugging her shoulders*) Oh, me . . . I
   love everybody!

FRÉDÉRICK: Well, then, what are we worrying about? That's perfect!
   I'm not jealous . . . But what about him, humph . . . 'the other
   man'? . . . I'm sure he's jealous!

YOUNG WOMAN: (*Smiling*) And what would you know about it?

FRÉDÉRICK: (*Peremptorily*) They all are . . . except for me.

Marcel Carné and Jacques Prévert, *Les Enfants du Paradis*   65

Men who pursue a multitude of women fit neatly into two categories. Some seek their own subjective and unchanging dream of a woman in all women. Others are prompted by a desire to possess the endless variety of the objective female world.

The obsession of the former is *lyrical*; what they seek in women is themselves, their ideal, and since an ideal is by definition something that can never be found, they are disappointed again and again . . .

The obsession of the latter is *epic*, and women see nothing the least bit touching in it: the man projects no subjective ideal on women, and since everything interests him, nothing can disappoint him.

Milan Kundera, The Unbearable Lightness of Being

GARANCE: Well, *au revoir*, Frédérick.

FRÉDÉRICK: (*Disappointed*) Don't you like me?

GARANCE: I didn't say that, but I've got an appointment.

FRÉDÉRICK: (*Put out, but carrying it off very well*) Come on Garance, you can't abandon me like that, leave me all alone in the 'Street of Many Murders' . . . at least tell me when I can see you again?

GARANCE: (*Sceptical*) Soon, perhaps? . . . who knows what chance will bring?

FRÉDÉRICK: Oh! What do you mean, chance? Paris is a big place, you know!

GARANCE: No, for those who love each other with such a *grand passion*, Paris is very small!

(*With a last smile at* FRÉDÉRICK *she turns her back and walks away. The camera pans to follow her. Cut back to* FRÉDÉRICK *in close shot: he is obviously crestfallen, but cannot repress a little smile. Shot of* GARANCE *disappearing into the crowd. Shot of* FRÉDÉRICK *watching her go.* GARANCE *is out of shot.*)

(*Suddenly a broad smile spreads over his face. Shot of a pretty young girl walking towards him. She takes* FRÉDÉRICK*'s smile as a homage to her beauty, and smiles back at him . . .* FRÉDÉRICK *rushes towards her.*)

FRÉDÉRICK: Ah! Yes, yes, you did – you smiled at me – you can't deny it . . . Life is beautiful, you smiled . . .

(*He takes the young girl by the arm and walks off with her. Both of them disappear into the crowd.*)

Marcel Carné and Jacques Prévert, Les Enfants du Paradis

To a foreigner, half an hour spent on the boulevards . . . has the effect of
an infinitely diverting theatrical performance.

Augustus Hare

Now the great function of the city is . . . to permit, indeed to encourage
and incite the greatest possible number of meetings, encounters,
challenges, between all persons, classes and groups, providing, as it
were, a stage upon which the drama of social life may be enacted, with
the actors taking their turns as spectators, and the spectators as actors.

Lewis Mumford, *Landscape*

PUBLIC ROLES IN CITIES

The problem is one of *audience* – specifically, how to arouse belief in
one's appearance among a milieu of strangers . . .

The idea that men are like actors, society like a stage, was enshrined
in the traditional school of *theatrum mundi*, because in fact this common
problem of audience has in the past frequently been solved through a
common code of believable appearances . . . In mid-18th Century Paris,
for instance, both clothes for the street and costumes for the stage
treated the body as a neutral frame, an inanimate mannequin, on which
wigs, elaborate hats, and other adornments were to be placed: the body

67

aroused interest, and the character dressing his body belief, to the extent that the body was treated as an object to be decorated.

Richard Sennett, *The Fall of Public Man*

Man is least himself when he talks in his own person. Give him a mask and he will tell the truth.

Oscar Wilde, 'The Critic as Artist: A Dialogue, Part II'

The 19th century seems to leave little room for play . . . Never had the age taken itself with more portentous seriousness. Culture ceased to be 'played'. Outward forms were no longer intended to give the appearance, the fiction, if you like, of a higher ideal mode of life.

There is no more striking symptom of the decline of the play factor than the disappearance of everything imaginative, fanciful, fantastic from men's dress after the French Revolution. Long trousers, hitherto the typical garb of peasants, fishermen, and sailors in many countries . . . suddenly became the fashion for gentlemen . . .

From then on men's dress became increasingly colourless and subject to fewer and fewer changes. The elegant gentleman of former days, resplendent in the gala dress befitting his dignity, is now the serious citizen. Sartorially speaking, he no longer plays the hero, the warrior or grandee. With his top hat he crowns himself, as it were, with the symbol of his sobriety . . . Gay colours vanish completely, and rich fabrics are replaced by some bleak and serviceable cloth of Scottish make. The tail coat, once the essential item in a gentleman's wardrobe, ended a career of many centuries by becoming the garb of waiters . . .

This levelling down and democratisation of men's fashions is far from unimportant. The whole transformation of mind and society since the French Revolution is expressed in it.

Johan Huizinga, *Homo Ludens*

Regarding the attire, the covering of the modern hero . . . does it not have a beauty and a charm of its own? . . . Is this not an attire that is needed by our epoch, suffering, and dressed up to its thin black narrow shoulders in the symbol of constant mourning?

The black suit and the frock coat not only have their political beauty as an expression of general equality, but also their poetic beauty as an expression of the public mentality – an immense cortège of undertakers, political undertakers, amorous undertakers, bourgeois undertakers. We all observe some kind of funeral.

Charles Baudelaire, *Œuvres II*

Bourgeois existence is the regime of private affairs. The more important the nature and implications of a mode of behaviour, the further it is removed from observation ... Mundane life proclaims the total subjugation of eroticism to privacy. So wooing becomes a silent, dead-serious transaction between two people alone, and this thoroughly private wooing, severed from all responsibility, is what is really new in flirting.

Walter Benjamin, 'Betting Office'

Arcadia

Paris, the French agree, is a place to drink and eat in, and to walk and talk. It is a setting for the life of *consumption*, not of accumulation.

Gillian Tindall, 'Expatriates' Paris'

[In Paris] genuine feelings are the exception: they are broken by the play of interests, crushed between the wheels of the mechanical world. Virtue is slandered here; innocence is sold here. Passions have given way to ruinous tastes and vices; everything is sublimated, is analysed, is bought and sold. It is a bazaar where everything has its price ...

Honoré de Balzac, *Scènes de la vie parisienne* (1836)

As industry expanded, it needed more and more outlets for its manufactured goods ... Cities changed from being periodic districts for market produce to permanent shopping centres selling manufactured goods. Regent Street and the Rue de Rivoli were elegantly colonnaded to protect their fashionable clients from the weather, and pedestrian shopping streets, completely roofed over with iron and glass vaulted arcades, became quite common in the larger cities.

Bill Risebero, *The Story of Western Architecture*

An arcade is a city, even a world, in miniature.

Galignani (ed.), *New Paris Guide* (1834)

Between 1830 and 1838, in the Paris of Louis-Philippe, the bourgeois monarch, the interior developed its characteristic role in consumer society as the realm of private feeling, private wish fulfilment, and private display of private life.

DECOR might provide what social revolution had failed to deliver – the possibility of each to realise his individual utopia by populating his

69

own interior world with the objects of his dreams, conveniently reproduced for him by the emerging industry of universal KITSCH.

Anthony Vidler, 'The Scenes on the Street'

The GALLERY STREET is certainly one of the most characteristic
organs of social architecture. It serves for great feasts and special
gatherings. Adorned with flowers like the most beautiful glass-houses,
decorated with the richest products of art and industry.

The first time you see it you think you are entering a fairy palace.
You find everything you could wish for here – spectacles, magnificent
buildings, promenades, fashions.

Charles Fourier

Vast and solid galleries, very well ventilated and planned with art, have
replaced those narrow, insanitary, muddy crossroads where, without
order or taste, the daily provisions for 200,000 people were heaped up.
Paris has become a manufacturing town, and the marketplace for all
the manufactures of France.

Dufey, *Mémorial d'un Parisien*

PARIS is a great market for consumption, an immense workshop, an
arena of ambition.

Baron Haussmann, *Mémoires du Baron Haussmann* (1890)

In 1852, Aristide Boucicault opened a small retail store in Paris called
Bon Marché. The store was based on three novel ideas. The markup
on each item would be small, but the volume of goods sold large. The
prices of goods would be fixed, and plainly marked. Anyone could
enter his shop and browse around, without feeling an obligation to buy.

In a market where retail prices float, sellers and buyers go through
all kinds of theatrics to up or lower the price ... In the Paris meat
markets of the 18th Century, hours could be spent on manoeuvres to
up the price of a side of beef by a few centimes.

Haggling and its attendant rituals are the most ordinary instances of
everyday theatre in a city, and of the public man as an actor ... The
stylized interplay weaves the buyer and the seller together socially: not
to participate actively is to risk losing money... Boucicault's fixed-
price system lowered the risk of not playing a role. His notion of free
entrance made passivity into a norm ...

As complement to the factory, as a product of impersonal

bureaucracy, the department store could not have succeeded without a mass of buyers . . .

Richard Sennett, *The Fall of Public Man*

How ugly Paris seems after an absence, as one suffocates in these dark humid corridors that one would rather call the streets of Paris, one thinks one is in a subterranean town, the atmosphere is so heavy, the darkness so deep. And thousands of men live, move, pass together in these liquid shadows like reptiles in a marsh.

Vicomte de Launay (1838)

After 1848 . . . Paris was about to become uninhabitable. The constant expansion of the railway network . . . accelerated traffic and an increase in the city's population. The people choked in the narrow, dirty, convoluted old streets where they remained packed because there was no other way.

Maxime du Camp, *Paris, ses organes, ses fonctions et sa vie* (1886)

Let these insanitary streets be torn down and spacious routes opened up! Let room be made for the sun in the darkest quarter; let lines be given to Paris where it feels it needs to breathe.

Louis Blanc (1842)

The Emperor was anxious to show me a map of Paris, on which one saw traced by himself, in blue, in red, in yellow and in green, according to their degree of urgency, the different new routes he proposed to have undertaken.

Baron Haussmann, *Mémoires du Baron Haussmann*

The second of December 1851 had two great victims; the Republic and Old Paris. We know today that the Republic was only wounded, but the old Paris, struck in the heart by Baron Haussmann, never rose again. Of the old picturesque city hardly anything remains save a few hotels dishonoured by advertising placards . . .

Raymond Escholier

In a space some thirty meters wide and up to two kilometers long, Haussmann concentrated the services and the circulation of the new commercial city.

Paved with new macadam, lit with the latest design of gas light, carefully planned to separate pedestrian, stroller, loiterer, ambling street vehicle, and fast moving carriage, planted with rows of trees to ensure shade in summer, provided with underground piping for rain water, sewage and gas, cleared with the aid of scientifically designed gutters, faced with the uniform height of the residences and stores of the *nouvelle bourgeoisie*, and carefully sited to point toward a monument or vista as the object of civic pride or aesthetic pleasure, the boulevard of Haussmann was in effect the . . . modern artifact par excellence.

In a very real sense, the street had become an interior.

Anthony Vidler, 'The Scenes on the Street'

The French are the first to have thoroughly understood the street and realised a concept of it which has become a model of excellence. By adding the commerce and density of the old Paris street to the greenery and spaciousness of the old boulevards, the new boulevard achieved a wholly new urban form: the perfected street, a concrete representation of urbanity itself.

Phillip Gilbert Hammerton, *Paris in Old and Present Times* (1892)

All is levelled, all is effaced, the types have disappeared, the characters have been dulled . . . The street no longer exists in Paris, and the street once dead, it is the reign of the boulevard and advent of the grand arteries.

Lacrai (ed.), *Illustrated Paris Guide* (1867)

Brief Encounters

CROWDS

It is not given to everyone to bathe in the multitude: to enjoy the crowd is an art . . .

Multitude, solitude: terms that to the active and fertile poet are equivalent and interchangeable. A person unable to people his solitude cannot know how to be alone in a busy crowd.

The poet enjoys the incomparable privilege, that he can, in his turn, be himself or someone else. Like those spirits that wander in search of a body, he enters, at his pleasure, the mind of any man.

The lone and pensive pedestrian derives a singular thrill from this universal communion . . .

What men call love is very small, very narrow and very feeble, compared to this unspeakable orgy, this holy prostitution of the soul that surrenders itself, utterly, to the unforeseen encounter, to the stranger passing.

Charles Baudelaire, Petits Poèmes en Prose

TO A PASSER-BY

The deafening street was howling round my head.
Lofty, slender, in majestic mourning black,
A woman passed, whose delicate hand
Waved and swayed the flounces of her hem;

Deftly, elegantly, with alabaster limbs.
Meanwhile, contorted like some idiot, I
Drank from the storm-clouds gathered in her eyes
The charm that enraptures, the pleasure that kills.

Lightning! Then night! – Your fugitive beauty
One glimpse of which stirred this sudden rebirth,
Will I not see you again until eternity?

Far away. On some far off day. Maybe, not at all!
Because neither of us knows where we're going to . . .
O you would have been my love (and you knew it too).

Charles Baudelaire, Les Fleurs du mal

The delight of the urban poet is love – not at first sight, but at last sight. It is the farewell forever that coincides with the moment of enchantment. This is the look . . . of the object of love which only a city-dweller experiences, which Baudelaire captured for poetry, and of which one might not infrequently say that it was spared, rather than denied, fulfilment.

Walter Benjamin, On Some Motifs in Baudelaire

What did these boulevards do to the people who came to fill them? Baudelaire shows us some of the most striking things. For lovers . . . the boulevards created a new primal scene: a space where they could be private in public, intimately together without being physically alone. Moving along the boulevard, caught up in its immense and endless flux, they could feel their love more vividly than ever as the still point of a turning world. They could display their love before the boulevard's endless parade of strangers – indeed, within a generation Paris would be famous for this sort of amorous display – and draw different forms of joy from them all. They could weave veils of fantasy around the multitude of passers-by: who were these people, where did they come from and where were they going, what did they want, whom did they love? The more they saw of others and showed themselves to others – the more they participated in the extended 'family of eyes' – the richer became their vision of themselves . . .

From this moment on, the boulevard will be as vital as the boudoir in the making of modern love.

Marshall Berman, All That is Solid Melts into Air

THE FAMILY OF EYES

We had spent a long day together, one which had seemed all too short to me . . .

In the evening, a little tired, you wanted to rest in front of a new café on the corner of one of the new boulevards, still strewn with rubble and already proudly showing its unfinished splendours. The café dazzled. The gas burnt with all the brilliance of an opening night, shining against the blinding whiteness of the walls, the glittering expanse of mirrors, the gold mouldings and the cornices . . . the nymphs and goddesses carrying fruits, pâtés and game on their head . . . all history and mythology put to the service of greed.

Right in front of us, on the pavement, stood a man of some forty years with a haggard face, a greying beard, holding a small boy by one hand, carrying a baby too young to walk in the other . . .

They were all in rags. Their three faces were extraordinarily serious, and those six wide eyes stared at the new café with equal admiration, only the nuance changing according to age.

The eyes of the father said: 'How beautiful it is! How beautiful! You'd think the gold of this whole poor world had been put in its walls.' The eyes of the little boy: 'How beautiful it is! How beautiful! Yet this place is closed to the likes of us.' – As for the eyes of the youngest, they were too fascinated to express anything but a stupid and profound joy.

Singers say pleasure softens the heart and is good for the soul. The song was right that night, or at least it was for me. I was not only touched by this family of eyes, but slightly ashamed by our glasses and carafes bigger than our thirsts. I turned my eyes to yours, my love, to read *my* thoughts there; I plunged into those beautiful and strangely soft eyes, into your green eyes, inhabited by Caprice and inspired by the Moon, when you said to me: 'Those people are unbearable, gawping with their saucer-eyes. Can't you ask the manager to tell them to go away.'

It is hard to understand, my angel, how incommunicable thoughts are, even between people in love.

Charles Baudelaire, Petits Poèmes en Prose

The boulevard cafés, often cited as triumphs of 'modern democracy' where 'a simple workman, for his thirty centimes, while having his coffee, is reflected in mirrors that Louis XIV would not have been able to procure' practised informal and effective segregation.

The Maison Dorée offered its fashionable customers special rooms facing the side streets so that they wouldn't have to mix with people who wandered in from the boulevard.

Donald Olsen, quoting César Dary in The City as a Work of Art

In Paris, it is first of all the general pattern that commands attention . . . The ever-present contrast between extreme luxury and extreme indigence, all these things are particularly striking.

Honoré de Balzac, Scènes de la vie parisienne (1836)

Why is it that, in a thriving city, the Poor are so miserable, while each such extreme distress is hardly ever experienced in those countries where there are no instances of immense wealth?

Jean-Jacques Rousseau, La Nouvelle Héloïse

Real poverty is that of cities, because it is there such a close neighbour to the excesses.

André Gide

The *laissez-faire* city is not only *founded* on social inequality: its main goal is to *intensify* it.

Franco Moretti, 'Homo Palpitans'

Window Shopping

Interpersonal relationships in big cities are distinguished by a marked preponderance of the eye over the activity of the ear.

George Simmel, 'The Metropolis'

No shop windows. Strolling, something which nations with imagination love, is not possible in Brussels. There is nothing to see, and the streets are unusable.

Charles Baudelaire, Œuvres

> Consumption can perfectly well be accomplished simply by looking.
>
> Roland Barthes, *Mythologies*

In the mid-19th Century there grew up in Paris and London, and thence in other Western capitals, a pattern of behaviour unlike what was known in London or Paris a century before, or is known in most of the non-Western world today. There grew up the notion that strangers had no right to speak to each other, and that each man possessed as a public right an invisible shield, a right to be left alone. Public behaviour was a matter of observation, of passive participation, of a certain kind of voyeurism. The 'gastronomy of eye', Balzac called it; one is open to everything, one rejects nothing *a priori* from one's purview, provided one needn't become a participant, enmeshed in a scene. This invisible wall of silence as a right meant that knowledge in public was a matter of observation – of scenes, of other men and women, of locales.

Knowledge was no longer to be produced by social intercourse.

Richard Sennett, *The Fall of Public Man*

The department store was more than a site for consumption, it was a *sight* of consumption: goods were graced with monumental splendour. Shopping was a perceptual adventure. From their beginnings, department stores were publicised as 'cathedrals' and 'palaces'. The department store surrounded practical concerns with a religious intonation, a touch of royalty, the promise that the mundane could become glamorous.

Innovators in the retail trade, new men such as R. H. Macey, Marshall Field, and John Wanamaker, built mammoth structures replete with rotundas, Grecian columns and grandiose courts where elaborate balconies and gas-lit chandeliers surrounded and dazzled their customers. As a theatre of goods, the department store combined sheer immensity with regal forms of display.

Wanamaker built a nearly life-sized replica of the Rue de la Paix in his store – 'a consolation for Americans who could not go to Paris'.

Stuart and Elisabeth Ewen, *Channels of Desire*

This extraordinary Paris with its new – I mean more and more multiplied – manifestations of luxurious and extravagant extension, grandeur and general chronic *expositionism* . . . it strikes me as a massive flower of national decadence, the biggest temple ever built to material joys and the lust of the eyes . . . It is a strange great phenomenon – with a deal of beauty still in its great expansive symmetries and perspectives – and *such* a beauty of light.

Henry James, Letter to Edward Warren (1883)

FOR SALE

For sale priceless Bodies, beyond the claim of any race, world, sex or family! Wealth piling up with each step forward! Sale of unmanageable diamonds! . . .

For sale home and migrations, sports, romances and total comforts, the noise, the movement, the future that they make.

For sale the uses of calculus and harmonic scales unheard of. New discoveries and unsuspected expressions to take home now.

A mad and limitless leap to invisible splendours, impalpable delights, each vice with its delirium of secrets, transports of abandon for the crowd.

For sale flesh, voices, wealth, vast and incontestable, what will never be sold. And the sellers are nowhere near the end of the sale! And adventurers can pay later!

Arthur Rimbaud, 'Génie'

I am a stranger to these new boulevards without turn, without incident or perspective, implacable in their straight lines, no longer feeling like the world of Balzac, but bringing to mind the American Babylon of the future.

Edmond de Goncourt, *Journals* (1851–1870)

GREAT COMPLAINT OF THE CITY OF PARIS

Ladies and gentlemen. Hear me out. This is Paris . . .

Established in . . . To Let. Awarded mentions and medals in all the exhibitions. Leasehold. In perpetuity. Wholesalers and retailers of happiness – a special reserve. Sole suppliers by appointment to a pile of majesties. Recommended. Prevents hair loss. By Lottery. Nationwide delivery. Open all year round. Purveyors of tediums, 100% free from humanity, in bulk or otherwise, catering for every occasion. Credit terms available on request, but always cash. Ah yes, my good people – cash!

And it is stocked up, import and export, by twenty stations and customs posts. In the rain, how sad the trains look. They bring for you gods, priestly robes, church furnishings, christening sweets – cults can be found on the third floor, you dumbstruck customers . . . O Chlorosis. Jewellery of the seraglio, furbelows, pocket mirrors, romances . . .

And what do they do on the other side of the world? They slave away for Paris to stock up.

Jules Laforgue, *Les Complaintes* (1885)

Man as artist is at home only in Paris.

Friedrich Nietzsche, *The Philosophy of Nietzsche*

Impressionism is an urban art, and not only because it discovers the landscape quality of the city and brings painting back from the country into the town, but because it sees the world through the eyes of the townsman and reacts to external impressions with the overstrained

12 Painting for sale in a Paris gallery window, 1987 – the author.

nerves of modern technical man. It is an urban style, because it describes the changeability, the nervous rhythm, the sudden sharp but always ephemeral impressions of city life . . .

The two basic feelings which life in such an environment produces, the feeling of being alone and unobserved, on the one hand, and the impression of roaring, incessant movement and constant variety, on the other, breed the impressionistic outlook on life in which the most subtle moods are combined with the most rapid alternation of sensation.

Arnold Hauser, The Social History of Art

As *flâneurs*, the intelligentsia came into the market-place. As they thought, to observe it – but in reality it was already to find a buyer.

Walter Benjamin, 'On Some Motifs in Baudelaire'

In the 1850s it was estimated that London had about 24,000 prostitutes but Paris, with almost half the population, was said to have 34,000 . . . Brothels always existed to cater for every class, but with time some became like department stores, offering mass produced luxury at a popular price.

Theodore Zeldin, Ambition and Love

So that she can have her shoes, she has sold her soul
But the Good Lord would laugh if, beside this whore,
I played the hypocrite, and looked at her down my nose,
I, who'd flog my thoughts, who would be an author.

Charles Baudelaire, 'Untitled Poem'

The avenue seemed unending. Hundreds of leagues ended in nothingness: the end of the road eluded him. The lanterns, lined up regularly spaced, with their short yellow flames, were the only life in this desert of deserts.

Émile Zola, The Belly of Paris (1869)

Paris is like a whore. From a distance she seems ravishing, you can't wait until you have her in your arms. And five minutes later you feel empty, disgusted with yourself. You feel tricked.

Henry Miller, The Tropic of Cancer

13 Street walker – Eugène
Atget.

Step right up, step right up! See beautiful girls! See it all! Step right up!

14 Dancers on display in front of their booth – André Brassaï.

At the spring street fair at the Place d'Italie, out of a tent bearing the sign 'Her Majesty; Woman' the girls appeared before the gathering crowd, dressed in their multicoloured pyjamas.

'Step right up, gentlemen. Unbelievably real *tableaux vivants*.' An enormously fat woman spoke in a megaphone, her voice hoarse. 'The Naked Idyll, Lesbos, the Naked Libertines, the Midnight Sun, Eve and the Snake, Diana the Huntress, and many more. Sensational, passionate, exciting. If you like flesh, if you like lovely bodies, if you like sex, you've got to see this! The best in the world.'

André Brassaï, *The Secret Paris of the 30's*

Gazing on other people's reality with curiosity, with detachment, with professionalism, the ubiquitous photographer operates as if that activity transcends class interests, as if its perspective is universal. In fact, photography first comes into its own as an extension of the eye of the middle-class *flâneur*, whose sensibility was so accurately charted by Baudelaire. The photographer is an armed version of the solitary walker reconnoitring, stalking, cruising the urban inferno, the voyeuristic stroller who discovers the city as a landscape of voluptuous extremes.

Susan Sontag, *On Photography*

Spoilt for Choice

The SPECTACLE is the moment when the commodity has attained the total occupation of social life ... the world one sees is its world ...

Guy Debord, The Society of the Spectacle

BLOOM AT THE BUTCHER'S

He halted before Dlugacz's window, staring at the hanks of sausages, polonies, black and white ... A kidney oozed bloodguts on the willow-patterned dish: the last. He stood by the nextdoor girl at the counter. Would she buy it too, calling the items from a slip in her hand ...

The porkbutcher snapped two sheets from the pile, wrapped up her prime sausages and made a red grimace.

– Now, my miss, he said.

She tendered a coin, smiling boldly, holding her thick wrist out.

– Thank you, my miss. And one shilling threepence. For you, please?

Mr Bloom pointed quickly. To catch up and walk behind her as she went slowly, behind her moving hams. Pleasant to see first thing in the morning. Hurry up, damn it. Make hay while the sun shines. She stood outside the shop in sunlight and sauntered lazily to the right ...

– Threepence, please.

His hand accepted the moist tender gland and slid it into a side-pocket. Then it fetched up three coins from his trousers' pocket and laid them on the rubber prickles ...

– Good morning, he said, moving away.

– Good morning, sir.

No sign. Gone. What matter?

James Joyce, Ulysses

It is worth remembering that Joyce insists on the fact that Bloom is an advertising agent. And advertising ... becomes an indispensable aid to modern trade precisely at the time of *Ulysses*, because of the definitive crisis of the automatic balance between supply and demand ...

> What were habitually his final meditations?
> Of some one sole unique advertisement to cause passers to stop in wonder, a poster novelty, with all extraneous accretions excluded, reduced to its simplest and most efficient terms not exceeding the span of casual vision and congruous with the velocity of modern life.

Here we find precisely the randomness, rapidity, discontinuity, uncontrollability and depth of the stream of consciousness. And these passages demonstrate that the associations of the stream of consciousness are by no means 'free'. They have a cause, a driving force, which is *outside* the individual consciousness: even syntactically, the subject of the last passage quoted is advertising: the individual psyche is only the necessary buttress of its effectiveness.

Franco Moretti, *Signs Taken for Wonders*

REJECTION

When I meet a pretty girl and beg her: 'Be so good as to come with me,' and she walks by without a word, this is what she means to say:

'You are no Duke with a famous name, no broad American with a Red Indian figure, level, brooding eyes and a skin tempered by the air of the prairies and the rivers that flow through them, you have never journeyed to the seven seas and voyaged on them wherever they may be, I don't know where. So why, pray, should a pretty girl like myself go with you?'

'You forget that no automobile swings you through the street in long thrusts: I see no gentleman escorting you in a close half-circle, pressing on your skirts from behind and murmuring blessings on your head: your breasts are well laced into your bodice, but your thighs and hips make up for that restraint; you are wearing a taffeta dress with a pleated skirt such as delighted all of us last autumn, and yet you smile – inviting mortal danger – from time to time.'

'Yes, we're both in the right, and to keep us from being irrevocably aware of it, hadn't we better go our separate way home?'

Franz Kafka, *Meditation*

The conditions of everyday social intercourse, in societies based on mass production and mass consumption, encourage an unprecedented attention to superficial impressions and images, to the point where the self becomes almost indistinguishable from its surface. Selfhood and personal identity become problematic in such societies ... When people complain of feeling inauthentic or rebel against 'role-playing', they testify to the prevailing pressure to see themselves with the eyes of strangers and to shape the self as another commodity offered up for consumption on the open market.

Christopher Lasch, *The Minimal Self*

Avenues of Desire

PUBLICITY; does not only provide an ideology of consumption – it is based on the imaginary existence of things . . . A display window in the Faubourg Saint-Honoré or a fashion show, are rhetorical happenings, a language of things.

Henri Lefebvre, Everyday Life in the Modern World

THE FETISHISM OF COMMODITIES
AND THE MYSTERY THEREOF

A commodity appears, at first sight, a very trivial thing, and easily understood. Its analysis shows that it is, in reality, a very queer thing, abounding in metaphysical subtleties and theological niceties.

15 Wig shop window –
Eugène Atget.

There is a physical relation between physical things. But it is different with commodities ... There is a definite social relation between men, that assumes in their eyes, the fantastic form of a relation between things.

Karl Marx, *Das Capital*, Vol. I (1867)

16 Corset shop window – Eugène Atget.

Avenues of Desire

UNSUITABLE SUBSTITUTES FOR THE SEXUAL OBJECT – FETISHISM

What is substituted for the sexual object is some part of the body (such as the foot or hair) which is generally very inappropriate for sexual purposes, or some inanimate object which bears an assignable relation to the person whom it replaces ... Such substitutes are with some justice likened to the fetishes in which some savages believe their gods are embodied. The situation only becomes pathological when the longing for the fetish ... actually *takes the place* of the normal aim, and, further, the fetish becomes detached from a particular individual and becomes the *sole* sexual object.

Sigmund Freud, *Three Essays on the Theory of Sexuality* (1905)

17 Edward G. Robinson gazes at a portrait – still from Fritz Lang's *Woman in the Window* (1947).

ZONE
You read the handbills the catalogues the high-pitched singing
   posters
That's poetry this morning and as for prose it's in the papers
The latest crime instalments for twenty-five centimes
Portraits of the famous and other assorted titles . . .

And now you are walking in Paris alone among the crowds
Herds of trumpeting omnibuses stampeding roundabout
And the anguish of love is choking you in
As if you will never be loved again . . .

Guillaume Apollinaire, Œuvre Poétique

Freedom is every new face, so long as it cannot speak to you. Freedom is
everyone before you who doesn't know you. Freedom is the populated
space that does not yet contract, in which you do not suffocate. You are
free as long as you do not enter other people's reckonings. You are free
wherever you are not loved.

Elias Canetti, The Human Province

The inhabitant of the great urban centres reverts to a state of savagery –
that is, of isolation. The feeling of being dependent on others, which
used to be kept alive by need, is gradually blunted in the smooth
functioning of the social mechanism.

Paul Valéry, Œuvres Complètes

Think of Baudelaire's *flâneur* and the intense society of Haussmann's
boulevards, of Toulouse-Lautrec's bars and bordellos, Degas's circus
crowds, and Seurat's bathers at Neuilly, each couple sitting separately
by the water's edge, alone and yet together, sharing civic space in the
silence of the painter's eye. In these images of civic life, loneliness and
belonging, togetherness and estrangement live cheek by jowl; every
exchanged glance, every instant of pleasure, is tinged with portents of
loss.

Michael Ignatieff, The Needs of Strangers

In the Passage de l'Opéra, [there are] so many female strollers of all
kinds . . . They are of varying ages and degrees of beauty, often vulgar,
and in a sense already depreciated, but women, truly women, palpably
women . . . so many women, in league with these arcades they stroll
along, are content to be solely women that the man who is still irresolute

and solitary in his conception of love, the man who does not yet believe in the plurality of women, the child seeking an absolute for his nights has no business in these parts. How sad it is to see those groups of flushed students jostling each other on the way to the Théâtre Moderne: once inside, how could they ever come to a decision?

Louis Aragon, Paris Peasant

A culture organised around mass consumption encourages narcissism . . .

Partly because the propaganda surrounding commodities advertises them so seductively as wish-fulfilments, but also because commodity production by its very nature replaces the world of durable objects with disposable products designed for immediate obsolescence, the consumer confronts the world as a reflection of his wishes and fears. He knows the world, moreover, largely through insubstantial images and symbols that seem to refer not so much to a palpable, solid and durable reality as to his inner psychic life, itself experienced not as an abiding sense of self but as reflections glimpsed in the mirror of his surroundings.

Christopher Lasch, The Minimal Self

BAPTISTE: Garance! Garance!

(*High angle medium shot, panning to follow* BAPTISTE *as he loses himself in the crowd. Several shots of the passers-by, some of them dressed in the* PIERROT *costume that* BAPTISTE *has made famous . . . Medium shot of* GARANCE *disappearing in the crowd while another group of* PIERROTS *confronts* BAPTISTE, *and holding each other round the waist in dance formation they bar his way.*)

BAPTISTE: (*Screaming*) Garance, Garance!

(*Medium shot of* GARANCE *who hails a cab and climbs into it. Cut back to* BAPTISTE *who hurls himself forward, thrusting his way through the crowd.*)

BAPTISTE: Garance! Garance!

(*Cut back to* GARANCE, *as seen by* BAPTISTE. *Without hearing, she gets into the carriage which immediately drives off . . .*)

BAPTISTE: Garance!

(*The camera tracks backwards, and frames him, swamped by the crowd. A group of* PIERROTS *dance in a chain around him . . .*)

(*The hubbub and music rise to a crescendo over a shot of* BAPTISTE *swamped in the crowd . . . General shot of the Boulevard, which is now being invaded by an enormous crowd, an indescribable hurly-burly of people, dominated by the white figures of hundreds of* PIERROTS, *who shout and laugh at one another, and sing and enjoy themselves.*)

Marcel Carné and Jacques Prévert, Les Enfants du Paradis

The Other Side of the Street

To be a woman is to be constantly addressed, to be constantly scrutinised, to have our desire constantly courted – in the kitchen, on the streets ... Desire is endlessly defined and stimulated. Everywhere female desire is sought, bought, packaged and consumed.

Ros Coward, *Female Desire*

18 Woman appears by her portrait – still from Fritz Lang's *Woman in the Window* (1947).

If the worker sells himself in the sense that he is selling his life by selling his time, the model is selling her time because she is selling herself.

Rosetta Brookes, 'The Night of Consumerism to the Dawn of Stimulation'

SEPARATION is the alpha and omega of the spectacle ... In the spectacle, one part of the world *represents itself* before the world and is superior to it.

Guy Debord, *The Society of the Spectacle*

THE MODELS
They are stillness in the midst of chaos ... all around them a mosaic of activity, of being, of animated expression, character, and vitality. And

89

such is the contrast between the stark stillness of these two women, the rigidity, therefore, of their bodies, the posed carriage of their spines, the composed smoothness of their almost expressionless (one might say *serene*) faces, and this sea of human variation and unpredictability behind them and around them that they themselves appear to be two-dimensional cutouts placed against a three-dimensional background . . .

But this two-dimensionality goes beyond mere posture and enters into the absence of meaning. The look of disinterest on these faces is notable. Here, certainly, along with serenity, is zero, coldness, a void where sexual feeling would lie . . . Here the idea of composure becomes literal. The perfection of the line of her shoulders, her long neck, her precisely drawn eyebrows, suggests above all that rather than a subjective soul we find here a *made object*, a *construct*. Yes, the expression of her face is impermeable, but something about her pose tells us that behind this impermeable mask would be nothing, and thus any curiosity regarding the unique identity of this being would be wasted. One looks then at her gown.

This is a gown that exists to be envied. It will be copied by other women. And this woman in her nothingness is also to be envied. For this is one of the meanings of the word 'model': a model is something we emulate. And like any model, this woman presents to us a whole set of rules for our behaviour. And these rules come to us more powerfully because they are not spoken but rather communicated implicitly through this flesh-and-blood symbol of propriety. *This is how you ought to be*, we hear. *Imitate me.*

Susan Griffin, Pornography and Silence

The spectator–buyer is meant to envy herself as she will become if she buys the product. She is meant to imagine herself transformed by the product into an object of envy for others, an envy which will then justify her loving herself.

One could put this another way: the publicity image steals her love for herself as she is, and offers it back to her for the price of the product.

John Berger, Ways of Looking

The windows slowly went by one after another. Scarves, clips, chain-bracelets, jewels for millionaires – a diamond and ruby choker, a long rope of black pearls, sapphires, emeralds, gold bracelets, bracelets made of precious stones – more modest toys, rock crystal, jade,

19 A mannequin studies its own reflection in a Paris shop window, summer 1987 – the author.

rhinestones, glass bubbles with brilliant ribbons inside them, twirling in the light, blown glass bottles, thick crystal glasses for the single rose, white and blue opaline jars, china bottles, bottles made of lacquer, gold powder-compacts, others inlaid with jewels; scent, lotions, atomizers, feather waistcoats, pale pullovers made of wool and camel hair, the frothy coolness of the underclothes, the softness, the downy softness of the housecoats in pastel shades, the richness of lamé, cloqué, brocade, gaufré, the filmy woollens frosted with metallic threads, the muted red of Hermès's window, the contrast of leather and fur in which each sets off the other, clouds of swansdown, foaming lace. And all those eyes shining with the desire to possess, the men's as well as the women's.

My eyes used to shine like that: I loved going into the shops, gazing at the flowers: through my hands there used to flow the softness of mohair and angora, the coolness of linen, the charm of lawn and the sensuous warmth of velvet . . .

91

20 Capital of Desire: Capital of Fashion, advertisement for Galeries Lafayette, Paris, 1987 – the author.

She scented the humbug: and all these pretences and subtleties tired her – in the end, indeed, they angered her. I shall finish by becoming detached from everything ... Nevertheless she stopped in front of a suède jacket of a colour without a name – the colour of mist, of time, of fairy tales.

'What a lovely thing.'

'Buy it. But that's not my present. I want to give you something wholly useless.'

'No, I don't want to buy it.'

The urge had left her already: the jacket would no longer have the same shade nor the same velvety texture once it was no longer next to the three-quarter length coat the colour of dead leaves, no longer among the smooth leather overcoats and the brilliant scarves that surrounded it in the window: it was the whole display that one coveted through each of its component objects.

Simone de Beauvoir, Les Belles Images

A capitalist society requires a culture based on images. It needs to furnish vast amounts of entertainment in order to stimulate buying and anaesthetise the injuries of class, race, and sex ... Social change is replaced by a change in images. The freedom to consume a plurality of images and goods is equated with freedom itself.

Susan Sontag, On Photography

In a simpler time, advertising merely called attention to the product and extolled its advantages. Now it manufactures a product of its own: the consumer (perpetually unsatisfied, restless, anxious, and bored).

IS YOUR JOB BORING AND MEANINGLESS?
DOES IT LEAVE YOU WITH FEELINGS OF FUTILITY? FATIGUE?
IS YOUR LIFE EMPTY?

Christopher Lasch, The Culture of Narcissism

I'm all lost in the supermarket
I can no longer shop happily
I came here for that special offer
Guaranteed Personality.

The Clash, 'Lost in the Supermarket'

Advertisements are selling us something beside consumer goods: providing us with a structure in which we, and those goods, are interchangeable, they are selling us ourselves.

Judith Williamson, Decoding Advertisements

There is a part of Montreal which is our Soho if you like, it's called the Main, Main Street, St Lawrence Street. And it's always been the cheap dream of the French Canadians, of the Quebecois people ... So, for women for instance, there was always only two endings to their lives, they would become mothers, or whores.

93

So all my characters, when they can't just be mothers or fathers . . . they go to St Lawrence Street, to the Main. Because on the Main at least you can disguise yourself . . . The only way you could forget where you came from was to disguise yourself as somebody else.

Michel Tremblay

CHORUS: The neon lights are lit. The Main is empty. All is quiet. Night falls as fast as the day began. Greta the Old crosses La Catherine as fast as she can. She goes into the five and dime. Her best set of nails has disappeared. Meanwhile, Greta the Young is blowing on her cutex. Her spidery fingers spread wide. Bambi can't get her second eye to match the first. She curses. I saw Hosanna in her window. Hosanna won't come tonight. She's too proud. But she'll spend her whole evening with her nose glued to the pane. Betty Bird has closed her pig sty. Purple has bought a new pair of stockings. Catherine the Great depilates. Big Pauline de Joilette has tried her new platform shoes, the ones with the six inch soles. Tonight. Big Pauline de Joilette will be seven feet tall. Sandra and Rose-beef are pacing outside the club.

Michel Tremblay, *Sainte Carmen of the Main*

The abolition of prostitute regulation by the police naturally didn't wipe out prostitutes. And the closing of the bordellos in 1946, sending thousands of girls out onto the streets, also led to an increase in their number, estimated to have been around a half-million at the time. The character of prostitution, however, has changed enormously.

The sexual revolution took away the younger clientele. Today, in the Quartier Latin, for example, there are practically no prostitutes at all. And the streetwalkers who are still working the sidewalks attract only the old, the ugly, the solitary, foreigners, perverts. In place of a trade whose practice was perhaps too visible, too provocative, there has gradually grown up a hidden, but nonetheless flourishing, prostitution. And more often than not in the better neighbourhoods. Today, the girls prefer to hang out in bars or cafés, where they are backed by the owners, the waiters, or the doormen and the desk clerks in the larger hotels. Some of them work out of their houses, or in places where they are tolerated by the police.

Nowadays, their main tools are the telephone, the address book, the automobile, and nude photographs of themselves in seductive poses.

André Brassaï, *The Secret Paris of the 30's*

Idris had not finished with shop windows. That evening coming from the Boulevard Bonne-Nouvelle, he had turned into the Rue Saint-Denis, and he became aware of the call and smell of sex coming up from all sides . . . *Sex Shop. Live Show. Peepshow.* These words kept on repeating themselves in flashing lights over the shop fronts. Their triple red grimace promised the young unmarried man, condemned to chastity by solitude and poverty, the satisfaction of his virile needs among showers of obscene images. He passed three small shops, and then pushed aside the doorway of the fourth. At first he thought he was in a bookshop. The walls were covered with books with garish covers and enigmatic titles. *My Wife is a Lesbian, Mixed Doubles, X Nights, Three Vestas for one Cigar, Heads with Tails, Loves, Delights and Orgasms, Woman Descends from Ape, The Hidden Face of the Moon.*

With some difficulty, Idris deciphered these words which meant nothing to him. The photos on the covers, on the other hand, displayed a brutal, puerile eroticism that spoke more of abjection and burlesque than of beauty or seduction. Yet Idris could well see what reduced the violence of these images: the more completely the anatomical details of the genitals were revealed, the less the faces appeared. In many of the photographs they were totally invisible. There was a kind of compensation on this. It seemed that by abandoning only the lower part of their bodies to the photograph, both men and women managed to deprive it of the essence of their real selves.

Michel Tournier, La Goutte d'Or

But the woman, the woman: she was completely drawn into herself, her face in her hands. It was on the corner of the rue Notre Dame des Champs. I started walking softly as soon as I saw her . . .

The street was too empty, and the tedium of its emptiness snatched my steps from under my feet, clattered up and down in them as though they were wooden clogs. Startled, the woman was drawn out of herself too suddenly, too vehemently, so that her face was left in her two hands.

I could see it lying there, its hollowed out form. It took an indescribable effort on my part to focus on those two hands, and not to look at what had been snatched out of them. Though I shuddered to see a face from the inside, I was much more afraid still of the raw, flayed, faceless head.

Rainer Maria Rilke, The Notebooks of Malte Laurids Brigge

Eye to Eye

You can't keep living in a truly beautiful city: it drives out all your yearning.

Elias Canetti, The Human Province

In Chloe, a great city, the people who move through the streets are all strangers. At each encounter, they imagine a thousand things about one another; meetings which could take place between them, conversations, surprises, caresses, bites. But no one greets anyone; eyes lock for a second, then dart away, seeking other eyes, never stopping . . .

Thus when some people happen to find themselves together, taking shelter from the rain under an arcade, or crowding beneath the awning of the bazaar, or stopping to listen to the band in the square, meetings, seductions, copulations, orgies are consummated among them without a word being exchanged, without a finger touching anything, almost without an eye raised.

Italo Calvino, Invisible Cities

What we love in human beings is the hoped-for satisfaction of our desire. We do not love their desire. If what we loved in them was their desire, then we should love them as ourself.

Simone Weil, First and Last Notebooks

To make the object one with us, we must become one with the object – ergo, *an object.*

S. T. Coleridge

In the crowd, I catch the eyes of girls – that rapid, casual, essentially urban interrogation: a glance held between a man and a woman fixes each for a moment, gives them back at least the minimal identity of their sex. The train pulls away from the platform, and she too, behind the double glass of the carriage window, but we have made each other exist for an instant; another belonging, of a kind. A big city is an encyclopaedia of sexual possibility, and the eye-language of the crowd asserts this possibility without the risk of real encounters . . . These are not invitations to an assignation. They are simply the small, reassuring services which men and women can render for each other . . .

Jonathan Raban, Soft City

The people I pass in the Avenue des Champs-Élysées appear to me like marble figures moved forward by springs. But let their eyes meet mine, and at once these walking and gazing statues become human.

Two persons, looking each other in the eye, see not their eyes but their looks.

Robert Bresson, Notes of a Cinematographer

A host of perceptions suddenly come together to form a dazzling impression (to dazzle is ultimately to prevent sight, to prevent speech): the weather, the season, the light, the boulevard, the Parisians out walking, shopping, all held within what *already* has its vocation as memory . . .

All Paris is within my grasp, without my wanting to grasp it; neither languor nor lust. I forget all the reality in Paris which exceeds its charm: history, labour, money, merchandise – all the harshness of big cities: here I see only the object of aesthetically *restrained* desire . . .

I encounter millions of bodies in my life; of these millions, I may desire some hundreds, but of these hundreds, I love only one. The other with whom I am in love designates for me the specialty of my desire.

Roland Barthes, A Lover's Discourse

Street as Market

The Magic of the Marketplace

One of the other great myths of the city – just as great as that of poverty and darkness – is that the streets offer fame and fortune to the adventurer. There he can win his booty, find his princess. Behind this myth is the fact that change and exchange are central functions of the metropolis, as it manufactures desires for a new identity, a new partner, a new future, a new life.

The analogy between bodies and commodities, romance and markets is by no means merely rhetorical. Round the market-places of the great cities, such as Covent Garden and Les Halles, other more personal services have historically been traded: entertainments, amusements, arts, sex. As these markets expanded, the terms of trade we adopt for our economic life and our other everyday social transactions become more interlocked. On the consumerist street, in the eyes of strangers, all of us in more or less obvious ways adopt clothes, styles, attitudes, manners with which to make ourselves desirable or presentable. To do this, we use these same commodities we see in the shop windows or pictured on the hoardings. One of the hallmarks of modern metropolitan markets is that they attempt to furnish not only the physical necessities, but the imaginative requirements of existence: fantasy, escapism, glamour, magic, romance.

Though we may resist the analogy between romance and commodities it doesn't seem to be able to resist us.

All the Fun of the Fair

Cities are charged with erotic potential. The street is essentially an intercourse of bodies. Pressed close on trains or buses, rubbing shoulders in queues, you are surrounded by an abundance of flesh. An appreciation of this fact need not be sexually fixated. Often, even when attention is focused on one person, it can be a celebration of the beauties of the species, an appreciation of the nape of a neck, a finger, a leg, quite apart from other notions of desirability such as wealth, style and power. In summer particularly, when status-bearing clothes are shed, and limbs appear from T-shirts, shorts and skirts, this general sensuality begins to break down our usual erotic categories. How many have admired a member of the opposite sex on such occasions, until they heard them speak? How many have desired someone momentarily from behind, only to be taken aback when they realize they have mistaken the gender?

Developed sexuality is highly specific about its object, both in terms of who is considered acceptable and what part of the body is considered erotic. But in the 'unspeakable orgy' of the crowd, as Baudelaire called it (see pp. 72–3), we can lose ourselves, our social standards, our desires for coition and possession. We become part of humankind's collective body, and experience the festive joy of this limitless life.

One of the traditional sources for the city's carnivals is the market, the street market, where buyers and sellers can meet eyeball to eyeball between trestles, with the clamour of voices and palpable abundance of goods. It is the riot of *things*, their density and visibility. At carnival time, the market has also been a place of important civic freedoms and licences, much suspected by Church and state. During fairs, when donkeys were dressed as prelates, barrow boys made 'kings for the day', the market turned the world upside down. By the nature of its bargaining and haggling, the market transmuted fixities, and showed that values were not absolute but relative.

In the street fair on the Boulevard du Temple (recreated in Carné and Prévert's *Les Enfants du Paradis*), a peepshow offers its punters glimpses of 'The Naked Truth'. But inside the booth Garance sits in a bathtub regarding herself in the mirror, with the water discreetly covering her flesh. There is no 'naked truth' in the market, but disguise, deceit, play.

The Comfort of Strangers

If the street is the urban substitute for the village green, a place of brief encounters and romantic rendezvous, it is important to notice how its mass of shifting strangers determines the conventions of courtship.

On the Boulevard du Temple, Frédérick Lemaître, aspiring actor and epic lover, spies Garance, the woman who had been playing the 'naked truth'. Ironic, hyperbolical, he hurriedly protests to her his undying love, and when that doesn't work, he tries exactly the same tactic on someone else (p. 66). With its exaggerated manners, the street appears as a stage, with men and women playing their stylized roles (cf. Mumford, Sennett, pp. 67–8). The theatrical metaphor is illuminating, for given an audience of strangers and the protagonists' uncertainty about each other, truth is a matter of external perform- ance rather than inner integrity. Street credibility is a matter of dis- play. Throughout the film, Frédérick comes to represent this spirit of play and ironic self-distance – he is a paragon of 'urbanity'. And what makes his courtship both urbane and urban is the recognition that 'Paris is a big place' (p. 68) and no matter how intense their attrac- tions are, the relation between these two passers-by is provisional, tentative, conditioned by the multiplicity of other opportunities around them, other lives, other loves. The flirtation between Frédérick and Garance is like a public act of bargaining. Their values are found in the process of negotiation, forged on the street, *among* people not *within* them.

One of the greatest critics of urbanity, its manners and *mœurs*, is Jean-Jacques Rousseau (see pp. 63–4). In his famous antithesis, love of self (*amour de soi*) is the natural instinctive sense of being and self- preservation, but selfish love (*amour-propre*) is a relative and factitious feeling that arises only in the state of society, and leads the individual to set himself above others. Thus the 'natural man' lives *in* himself, finding his way by some internal compass, whereas the metropolitan man lives *out* of himself, assessing his position from others like a radar. It is no surprise that the two places Rousseau severely condemns for their display, emulation and relativity of values are the theatre and the market. For the old market is both theatrical and urbane: the leger- demain of the street seller makes his goods like props in the hands of an actor. In the tradition of haggling, a certain amount of histrionics is vital in setting the price. In personal terms, the market, the theatre, the big city itself, are the major sources of corrupt *amour-propre*.

Beneath Rousseau's invective against the social whirlwind of the city is a distrust of the public domain. His elevation of intimate *amour de soi* effectively privatizes eroticism, making it a matter of the boudoir rather than the street, or even better, the noble savage in the solitude of a forest (cf. Benjamin, p. 69). But one of the paradoxes of making a public standard of privacy is that it leads to its violation. Like Madame Bovary, who attempts to respond to impulse rather than manners, to the spontaneity of the heart rather than the conventions of society, the more she tries to be her most intimate self the deeper the clichés of spontaneity and impulse penetrate. As one of its great explorers, Rousseau had opened up the pyschological interior, and the merchants and traders quickly followed. It is precisely these terms, 'spontaneity', 'romance', 'impulse', that the new market makers, particulary in the fashion world, sought to exploit. And as urbanity, a sense of distance between the self and its presentation in public, is increasingly lost in a favour of 'being yourself', the protective distance between inside and outside is lost.

As Danton says in Buchner's *Danton's Death*, tear off the mask and the skin comes away with it.

Les Enfants du Paradis itself seems to travel this distance between the urbane and sincere conceptions of the self: from the opening playful theatrical scenes to a more modern anxiety about the inauthenticity of the street. The film concludes with an image of its other hero, the lyrical lover Baptiste, prevented from pursuing Garance by a chain of dancing pierrots, people dressed in the costume he has made famous (p. 88). Even his appearance, his pierrot costume, has become a trap; mass marketed, the fashion equivalent of a cliché. And the crowds are no longer an audience to play to. They have become a mass that obstructs. The street is less a meeting place than a wilderness of mirrors, offering no route to erotic happiness.

Shop and Stop

As its range became too vast, its economics too important to be left to the old open market, Paris invented a new kind of urban institution to house its consumerism, the arcade (p. 70). Requiring large capital investment, built with the latest technology, the arcade is an enclosure of the open market, both literally and economically. Leased to the new luxury *négociants*, it appealed to the respectable 'client' or 'customer', and under its iron and glass the new shopper is freed from the clamour of the stallholders, their haggling and deceit. Indeed, the seller himself retreats behind shop windows, and the shopper is free to contemplate the displayed produce without the crowds pushing him on. Consumption becomes spectacle rather than theatre, a question of individual imagination rather than dialogue.

If there is an Arcadian element in the arcades it is because these *rues intérieures* reflect one of the Utopian promises of the Revolution: that it could deliver some form of heaven on earth and democratize those aristocratic pleasures once enjoyed by the few. Of course, the arcades could no more deliver universal satisfaction than they could give their commodities away gratis. But what they could offer to anyone who entered is an illusion of riches, an endless titillation of choice. The pursuit of commodities – 'shopportunities' – becomes, like the aristocratic hunt, as much part of the pleasure as the feast. And with the advent of a fixed price in Boucicault's department store Au Bon Marché (soon to be followed by stores such as Samaritaine, Printemps, Galeries Lafayette) commodities are no longer props in the hands of the vendor. Value, instead of being created directly in the act of buying and selling, is made an intrinsic property of the objects themselves (cf. Marx, pp. 84–5). Bathed in light, behind glass, for all their exotic allure what these goods conceal is that they are actually becoming more standardized.

A prophetic vision of the contradiction of the arcades is to be found in the works of the nineteenth-century Utopian Socialist, Charles Fourier. Unlike that of his fellow-visionary Saint-Simon, Fourier's ideal community – Harmony – is not devoted to production but consumption. The communal focus is the Phalanstery, an arcade-like structure which caters for the pleasures of the citizens, from sweet *compotes* (thought to combine the most satisfaction with the least effort), to matching different sexual proclivities to please every taste. But behind this confection of dreams is something more sinister. To make this Utopia work, Fourier must quantify the unquantifiable, joy; he has to calculate relentlessly the factors of desire and process them through complex mathematical equations. There is a parallel between this and the 'psychosocial' research behind the seductive launch of some new product today. For what the real arcades and shopping malls of the city share with the projected Phalanstery is that they mechanize desire, they standardize fantasy. To the extent that, in the modern consumerist dream, our instincts are also put on the assembly line, our lifestyles manufactured, our dreams and romances marketed and targeted, to that extent we still live in the arcades today.

Contraflow

Fourier's ideal community was a small one, some twelve thousand people, and Paris, whose population had in the sixty years from 1801 to 1861 tripled to 1.75 million, was not about to be made into one vast arcade. Not quite. But given the immense overcrowding in the centre, the spilling of markets into streets and the terrific congestion of its traffic, the Préfet of Paris attempted the next best thing.

Under direct orders from the Emperor Napoleon III, Baron Georges-Eugène Haussmann set about the most radical transformation of Paris ever attempted. In a typical Second Empire alliance of new finance and central government powers, he proceeded to blast miles of new streets through the historic centre of the city, to bulldoze through the often rebellious working-class quarters. And as well as providing access to this new *centre du plaisir*, Haussmann's boulevards themselves were to be a civic equivalent of the arcades, with consistent façades *à l'ordonnance*, wrought-iron street furniture and broad esplanades (see pp. 71–2). Both in appearance and financial function, they were a massive attempt in city planning to stimulate and drive desire.

It has often been asserted that the primary purpose of Haussmann's boulevards was military: to provide easy access for troops, prevent the building of barricades, allow long ranges for artillery, with *rond-points* from which they could control whole quarters. But Donald Olsen, in his recent book *The City as a Work of Art*, argues against this emphasis and instead focuses on the aesthetic beauties and economic merits of Haussmann's plan. His boulevards not only stimulated a retail boom in the Parisian economy but also provided long vistas for its promenading shoppers, each culminating in the view of a monument or spire. But these three purposes, economic, aesthetic, strategic, might be inextricably related.

What was attempted in Paris in the nineteenth century, as in London at about the same time (pp. 43–5), was the rationalization of the chaotic street plan of the old centre and, through avenues and boulevards, the imposition of a quattrocento perspective. The political content of that perspective is classically expressed in the view from the palace of Versailles. Space is possessed like property, parcelled up, regimented, made visible yet distant, subordinate to a fixed observer who stands outside the scene. And the relation between these lines of sight and military power is even more direct. David Hockney has pointed out that the development of closed perspective in painting accompanies the development of artillery. Both use trigonometry to assess ranges and distance: a line of sight can also be a line of fire. Haussmann's boulevards were an adaptation of the Versailles vantage point to a more plural and mobile society: the new Paris allowed a whole series of vistas, a whole class who could move through from one view to another. But the emphasis on the closed perspective remains. Like Baudelaire's *flâneur*, the bourgeois 'man about town' remains a voyeur, an observer of scenes rather than a participant in them. And his ability to consume the city visually, to move in and out of the old working-class faubourgs via the boulevards, presupposes that these districts can also be more effectively inspected, controlled, and if necessary, bombarded. An economic matrix, a political pattern, a strategic formula – all these are contained in that aesthetic effect.

This relation between urban planning and politics is more fully explored in the chapter on Leningrad (pp. 159–62, 167–8), but it might be worth stressing some of its contradictions here. For Paris is also a capital of revolution as well as consumption, and a decade after Haussmann started his rebuilding, those same streets of the Second Empire set the scene for the Paris Commune. Ironically, government troops actually avoided the *grands boulevards* when fighting the Communards as they found the long, straight avenues also provided ideal opportunities for the sniper: the lines of sight work both ways. But what is more curious is that Paris, at the end of the previous century, should have given rise to the Revolution at all.

Apart from Leningrad, few other Western capitals exhibit such monarchical structure; the long view down the Champs-Élysées past La Place de la Concorde to the Louvre seems to epitomize the vista of absolute kingship. But by making its power lines so visible, the French monarchy was also enfranchising its subjects with the same view. Virtually anyone could stand along that line and, for a moment, visually command the city, feel king for a day. For a brief while in the nineteenth century, before they were taken over by corporate headquarters and banks, the Champs-Élysées themselves, crowded with popular amusements and *marchands de luxe*, cheap hairdressers and theatre shows, did seem to contain this promise of democracy in an entirely different urban form.

Street Beat

The effect of these boulevards on the codes of courtship and self-display is shown in the works of that first great lyric poet of the modern city, claimed as the forerunner of Dada and surrealism, the first beatnik, the first punk on the street: Baudelaire. Hitherto, the novel seemed to be the main literary form of the city, requiring its printing technology, large readership, and reflecting the vastness and diversity of its social form. With Balzac and Hugo, as with Dickens, narrative seems best fit to capture the picaresque adventures, the interweaving destinies of individuals, the life of different quarters and classes. But instead of the vast objective canvas of the epic, Baudelaire's Paris seems best expressed in the subjective lyricism of his *Spleen et Idéal*, or his *Petits Poèmes en Prose*, which combine reportage with intense inwardness.

What may not immediately be apparent, but is striking when one compares his streets with those in Hugo and Balzac, is the absence of the crowd. But as Benjamin points out, though they are nowhere described in his work, crowds permeate it, just as wind determines a sail. The crowd has accelerated, become less an identifiable community than an amorphous mass, a blur, exerting its pressure on the inner pace and rhythm ('To a Passer-by', p. 73). In courtship, instead of being an audience to play to, the crowd is the force that carries away the beloved, that makes her into an elusive ideal. Many modern urban love stories revolve around this conflict between the one and the many, in which, among the vast numbers of citizens, love at first sight is likely to be love at last sight. But distance breeds idealism. Through their unconsummated eye language the lovers are free to fantasize about each other and the lives they would have led together. In place of the desire for the present object, the concrete affirmable flesh, the urban lover seems to be possessed by the more burning desire for the absent object which can remain in the imagination without the dangers of disillusion.

The difference between Baudelaire's brief encounter as a *flâneur* and Frédérick's casual courting of Garance is nearly identical to the shift from the open market to the arcade. Both shopper and lover now posit an invisible wall of silence, the right to remain undisturbed in reverie (cf. Sennett, Ewen, p. 76). This intrusion of commercial spectacle into emotional life is made evident in Baudelaire's prose poem 'The Family of Eyes' (see pp. 74–5) when, having walked all day, Baudelaire and his companion stop to rest in one of the new cafés opening up on Haussmann's boulevards. The famed Parisian café, which allows a kind of dual consumption, both to eat and watch, to sample the cuisine and enjoy the sights, adds to the romance of 'being in love in Paris'. To intensify and sustain their passion the lovers have to *be seen* to be in love, and in the café window the very publicity of their intimacy makes their desire desirable. Love isn't a performance, it's a pose. And it requires its captive spectators. As a poor family come to admire and envy the glittering world of these lovers, it becomes apparent that the happiness of one is at the expense of another.

Baudelaire's prose poem shows how consumption – of romance as well as commodities – is necessarily based on making inequalities visible, as one half of the world represents itself to the other, and is held superior to it. Haussmann's new avenues were to stir up a tremendous tension between the imaginary availability of their riches and romances, and their real ownership, tensions that would explode again with revolutionary fervour in the Commune.

Such tensions are a crucial part of the modern commercial metropolis, and sometimes the juxtapositions it makes seem obscene: a hoarding for five-figure sports cars in a run-down neighbourhood, an advertisement showing long female legs in a subway where a woman has been raped. But that is the function of the spectacle: to stimulate desire and dissatisfaction. The shop windows vaunt their wares so shamelessly, they incite an attitude of smash and grab. In the early eighties, many town centres in Britain experienced copy-cat riots, of which the majority were in fact more a confirmation of, rather than a rebellion against, market values. In the provincial town where I lived at the time, I remember young lads stalking the shopping centre and the market square, eyeing the sleek stereos in the window displays, pressing close against that brittle convention of glass which stands between consumerism and looting.

Personal Services

By leading the way in the style of appearances Paris gained the reputation of being the international centre of *haute couture*, where fashion suppliers such as Worth would attract a worldwide clientele who, if not in possession of an aristocratic pedigree, could buy the look of one. Paradoxically, the era of *Paris de luxe* also attracted a quite different kind of tourist: the *bohèmes* of Montmartre and Montparnasse, the struggling artist in his or her atelier in the Latin Quarter. Paris in the Belle Époque provided all kinds of markets, and not least in poetry and the visual arts. Toulouse-Lautrec painted posters for the Moulin Rouge. And in this image-conscious city there was always a grey area between fashion, advertising, commercial and salon art, inhabited by what today would be called, in the ad-man's jargon, 'style-formers, opinion-leaders, trend-setters'.

Yet there is another reason why Paris, for all its chic, could embrace artists with less pecuniary motives. Despite Haussmann's dishousing, it could still accommodate the aesthetic of the Bohemian life in its remaining backwaters, the celebrated *vie du quartier*. One thing stands out which seems particularly Parisian in this respect – an obsession with prostitution (cf. illustration 13, p. 80). In the hot-spots of Paris, the streetwalker and the Bohemian stroller seem to share (at least in the latter's eyes) some kind of identity. This is a running theme from Baudelaire, Verlaine and Rimbaud, to Brassaï, Miller and Prévert in the thirties (cf. Brassaï, p. 94). Often the association was thought to be a protest against bourgeois values of possession, propriety and mono-gamy. But early on Baudelaire makes a more profound comment about the affinity of the artist and the whore: how can he condemn her for selling her body when he is trying to sell his soul (see p. 79)? In Paris the writer, the painter and the photographer, like the subculture of pimps, prostitutes and drug peddlers which fascinated them, were also in the business of trafficking in dreams, of peddling romances to their customers.

Empire of Eyes

Paris's style was international, the commercialism of its boulevards a model for city development for metropolises as diverse as Brussels and Chicago, Vienna and Edinburgh, Berlin and Washington. In fact few Western city centres would be free from the impact of the arcades and the department stores which it developed. And this sophisticated spectacle of images, in the diverse forms of entertainment, advertising and retail, sums up the bright lights of modernity.

The profusion of images on the street has deep repercussions on the language of our loves and lusts. We see a leg, we assess it in relation to other legs. We check its taste and refinement by its shoes. We compare that leg with the other giant legs on the posters or shop windows near by. We go on to construct the desirability of its owner within the whole economy of legs, their scarcity, their style. So deeply is the art of commerce embedded in our notions of desire, that it seems to have invaded our dreams.

The street, with its shop signs, has always had an oneiric quality: the barber's pole being a dream condensation of his blood and bandages, the chemist's giant pestle and mortar a dream displacement. But in modern advertising and marketing the images are both more verisimilar and more fantastical. Dismembered parts of bodies are posted up which seem to bear only oblique relation to the products they are trying to sell, from financial services to CDs. The city, if we looked closely at its film posters, mannequins and hoardings, would seem to make a nightmarish appeal to our weirdest wish fulfilments. With its truncated torsos and strange associations, giant cigarette packets towering over desert islands or skyscrapers, mechanical legs doing the can-can above a shop display, the visual vocabulary of the modern city may be best described as surreal (cf. Leningrad, pp. 162–3, New York, pp. 222–3).

Leopold Bloom, in his Bloom's day in Dublin, is one of the most striking embodiments of this surreal, fragmented urban consciousness, as well as being probably the first ad-man hero in literature (p. 82). The so-called 'free association' of his thoughts is no more free than the free market of a society busily selling itself to itself. During the hallucinatory Nighttown episode in Dublin's red-light district, Bloom even sees a bar of soap rise like the sun over the city, singing: 'We're a capital couple Bloom and I/He brightens the earth, I polish the sky.' This is the apotheosis of the new technique of 'branding' in which ordinary products, such as processed hog fat (i.e. soap), are magically given an identity or supernatural attributes.

If advertising seduces us into seeing objects as people, it also tends to make us see people as objects. Bloom's sexuality is not just a natural appetite for flesh. When he sees the woman customer at Dluglacz the butcher's, and licks his lips at her 'moving hams', his materialism is more akin to the dicta of the trade journal, 'Sell the sizzle, not the steak', than to straight hunger or lust. The image is savoured more than the thing itself: a part of a woman – which is merely a sign of her sexuality – is taken for the whole (cf. illustrations 15 and 16, pp. 84 and 85). This way of seeing others, spurred on by the language of advertising, not only sells them short; it also offers no real satisfaction (cf. Freud, p. 86).

The buying and selling which, as Dennis Potter has said, used once to stop at the street now goes on inside your head.

Free Choice

The city thrives on the belief in free choice. Like some vast department store, it offers us a new partner, a new identity, a new life. But in promoting happiness as a series of limitless futures, the city also conceals the actual cost. For free choice lies behind the anxiety of modern love in cities. The characteristic *Angst* of the advertising age is not the unavailability of the beloved, but the sense that by selecting one partner you are missing out on the rest. How can any individual romance live up to its endless images? With so many possibilities vaunted everywhere, how can you ever make a choice (cf. Kafka, p. 83, Aragon, pp. 87–8)?

Free choice: the notion, in the new consumer theology, has been extended to so many aspects of the self, society and politics that it has become the modern equivalent of the scholastic justification of free will. But free will implies that you have capacity to *do* what you want, not *have* what you want. Choice is not free if it depends on how much you have in your pocket. Even then, the freedom to choose is impeded by what is on offer. In America most homes have at least two televisions, each able to tune into dozens of stations, all of which show basically the same thing. About the only real freedom you have is not to choose at all. Besides, the notion itself is a contradiction in terms, a trick, for every choice has its cost, implies a loss, and thereby a constraint of freedom (cf. Canetti, p. 87). The 'free' in free choice is as deceptive as the 'free' in free market: it no longer means that people are free to enter and leave the market, but that it is free to enter and leave them.

Model Citizens

Today few are free from the attention of the market, but women – either as buyers and sellers – have historically been a special target of the image industry. On the streets they are expected both to desire and be desirable, exploited by the market and encouraged to exploit themselves (cf. Brookes, Coward, p. 89).

Until recently, the freedom of the city was predominantly a male prerogative: a woman 'on the street' was either destitute or a whore. For the middle-class *femme d'intérieur*, caged in the domestic space, shopping provided most of the rare excursions into the public domain. Thus, acquisition could become one of a woman's few imaginative outlets – a fact manipulated by the market as a box of chocolates comes to represent magic, a scarf spontaneity, a perfume mystery. But since these commodities can never bring the benefits they promise, the pleasure of purchase is rapidly succeeded by some kind of 'post-consumption *tristesse*'. One of the few ways of staving off impending dissatisfaction is to quickly go and buy something else.

Simone de Beauvoir's heroine in *Les Belles Images* follows the logic of the shop windows to its conclusion, and realizes that to capture the fairy-tale romance of the windows, you would have to take home everything in them (p. 93). Indeed, why bother? Why not live in the shop window itself? For just as the window's displays are often designed to represent ideal interiors, so the home itself aspires to become an ideal showroom. Buying the right furniture, the right clothes, the right lifestyle, aspiring to emulate the 'beautiful people' with their beautiful interiors, who hasn't, even at the most intimate moments, sensed that he is being regarded, assessed? It is as though, our emotional lives having been turned inside out, we do indeed inhabit showrooms, a glass wall between us and the street, with the whole world looking on (cf. New York, pp. 225, 227–8).

Women have had both to buy and be bought on the street, and their experience becomes increasingly the norm for everyone when personality rather than skill, appearance rather than performance becomes a larger part of work as well as play (cf. Lasch, The Clash, Williamson, p. 93). Susan Griffin, in her discussion of *The Models* (see pp. 89–90), shows how this experience of visibility determines self-presentation. Women constantly photographed, constantly gazed at, don't assume a mask (which implies it can be taken off) but an *attitude*. The attitude is of disengagement, of a certain kind of flatness. These models are themselves beginning to resemble mannequins. Of course, as we aspire to live in shop windows, we are bound to become mannequins. And it's not that the mannequins are necessarily more still and composed than we are. Fashions, styles, attitudes and platitudes change. On today's posters they can be more acrobatic, more carefree or even more dissolute – but always *more*: the one necessary attribute of the mannequins, they must always be better, in order to incite dissatisfaction and demand. Thus the Frankenstinas with spiky hair, and, increasingly, the Frankensteins in Italian suits, their legs smoother, their muscles harder, have always the same look in their eyes: one which says *you can look at us, but we can see straight through you* (see illustration 19, p. 91).

Any visitor from outer space, seeing the brightly lit shop windows the mannequins inhabit, might think that our cities are made for them and not us. They all live in the world of light; and we alone stand lingering here, our noses to the plate glass, seeing our shabby selves reflected back; they seem to be the masters now. Science fiction writers once imagined our cities being overrun by robots, but who would have foreseen the rule of the mannequins? We worship our creations as if they created us. They now occupy the spaces vacated by the gods.

The Combat Zone

Where once were the crowds and street cries of the market of Les Halles, today you can find the Forum, a glittering underground arcade of boutiques. Its concourses are filled with a quiet hush of strangers who ignore one another in favour of the displays behind the thick plate glass. A few hundred metres away, in the former working-class area of Beaubourg, the square has been converted to a playground for that global consumer, the tourist. Like Covent Garden, its London counterpart, the piazza around the Centre Pompidou (itself a repository of images) has a residual theatre: hypnotists, clowns, hawkers and magicians peddle their wares. But even the theatre is increasingly like a spectacle, and the last time I was there, the largest crowds gathered round a group of young Arab men performing robotics, copying slow-motion filmic effects to the accompaniment of taped electronic music. Heirs to the tradition of Baptiste Debureau, they imitated not the expressive slow movements of street mime, but the hydraulic mechanics of high tech. And with their blank, expressionless faces they resembled less robots than mannequins.

Cool, distance, self-control are particular stretgies of resistance in the modern city (cf. Warhol, p. 210). Study the eye language in a place like the métro, its cursory glances and fixed stares, and the faces of men and women who are used to being looked at are aloof, frozen, unmoved. Outside the Beaubourg centre, watching these men making marionettes out of their own bodies, I'm undecided whether robotics is a parody of modern self-fashioning or an extreme emulation, counter-culture aspiring to become shop-counter culture. It even seems ridiculous looking for deeper significances in designer phenomena like these: they are 'fun', they 'look good' – and that's all. Indeed, the term 'designer', which ten years ago started with a fad for the conspicuous sporting of brand names – Lacoste, Yves St-Laurent, Gucci, Fiorucci – now extends over such a range of image-making, from graphics to film, that it seems to mean precisely the opposite of labelling: *de-*signed, the image is sundered from its significance: the aesthetic floats free, purged of any ethical content.

A logical route leads from the glitter of these arcades to the red light districts of the city. Given the ultimate, enervating banality of the consumer scene, the desire for the *ob*scene, beyond the spectacle, beyond illusion, is a reaction against the market as much as its extension.

In Amsterdam prostitutes actually sit in shop windows, and the porn shops on the Boulevard St-Denis still try to hawk 'the naked truth' just as they did on the Boulevard du Temple in the days of Frédérick Lemaître (cf. Tournier, p. 95). Pornography represents the ultimate attempt to go behind the mask, to unveil and probe the deepest intimacies. Not only does it offer the secrets of sex without the risk of real contact, but the violent insights of hard-core porn can be seen as a kind of perverse attempt to strip away the images that colonize our inner lives, to tear off the veil of culture, to find the 'natural', the authentic, the real thing, the *vrai de vrai*, in the extremity of pain or orgasm. Of course, the more we eschew the artifices of appearance for our deeper selves, the more we expose our privacy to assault. I suspect that even the obscenities of the peepshows, the strip clubs, the massage parlours and the magazines, with their poses and role reversals, are still less a promiscuity of bodies than a promiscuity of images (cf. Tremblay, p. 94).

Tear away the mask, and the skin comes away with it; nothing is left but a raw faceless head (cf. Rilke, p. 95).

Narcissus in the City

It has been said that the problem of urban life today is narcissism. The city is like a vain wilderness of mirrors, a massive campaign of self-congratulation. Our problem, it is said, is that we have come to love ourselves too much. But the fact of the matter is that, when Narcissus fell in love with his reflection in the water, he wasn't being vain – he didn't know it was himself; he thought it was someone else. So Narcissus's problem wasn't that he loved himself too much, but that he didn't realize his image belonged to him. In short, he didn't love himself enough.

The main argument of this chapter has been to show that it is not self-regard itself which vitiates our public lives in the city, but the way it is elevated and set up against us. Increasingly on the street, instead of individuals *presenting* themselves through images, the images increasingly *represent* them. The production of images is not to blame, but the fact that their production is no longer ours. Instead they are reproduced by a vast and powerful image industry, an international closed market, with the means of representation monopolized by the few. Self-regard has been taken out of our hands and, as Berger says, sold back to us for the price of the product (see p. 90).

So when it is said that the modern city is a place of excessive desire, of everyone wanting too much, I begin to wonder whether the same formula might not apply. Watching while the crowds mill outside the shop windows, trying to recapture magic, glamour, romance with a new shirt, a box of chocolates, a porn magazine, maybe our problem isn't that we desire too much – maybe we don't desire enough.

LENINGRAD
Crowds and Monuments and Power

Between the back alleys of memory and the avenues of desire, between the city's historical poverty and its possible riches, a growing antagonism exists. When all other channels of political exchange fail, the street becomes the only forum to redress these differences. 'Crossroads' is about this – the political dimension of our public urban spaces, a dimension which extends from the everyday power plays of individuals asserting their rights of way, through the protests and placards of massed demonstrations, to barricades, urban guerrillas and civil guards. Set in pre-revolutionary St Petersburg, it shows the personal politics of the pavement as a generation of poor clerks experience an illusion of freedom on the Nevsky Prospect, only to be tripped up by the feudal inertia that underlies it. The chapter then follows the individual demonstrations of these 'underground men' to the collective actions of 1905 and 1917. Throughout, beneath these historical currents, it also looks at the more general conflict between the flux of the urban crowd, and the hard monumental structures of the city, which both provoke and rebuff demands for social change.

Crossroads

And whoever becomes ruler of a city accustomed to living freely and does not destroy it, let him expect to be destroyed by her, because as refuge for her rebellious sons she always has the name of liberty and her old customs, which neither through the length of time nor for any good deed will be forgotten.

Niccolò Machiavelli, The Prince

The place itself, the Place Louis Quinze, the Place de la Révolution – had given him a sensible emotion from the day he arrived: he had recognised so quickly its tremendous historic character . . . The great legend of the French Revolution, a sunrise out of a sea of blood, was more real to him here than anywhere else; and, strangely, what was most present was not its turpitude and horror, but its magnificent energy, the spirit of creation that had been in it, not the spirit of destruction . . .

Henry James, The Ambassadors (1883)

Universal history is born in the cities and comes of age at the moment of the decisive victory of city over the country. Marx considered it one of the greatest revolutionary merits of the bourgeoisie that 'it subjected the village to the city', *itself* an emancipation.

But if the history of the city is the history of liberty, it is also the history of tyranny, of state administration which controls the country and city itself.

Guy Debord, The Society of the Spectacle

Petersburg is more original than all American cities because it is a new city in an old country, consequently it is a new hope; the marvellous hope of this country.

Vissarion Belinsky

Moscow – ancient, Slavic, with its Kremlin and its ring of walled monasteries at the periphery, the rest consisting of private homesteads, complete with vegetable gardens, service structures, and domestic animals – had the appearance of an overgrown village, where streets had to go round the private lots, with no municipal restrictions, and often led nowhere.

St Petersburg – preplanned, classical, with aligned streets, stone palaces, clearly zoned districts, and the Winter Palace dominating the space at the intersection of its three main radials – is essentially a Western aristocratic city, the centre of a vast governmental bureaucracy, its principal streets connecting the various regimental quarters to the palace to facilitate quick military action.

Lazar El Lissitsky, *An Architecture for World Revolution*

There is an entire series of utopias or projects for governing territory that developed on the premise that a state is like a large city; the capital is like its main square; the roads are like its streets. A state will be well organised when a system of policing as tight and efficient as that of the cities extends over the entire territory. At the outset, the notion of police applied only to the set of regulations that were to assure the tranquility of a city, but at that moment the police became the very *type* of rationality for the government of the whole territory. The model of the city became the matrix for the regulations that apply to a whole state.

Michel Foucault, 'Space, Knowledge and Power'

The Fabric of Dreams

Petersburg is not half what I expected – I had thought of it as much more beautiful, magnificent, and it seems people have been spreading false rumours about it ... everything seems to be crushed under a great weight, everyone is drowned in the trivial meaningless labours at which he spends his useless life.

Nikolai Gogol, *Diary*, 1828

I remember once on a wintry January evening I was hurrying home from the Vyborg side. I was still very young then. When I reached the Neva, I stopped for a minute and threw a piercing glance along the river into the smoky, frostily dim distance, which had already turned crimson with the last purple of a sunset that was dying out on the hazy horizon. Night lay over the city ...

Frozen steam poured from tired houses, from running people. The taut air quivered at the slightest sound, and columns of smoke like giants rose from all the roofs on both embankments and rushed upward through the cold sky, turning and entwining on the way, so that it seemed new buildings were rising above the old ones, a new city was forming in the air . . .

It seemed, finally, that this whole world with its inhabitants, strong and weak, with all their domiciles, the shelters of the poor or gilded mansions, resembled at this twilight hour a fantastic, magic vision, a dream which would in its turn vanish immediately and rise up as steam toward the dark blue sky.

I suppose that my existence began from just that minute . . .

Fyodor Dostoevsky, 'Petersburg Visions'

Beyond the bridge, against the background of St Isaacs, a crag rose out of the murk. Extending a heavy patinated hand, the enigmatic horseman loomed . . .

21 Equestrian statue of Peter the Great, Leningrad.

From that fecund time when the metallic horseman had galloped hither, when he had flung his steed upon the Finnish granite, Russia was divided in two. Divided in two as well were the destinies of the fatherland. Suffering and weeping, Russia was divided in two, until the final hour.

Andrei Belyi, Petersburg (1916)

The Tzar, riding up a rocky slope, has his face turned to the Neva, and points with his right hand towards the scene of his labours. The horse is balanced on its hind-legs and tail, while its hoofs trample on a writhing snake. The statue is 16½ft. high. The sculptor *E. M. Falconet* (1716–91) made the model in 1769 and supervised the work of casting it (1775) . . . The monument was unveiled in August 7, 1782, and cost 425,000 rb.

Karl Baedeker, Russia: A Handbook for Travellers

Pushkin is in the same measure the creator of the *image* of Petersburg as Peter the Great was the builder of the city itself.

N. P. Antsiferov, Dusha Petersburga

THE POOR CLERK AND THE BRONZE TSAR

Evgeny trembled. And his thoughts became
Terribly clear to him. He *knew* this place
Here, where the flood had swept, and rapacious waves
Had rioted around; he knew the lions,
The square, and the silent figure which still
Held its bronze head high in the gloom,
Him whose fateful will had established
This city on the sea . . . How awful he seemed
Wrapped round in mists! What thoughts were engraved
Upon his brow. What force concealed within!
And in that steed, what fire! Where are you charging,
Imperious steed? Where will you plant your feet?
You, who mastered destiny with force! Was it not
Thus that you rode to the brink of the precipice,
And reared up Russia with an iron rein?

Around the pedestal the poor clerk prowled
And cast his frantic glances up toward
That icon of the lord of half the world.
Chest tightening, pressing his forehead against

The cold iron railings with clouded eyes,
Flames flickered in his heart and his blood boiled.
Darkly he confronted the statue, his teeth
Clenched together, his knuckles white, possessed
With spite and shaking with rage he hissed:
'All right then, wonder-worker, just you wait!'
And then started in a sudden headlong flight,

For at that moment it seemed that the bronze head
Of the long dead Tsar, stirred with wrath, began
Soundlessly turning . . . Through the empty square
He plunges and behind him – like a crash
Of thunder – he hears the metallic clang
Of hooves pounding the pavement at a gallop.
And in the pallid moonlight, an arm thrust out,
The dark mass of the Bronze Horseman bears
Down upon Evgeny with all its weight.
And all night long, wherever the poor clerk turns
The hammering hooves of the Horseman follow.

Aleksandr Pushkin, *The Bronze Horseman* (1833)

Petersburg . . . is the touchstone of a man; whoever, living in it, has not
been carried away by the whirlpool of phantom life, has managed to
keep both heart and soul but not at the expense of common sense, to
preserve his human dignity without falling into quixoticism – to him
you can boldly extend your hand as to a man.

Vissarion Belinsky

As it turned out, I spent my early childhood in Petersburg under the
sign of the most authentic militarism, but it was really not my fault: it
was the fault of my nurse and the Petersburg streets of that period.

And I say now, without a moment's hesitation, that at the age of
seven and eight all this – the whole massif of Petersburg, the granite
and wood-paved quarters, all the gentle heart of the city with its
overflow of squares, its shaggy parks, its islands of monuments, the
caryatids of the Hermitage . . . but especially the General Staff Arch,
the Senate Square, and all Dutch Petersburg I regarded as something
sacred and festive . . .

The Petersburg street awakened in me a craving for spectacle, and
the very architecture of the city inspired me with a kind of childish
imperialism . . . All this mass of militarism and even a kind of police

aesthetics may very well have been proper to some son of a corps commander with the appropriate family traditions, but it was completely out of keeping with the kitchen fumes of a middle-class apartment, to father's study, heavy with the odours of leather, kidskin and calfskin, or to Jewish conversations about business.

Osip Mandelstam, The Noise of Time (1925)

What means does civilisation employ in order to inhibit the aggressiveness which opposes it, to make it harmless, to get rid of it perhaps? . . . This we can study in the history of the development of the individual. What happens in him to render his desire for aggression innocuous? His aggressiveness is introjected, internalised; it is in point of fact, sent back to where it came from – that is directed towards his own ego . . . in the form of conscience.

Civilisation, therefore, obtains mastery over the individual's dangerous desire for aggression by weakening and disarming it and by setting up an agency within him to watch over it, like a garrison in a conquered city.

Sigmund Freud, Civilisation and its Discontents

Pedestrian Power

God! One could write a whole book about encounters on the Nevsky Prospekt alone!

Fyodor Dostoevsky, Collected Prose

The 17th Century State encroached upon festive life and turned it into a *Parade* . . .

Mikhail Bakhtin, Rabelais and his World

In the new city, or in the formal additions made to old centres, the buildings form a setting for the avenue, and the avenue is essentially a parade ground . . . The buildings stand on each side, stiff and uniform, like soldiers at attention: the uniform soldiers march down the avenue, erect, formalized, repetitive: a classic building in motion. The spectator remains fixed. Life marches before him, without his leave, without his assistance: he may use his eyes, but if he wants to open his mouth or leave his place, he had better ask permission first.

Lewis Mumford, The City in History

Nothing is finer than the Nevsky Prospect, at least not in Petersburg . . .

22 Nevsky Prospect,
Leningrad, today.

The Nevsky Prospect is the universal means of communication in
Petersburg . . . The only promenade that is a place of recreation for the
poor. No directory or information bureau will furnish such correct
information as the Nevsky. How cleanly swept are its pavements, and
how many feet have left their marks on them! The clumsy dirty
jackboot of the retired soldier beneath whose weight the very granite
seems to crack; the miniature slipper, light as smoke, of the young lady
who turns her head to the dazzling shop window like a sunflower to the
sun; the hopeful ensign's rattling sabre that draws a sharp scratch over
its surface – everything is marked on it by the power of strength or the
power of weakness.

Nikolai Gogol, 'Nevsky Prospect' (1835)

NEVSKI PROSPEKT is 115 ft. wide and 2¾ M. long . . . the longest
street in Petersburg. From the admiralty it runs in a straight line [to]
Znamenskaya Square where it trends slightly to the S. and runs
through a poorer quarter to the Alexander Nevski Monastery . . . it is
the busiest street in St Petersburg.

Karl Baedeker, *Russia: A Handbook for Travellers*

A GIRL SMILES AT PISHKAREV

The pavement rushed away beneath him, the carriages with their galloping horses seemed motionless, the bridge stretched out and broke in the middle of its arch, a house stood upside down, a sentry box toppled towards him, and the sentry's halberd, together with the golden letters of a shop-sign and a pair of scissors painted on it, seemed to glitter on the very lash of his eye.

Nikolai Gogol, 'Nevsky Prospect'

Nearly one-tenth of the male population of St Petersburg wear some kind of uniform, including not only the numerous military officers, but civil officials, and even students, schoolboys and others.

Karl Baedeker, *Russia: A Handbook for Travellers*

The harmony of uniformity; the absence of variety, of what is personal, whimsical, and wayward: the obligatory wearing of uniform, and out-ward good form – all develop to the highest degree in the most inhuman condition in which men live – in barracks. Uniforms and uniformity are passionately loved by despotism. Nowhere are fashions so respectfully observed as in Petersburg, and that shows the immaturity of our civilisation: our clothes are alien.

In Europe people dress, but we dress up, and are so frightened if a sleeve is too full, or a collar too narrow. In Paris all that people are afraid of is being dressed without taste: in London all they are afraid of is catching a cold; in Italy everyone dresses as he likes. If one were to show him the battalions of exactly similar, tightly buttoned frock coats on the fops of the Nevsky Prospect, an Englishmen would mistake them for a squad of 'policemen'.

Alexander Herzen, *My Past and Thoughts* (1869)

LIEUTENANT PIROGOV

He was very pleased with his rank, to which he had only recently been promoted ... once when he came across a copyist clerk in the street who seemed rude to him, he immediately stopped him and made him see in a few curt words that he had a lieutenant to deal with and nothing less – he tried to express this, and more eloquently, because at this moment two rather good-looking young ladies were passing.

Nikolai Gogol, 'Nevsky Prospect'

Here, in a typically offhand way, Gogol shows us what will become of the primal scene in Petersburg literature and life: the confrontation between officer and clerk. The officer, representative of Russia's ruling class, demands from the clerk a quality of respect that he wouldn't dream of giving in return ... The clerk promenading in the Prospect has escaped from the 'official' sector of Petersburg, near the Neva and the palace, dominated by the *Bronze Horseman*, only to be trampled by a miniature but malign reproduction of the Tsar even in the city's freest space. Lieutenant Pirogov, in reducing the clerk to submission, forces him to recognise the limitations of the freedom that the Nevsky confers. Its modern fluidity and mobility turn out to be an illusory display, a dazzling screen for autocratic power. The men and women out on the Nevsky might forget Russian politics – indeed, this was part of the joy of being there – but Russian politics was not about to forget them.

Marshall Berman, All That is Solid Melts into Air

... Russian Society ... contains within it, fresh forces seething and bursting to break out; but crushed by heavy repression and unable to escape, they produce gloom, bitter depression, apathy.

Only in literature, in spite of a Tartar censorship, is there still some life and forward movement ... That is why the writer's calling enjoys such respect among us ... The public ... sees in Russian writers its only leaders, defenders, and saviours from dark autocracy ...

Ivan Turgenev, Open Letter to Gogol, 15 July 1847

THE POOR CLERK DREAMS

But really, one does get ideas sometimes, and I wonder what would happen if I just sat down and wrote something? ... Just suppose for one minute that a book has been published. You pick it up and it says *Poems*, by Makar Devushkin! I can tell you one thing for sure, my dear: if that book were published, I'd never dare show myself on the Nevsky Prospect again ...

What, for instance would I do about my shoes then? Because, as perhaps you know, my shoes have been patched many times, and the soles tend to break away sometimes, which is a very unseemly sight. So what would happen if everybody realised that Devushkin, the author, had patched shoes? Suppose some duchess or countess noticed this, what would the dear lady say about me?

Fyodor Dostoevsky, 'Poor Folk' (1845)

In the medieval town the upper classes and lower classes had jostled together on the street, in the market place, as they did in the cathedrals ... Now, with the development of the wide avenue, the dissociation between the upper and lower classes achieves form in the city itself. The rich drive: the poor walk. The rich roll along the axis of the grand avenue ... The rich swagger; the poor gape.

Lewis Mumford, The City in History

I walked incognito down Nevsky Prospect. His Imperial Majesty drove past. Every single person doffed his hat, and I followed suit. However, I didn't let out that I was the King of Spain. I considered it improper to reveal my true identity right there in the middle of the crowd, because, according to etiquette, I should first be presented at court. So far, the only thing that had stopped me was not having any royal clothes. If only I could get hold of a cloak ...

Nikolai Gogol, 'Diary of a Madman' (1834)

Do you know what a dreamer is, gentlemen? It is a Petersburg night-mare ... On the street he walks with his head hung low, paying little attention to those around him, sometimes here forgetting reality: but if he notices anything, then even the most ordinary everyday trifle, the most empty routine matter, immediately assumes for him fantastic colouring. His glance is already attuned to see the fantastic in every-thing ... And is not such a life a tragedy! ... Is it not a sin and a horror! Is it not a caricature? And aren't we all more or less dreamers?

Fyodor Dostoevsky, 'A Petersburg Dreamer'

A CLERK DARES TO HIRE A CARRIAGE

As soon as the blue carriage had passed through the gates, Mr Golyad-kin rubbed his hands feverishly together and dissolved into inaudible laughter, like a wag of a fellow who had brought off a fabulous joke with which he is as pleased as punch. Immediately after this access of mirth, however, the laughter in Mr Golyadkin's face changed into a strangely anxious expression ... At the corner of the Nevsky Prospect and Liteiny Street, he started at a most unpleasant sensation ... A pair of dashing Kazan horses, very well known to Mr Golyadin, harnessed to a smart droshky, were rapidly overtaking his carriage on the right ... The gentleman in the droshky was Andrey Philipovitch, head of the section of the Department where Mr Golyadkin was also a member of staff ... Mr Golyadkin, seeing that Andrey Philipovitch had recog-nised him beyond doubt ... blushed to the roots of his hair. 'Ought I to bow? Should I speak to him or not? Ought I to acknowledge our acquaintance?' our hero wondered in indescribable anguish. 'Or shall I pretend it's not me but someone who looks like me, and look as if nothing's the matter?' said Mr Golyadkin, lifting his head to Andrey Philipovitch and not taking his eyes off him.

'I . . . It's all right,' he whispered, hardly able to speak, 'It's quite all right; this is not me at all, Andrey Philipovitch, it's not me at all, not me, and that's all about it.'

Fyodor Dostoevsky, *The Double* (1846)

In *The Double* the timid little man had been frightened by imperial Petersburg, which watches him with its vigilant eye and encircles him with mysterious forces. This is what drives him mad. Dostoevsky's hero had a predecessor with Pushkin's 'poor Yevgeni', who is chased by bronze Peter, symbol of the relentless and vengeful autocracy . . . The system of Nicholas I, with its oppressions and terrors, in fact produced many real persecution manias.

Leonid Grossman, *Dostoevsky: A Life*

In front of him, about fifteen yards away, the small black figure of a man hastening towards him was again visible. The man was hurrying, scurrying, almost running; the distance between them rapidly decreased. Mr Golyadkin was even able to examine the new belated passer-by closely – and when he did so, he exclaimed aloud in horrified bewilderment; his knees shook . . . There was, indeed, good reason for him to be so upset. The fact was that the unknown now seemed to him to be somehow familiar . . .

Mr Golyadkin turned the corner of Liteiny Street. His situation at that moment was like that of a man standing above a terrible chasm when the ground has begun to break away . . . Mr Golyadkin had recognised his nocturnal acquaintance. Mr Golyadkin's was none other than himself, Mr Golyadkin himself, another Mr Golyadkin, but exactly the same as himself – in short, in every respect what is called his double.

Fyodor Dostoevsky, *The Double*

After the uprising of 14th December 1825 the political police in Russia . . . were reorganised and reinforced. Informing was widespread and continued to increase and become more sophisticated until, on the threshold of the revolution of 1848, it had reached an incredible scale.

Leonid Grossman, *Dostoevsky: A Life*

What kind of man was Lopukhov? This is the kind of man he was. He was walking in the Kameny-Ostrovsky Prospect in a ragged uniform . . . Towards him comes a dignitary, taking a constitutional, and, like a dignitary, comes straight at him without moving aside. At that time Lopukhov practised the rule 'Except in the case of women, I will not move aside first for anyone.' They banged into each other's shoulders.

The individual, making a half-turn said, 'What's the matter with you, pig? Cattle!' and was about to continue in this tone, but Lopukhov turned fully toward the individual, picked him up bodily, and deposited him very carefully into the gutter. He stood over him and said: 'If you make a move, I'll push you in further.' Two peasants passed by, looked, and praised him. A functionary passed by, looked, did not praise, but smiled broadly . . .

Lopukhov stood for a while, then picked up the individual again – this time not bodily, but by the hand – raised him, drew him up the sidewalk and said 'Alas, dear sir, what have you done? I hope you did not hurt yourself. Will you permit me to wipe you off?' A peasant passed and helped to wipe him off, two townspeople passed and helped to wipe him off, they all wiped the individual and went their ways.

Nikolai Chernyshevsky, What is to be Done? (1863)

Independence and Dependence of Self-Consciousness Master and Servant

SELF-CONSCIOUSNESS EXISTS IN ITSELF AND FOR ITSELF, in that, and by the fact that it exists for another self-consciousness, that is to say , it *is* only by being acknowledged or 'recognised'.

G. W. F. Hegel, Phenomenology of Spirit (1807)

THE CLERK IS IGNORED BY AN OFFICER

Those people . . . who can avenge their wrongs and generally stand up for themselves – how do they do it? . . .

Oh, if only that officer had been the sort who would consent to fight a duel! But no, he was one of those gentlemen (long vanished, alas), who preferred to act with billiard cues or, like Gogol's Lieutenant Pirogov, through the authorities . . .

After the incident with the officer I was even more strongly drawn to the Nevsky Prospect; it was there that I met him most often, there I feasted my eyes on him. He also went there chiefly on holidays. Although he too moved aside for generals and important personages, and wriggled past them like an eel, he simply trampled over nobodies of my sort, or even better than my sort; he bore straight down on them as though there was a clear space in front of him, and never in any circumstances gave way . . .

It was a torture to me that even on the street I could not manage to be his equal. 'Why are you invariably the first to give way?' I nagged at myself sometimes, hysterical with rage, when I woke up at three o'clock in the morning. 'Why is it always you, not him? There's no law about it, is there? Nothing on the statute books?'

'What,' I thought, 'if I were to meet him and not step aside? Deliberately refuse to step aside, even if it meant running into him? What about that, eh?' This audacious notion took possession of me bit by bit, to such an extent that it gave me no peace. I dreamed of it, ceaselessly and vividly, and on purpose went oftener to the Nevsky Prospect, so that I could more clearly picture to myself how I would act when the time came. I was full of enthusiasm . . . I began a gradual approach to the deed itself. After all, I couldn't just decide on the spur of the moment and at the first opportunity . . . Once, when I had definitely made up my mind I ended up by simply falling under his feet, because my courage failed me in the very last second, when I was only about two inches away from him . . .

Suddenly, three paces away from my adversary, I unexpectedly made up my mind, scowled fiercely and . . . our shoulders came squarely into collision. I did not yield an inch, but walked past on an exactly equal footing! He did not even glance round, and pretended he had not noticed; but he was only pretending, I am certain of that. I am certain of it to this day!

Of course, I was the greatest sufferer, since he was the stronger, but that was not the point. The point was that I had attained my object, upheld my dignity, not yielded an inch, and publicly placed myself on an equal footing with him.

Fyodor Dostoevsky, Notes from the Underground (1864)

Man, to be really, truly 'man', and to know that he is such, must, therefore, impose the idea that he has of himself on beings other than himself: he must be recognised by the others (in the ideal, extreme case, by all others).

Alexander Kojève, Lectures on Hegel

Vox Populi: Vox Dei

CITIZEN

This public person, so formed by the union of all other persons, formerly took the name of *city* ... The real meaning of this word [citizen] has almost been wholly lost in modern times; most people mistake a town for a city. They do not know that houses make a town, but citizens a city.

Jean-Jacques Rousseau, The Social Contract (1762)

Meng-tse's (Mencius') thesis that the people's voice is 'God's voice' has a very specific meaning: if the people cease to recognise the ruler, it is expressly stated that he simply becomes a private citizen; and if he wishes to become more, he becomes a usurper deserving punishment.

Max Weber, The Sociology of Charismatic Power

A PARTICIPANT REMEMBERS THE FIRST STUDENT DEMONSTRATION

A sight like it had never been seen. It was a wonderful September day [in 1862] ... In the streets the girls, who were just beginning to go to university, joined in, together with a number of young *raznochintsy* [*déclassé* intellectuals] who knew us or merely agreed with us ... When we approached the Nevsky Prospect, the French barbers came out of their shops, and their faces lit up, and they waved their arms cheerfully, shouting *'Revolution! Revolution!'*

Quoted in Franco Venturi, The Roots of Revolution

In certain epochs, events occur which herald the coming of great historical changes, of great expectations and triumphs for humanity. At these points everything moves with a quickened pace. An air of vigour and power seems to pervade the social atmosphere ... It is as though an electric current were galvanising the whole society, uniting the feelings of temperamentally different individuals into one common sentiment, forging totally different minds and wills into one.

At such times the individual is brimful of confidence and courage because his feelings are reciprocated and heightened by the emotion of his common men. Citing but a few examples from modern history, such was the period at the end of the eighteenth century, the eve of the French Revolution. So also, but to a considerably lesser extent, were the years preceding the revolution of 1848. And such, I believe, is the character of our present era, which may be the prelude to events which will perhaps outshine the glorious days of 1789 and 1793.

M. A. Bakunin, 'The Revolutionary Temper and its Matrix'

At first sight, there is much that is still normal; things run smoothly, judges judge, the churches are open, the stock exchange hums with activity, armies manoeuvre, palaces blaze with light, but the soul of life has fled, everyone is uneasy at heart, death is at our elbow, and, in reality, nothing goes well. In reality there is no church, no army, no government, no judiciary. Everything has become the police. The police is guarding and saving Europe, under its protection stand thrones and altar. It is the galvanic current by which life is being unnaturally kept going in order to gain the present moment. But the consuming fire of the disease is not extinguished, it has only been driven inward, it has been concealed . . .

All those blackened walls and monuments which seem to have acquired with age the everlasting quality of rocks – are insecure.

Alexander Herzen, Letters from Another Shore

III

In those years the terrible dawn
had scarcely shown red in the East . . .
The Petersburg mob was drawn
to gawp at the tsar like a beast.
And, huge and blubby, the tsar
drives past with all his family . . .

Wherever you turn, the wind's a knife
at your ribs . . . 'It's a terrible life' –
avoiding a puddle – you mutter;
a dog gets under your feet,
light glitters on a spy's galoshes,
an acid smell blows from each back-street,
and the rag-and-bone man shouts 'Old dresses!'
And meeting a stranger's stare,
you would like to spit in his face
if only you didn't notice
the same expression there . . .

IV

But, crimson streaked, behind the ships
the day was already dawning,
and already the pennant tips
were waking to the winds of the morning,
and the measureless dawn already
was pointing a bloody finger
towards Tsushima and Port-Arthur
towards the ninth of January . . .

Alexander Blok, 'Retribution – 1881'

23 Alexander II assassinated by a bomb – engraving.

Yes. Reality is incomprehensible and abhorrent, but there is always the hope that it is nothing but a filthy covering behind which is a high mystery . . . Perhaps it is possible . . . at the very bottom of the 'abyss', to enter into a similar communion with the same external power which, itself beyond good and evil, yet promises to whirl man away from all hard decisions, troublesome rules, hesitations and anxieties . . .

It may even be, finally (Blok's third period) that the squall of revolution, whose approach can already be sensed, will, on closer inspection, turn out to be the onset of that very divine dance of the violent, wild and primitive element which is destined to burst like lava through the prosaic, boring crust of everyday life.

Anatoly Lunacharsky, First People's Commissar of Education

Dionysiac excitation is capable of communicating to a whole multitude the artistic power to feel itself surrounded by, and at one with, a host of spirits . . . what we have here is the individual effacing himself through entering a strange being. It should be made clear that this pheno-menon is not singular but epidemic: a whole crowd becomes rapt in this manner.

Friedrich Nietzsche, *The Birth of Tragedy*

While individualism lay on its death bed, the remorseless grip of capitalism was, against its own will, re-creating the collective, com-pressing the proletariat into a solid moral force . . . To individualists the emergence of this force seems a dark storm-cloud on the horizon. It frightens them in the same degree as the death of the body does, for them this force spells social death.

Maxim Gorky, 'The Disintegration of Personality'

Petersburg is surrounded by a ring of many-chimneyed factories. A many-thousand swarm plods towards them in the morning, and the suburbs are all aswarm. All the factories were then in a state of terrible unrest. The workers had changed into prating shady types . . .

24 Petrograd: construction of the Palace Bridge and factory smoke from the Vyborg side – engraving, Anna Ostroumova-Lebedeva (1919).

135

The agitation that ringed Petersburg then began penetrating to the very centres of Petersburg. It first seized the islands, then crossed the Liteiny and Nicolaevsky Bridges. On Nevsky Prospect circulated a human myriapod. However the composition of the myriapod kept changing; and an observer could now note the appearance of a shaggy black fur hat from the fields of blood-stained Manchuria [soldiers demobilized from the Russo-Japanese War]. There was a sharp drop in the percentage of passing top hats. Now were heard the disturbing antigovernment cries of street urchins running at full tilt from the railway station to the Admiralty waving gutter rags.

Such were the days. Have you ever slipped off at night into the vacant plots of city outskirts to hear the same importunate note, 'oo'? Oooo-oooo-ooo: such was the sound of that space. But was it a sound? It was the sound of some other world. And it attained a rare strength and clarity. 'Oooo-oooo-ooo' . . . But no factory whistle blew; there was no wind; and the dogs remained silent.

Have you heard the October song: of the year nineteen hundred and five?

Andrei Belyi, *Petersburg*

1905
Demonstrations and meetings. Took part in them. That was good. Thought of participants pictorially. Anarchists in black. Social-Revolutionaries in red. Social-Democrats in blue. Federalists in other colours.

Socialism – Speeches. Newspapers. Demand from them all un-familiar words and ideas. Demand from myself explanations. In shop windows, pamphlets . . . Lassalle appealed to me. Must have been because he had no beard. Young. Confused Lassalle with Demosthenes.

Vladimir Mayakovsky, *I Myself*

Spring has entered its full season. The snow yields to the rays of the sun and forms into rushing streams.

The pressure of water seeking escape has broken up the icy crust of the river, which threatens every moment to burst its banks – a sequence of shots.

In the factory yard, filled with striking workers – a meeting . . .

None of the administrative staff, no soldiers . . .

An earlier strike attempt has failed. Now, the attempt succeeds . . .

Vsevolod Pudovkin, *Mother*

25 *Meeting* – linocut,
Vladimir Kozlinsky (1919).

The peculiarity of the [1905] Russian revolution is that it was a
bourgeois democratic revolution in its social content, but a *proletarian*
revolution in its methods of struggle.

Vladimir Ilich Lenin, 'Lecture on the 1905 Revolution', January 1917

137

A special type of crowd is created by refusal . . . In our own time the best example of a negative, or prohibition crowd is the *strike* . . . The moment of standstill is a great moment, and has been celebrated in workers' songs. There are many things that contribute to the workers' feeling of relief at the start of a strike . . . It is as though their hands have all dropped at exactly the same moment and now they had to exert all their strength *not* to lift them again, however hungry their families. Stopping work makes all the workers equal. Their concrete demands are actually of less importance than the effect of this moment . . . Pickets guard the entrances to the place where the strike started, and the workplace itself is forbidden ground. The interdict on it lifts it out of its everyday triviality and endows it with special dignity. In its emptiness and stillness it has something sacred . . .

There is something deeply serious and worthy of respect about such an organisation and, when the ferocity and destructiveness of crowds are mentioned, one cannot help remembering the responsibility and dignity of these structures springing spontaneously from crowds.

Elias Canetti, *Crowds and Power*

Inside the building hung a saffron murk, illuminated by candles. Nothing could be seen here but bodies, bodies, and more bodies: bent, half-arched, bent hardly at all, and not bent. Bodies were sitting and standing everywhere. They occupied the tiers of seats running round the amphitheatre, and the lecture podium could not be seen.

'Oooo-oooo-ooo.' A humming filled the space of the hall and through the 'ooo' sometimes was heard:

'Revolution . . . Evolution . . . Proletariat . . . Strike . . .' Again 'Strike . . .' Yet again: 'Strike . . .'

And more humming.

Andrei Belyi, *Petersburg*

It is terrifying to think that our life is a tale without a plot or hero, made up out of desolation and gloom, out of the feverish babble of constant digressions, out of the delirium of the Petersburg influenza . . . Are you familiar with this condition? When it's just as if every object were running a fever, when they are all joyously excited and ill: banners in the street, posters shedding their skin, grand pianos thronging at the depot like an intelligent, leaderless herd, born for frenzies of the sonata and for boiled water . . .

Osip Mandelstam, 'The Egyptian Stamp' (1928)

The demonstration moves through the open factory gates into the street . . .

At the other end of the street, an old acquaintance – the policeman on duty – watches the demonstration as it moves through the gates . . .

He experiences a brief struggle between duty and fear for his own skin – and his majestic tread gradually changes to a jog trot, then to a run, at full speed, all his old fat policeman's dignity lost.

People pour into the street from houses on every side. Some join the demonstration. Some, the timid, stay close to their doors . . . and look on in alarm.

Getting ever larger and larger, the demonstration moves on.

Vsevelod Pudovkin, *Mother*

The Revolution cast the rugged idiom of the millions out on to the the the streets: the slang of the outer suburbs flowed across the avenues to the city centre: the enervated burbling of the intelligentsia . . . – all this kind of talk, once mouthed in the restaurants has been wiped out. A new element of language has been liberated.

Vladimir Mayakovsky, *How are Verses to be Made?*

Earlier poets were read, but Mayakovsky writes for an imaginary assembled throng of listeners. By their very nature his poems are appeals to a crowd . . . He is a poet-brawler, a poet-screamer, a street poet, a public poet – that's what I particularly like about him. It would be silly to call him a writer – his calling is not writing, but yelling. His medium isn't paper, but his own throat – which is natural for a poet of the Revolution. He is Isaiah in the guise of a hooligan. The thousand-voiced roar of today's revolutionary streets emerges from his throat, and is it his fault if he is as vulgar as a mother oath, as simple as a pistol-shot? Street language must be fierce, scandalous, sensational. You have to strike the street dumb to get its attention. It needs fireworks and monstrously stunning words. He is a man of the street and the meeting, all for the crowd, he is himself a crowd.

Korney Chukovsky, 'Akhmatova and Mayakovsky'

NEVSKY PROSPECT

All the shoulders formed a viscous and slowly flowing sediment. The shoulder of Alexander Ivanovitch stuck to the sediment, and was, so to speak, sucked in. In keeping with the laws of the organic wholeness of the body, he followed the shoulder and was thus cast out onto the Nevsky . . .

There the body of each individual that streams onto the pavement becomes the organ of a general body ... Individual thought was sucked into the cerebration of the myriapod being that moved along the Nevsky ... And wordlessly they stared at the myriad legs; and the sediment crawled. It crawled by and shuffled on flowing feet; the sticky sediment was composed of individual segments; and each individual segment was a torso.

Andrei Belyi, *Petersburg*

THE ATTRIBUTES OF THE CROWD

1. *The crowd always wants to grow* ... There are no institutions which can be absolutely relied on to prevent the growth of the crowd once and for all.

2. *Within the crowd there is equality* ... A head is a head, an arm is an arm, and the differences between individual heads and arms are irrelevant ... All demands for justice and all theories of equality ultimately derive their quality, ultimately derive their energy from the actual experience of equality familiar to anyone who has been part of the crowd ...

4. *The crowd needs a direction* ... Direction is essential for the continuing existence of the crowd. Its constant fear of disintegration means that it will accept *any* goal. A crowd exists so long as it has an unattained goal.

Elias Canetti, *Crowds and Power*

There were no people on the Nevsky, but there was a crawling, howling myriapod there. The damp space poured together a myria-distinction of words. All the words jumbled together and again wove into a sentence; and the sentence seemed meaningless. It hung above the Nevsky, a black haze of phantasmata.

Andrei Belyi, *Petersburg*

   – That is God
   Hooray! Ay! Whrrwhee!
   – What? Mr Deasy asked.
   – A shout in the street, Stephen answered.

James Joyce, *Ulysses*

Pouring through the streets, colliding with the enemy, pulling at the arms of soldiers, crawling under horses' bellies, attacking, scattering, leaving their corpses on the crossings, grabbing a few firearms, spreading the news, catching at rumours, the insurrectionary mass becomes a collective entity with numberless eyes, ears, and antennae ... The art of revolutionary leadership in its most critical moments consists nine-tenths in knowing how to sense the mood of the masses ...

Leon Trotsky, 'Five Days; February 23–27, 1917'

A popular insurrection, by its very nature, is instinctive, chaotic, and destructive ... and in moments of crisis, for the sake of self-defence or victory, they will not hesitate to burn down their own houses and neighbourhoods, and property being no deterrent, since it belongs to their oppressors, they develop a passion for destruction: this negative passion it is true, is far from being sufficient to attain the heights of the revolutionary cause: but without it, revolution would be impossible. Revolution requires extensive and widespread destruction, a fecund and renovating destruction, since in this way and only in this way are new worlds born ...

M. A. Bakunin, 'Statism and Anarchy'

Comrades,
To the barricades!
Barricades of hearts and minds ...

The streets shall be our brushes
Our palettes shall be the squares,
On the thousand pages of the Book of Time,
Are written the Songs of Revolution,
into the streets, Futurists,
drummers and poets, go!

Vladimir Mayakovsky, 'Order of the Day to the Army of Arts'

As we reread the old histories, memoirs and novels, or regard the old photos or newsreels, or stir our own fugitive memories of 1968, we will see whole classes and masses move onto the street together. We will be able to discern two phases in their activity.

At first the people stop and overturn the vehicles in their path, and set the horses free: here they are avenging themselves on the traffic by decomposing it into its inert original elements. Next they incorporate the wreckage they have created into their rising barricades: they are recombining the isolated inanimate elements into vital new artistic and political forms. For one luminous moment, the multitude of solitudes that make the modern city come together in a new kind of encounter, to make a *people*. 'The streets belong to the people': they seize control of the city's elemental matter and make it their own.

Marshall Berman, All That is Solid Melts into Air

The space that the barricades formed was the space of combat and ambush: they were an attempt to make an already impenetrable quarter an even more impenetrable labyrinth known only to its defenders ... Within the space closed off by the barricades, the street took on the air of communal property; an open air room adopted by the community as its own; cabarets were turned into guard posts, cafés into political and strategic headquarters.

26 Barricade in Moscow, 1905.

Indeed the building of a barricade was a serious business, and its construction became skilled as well as swift. First iron bars were wrenched from street rails, then the street paving was levered up: the base of the barricade was formed by an overturned cart or carriage, its contents (preferably casks) placed beneath the pile of paving stones. Other barrels were purloined and set beside the rest, while the whole *barrique* was buttressed by more stones and topped by beams stolen from nearby houses. The resulting rampart was taller than a man. Passing vehicles were added to the original pile from time to time.

Anthony Vidler, 'The Scenes on the Street'

Imagine the blade of a giant guillotine as long as the diameter of the city. Imagine the blade descending and cutting a section through everything that is there – walls, railway lines, wagons, workshops, churches, crates of fruit, trees, sky, cobblestones. Such a blade has fallen a few yards in front of the face of everyone who is determined to fight.

. . . At the barricades the pain is over. The transformation is complete. It is completed by a shout from the rooftops that the soldiers are advancing. Suddenly there is nothing to regret. The barricades are between the defenders and the violence done to them throughout their lives. There is nothing to regret because it is the quintessence of their past which is now advancing against them. On their side of the barricades it is already the future.

John Berger, *G*

27 Woman at the barricades
– still from Kozintzev's *The New Babylon* (1929).

First there are *close-ups* of human figures rushing chaotically. Then *long shots* of the same scene. The *chaotic movement* is next superseded by shots showing the feet of soldiers as they march *rhythmically* down the steps.

Tempo increases. Rhythm accelerates.

And then, as the *downward* movement reaches its culmination the movement is suddenly reversed: instead of the headlong rush of the *crowd* down the steps we see the *solitary* figure of a mother carrying her dead son, *slowly* and solemnly *going up* the steps.

Mass. Headlong rush. *Downward*. And all of a sudden – A *solitary* figure. Slow and solemn. *Going up*. But only for a moment . . .

The shot of the *rushing crowd* is suddenly followed by one showing a perambulator hurtling down the steps. This gives one more aspect of downward movement.

Close-ups give place to *long shots*. The chaotic rush of a mass is succeeded by the rhythmic march of the soldiers.

Many volleys of *many* guns give place to *one* shot from *one* of the battleship's guns.

Sergei Eisenstein, Battleship Potemkin

BLOODY SUNDAY, JANUARY 1905

As we lay thus another volley was fired, and another, and yet another, till it seemed as if the shooting was continuous. The crowd first kneeled and then lay flat down, hiding their heads from the rain of bullets, while the rear rows of the procession began to run away. The smoke from the fire lay before us like a thin cloud, and I felt it stiflingly in my throat. An old man named Lavrentiev, who was carrying the Tsar's portrait, had been one of the first victims. Another old man caught the portrait as it fell from his hands and carried it until he too was killed by the next volley. With his last gasp the old man said, 'I may die, but I will see the Tsar.' One of the banner-carriers had his arm broken by a bullet. A little boy of ten years, who was carrying a church lantern, fell pierced by a bullet, but still held the lantern tightly and tried to rise again, when another shot struck him down. Both the smiths who had guarded me were killed, as well as all those who were carrying the icons and banners; and all these emblems now lay scattered in the snow . . .

At last the firing ceases. I stood up with a few others who remained uninjured and looked down at the bodies that lay prostrate around me. I cried to them, Stand up! But they lay still. At first I could not understand. Why did they lie there? I looked again and saw that their

arms were stretched out lifelessly, and I saw the scarlet stain of blood upon the snow . . .

Horror crept into my heart. The thought flashed through my mind, 'And this is the work of our Little Father, the Tsar'. . . . Looking backward, I saw that our line, though still stretching away into the distance, was broken and that many of the people were fleeing. It was in vain that I called to them, and in a moment I stood there, the centre of a few scores of men, trembling with indignation amid the broken ruins of our movement.

Father Gapon, Mémoires (1915)

Let us have no illusions about it: a real victory of an insurrection over the military in street fighting, a victory as between two armies, is one of the rarest exceptions . . . since 1848 the newly built quarters of the big towns have been laid out in long, straight, broad streets, as though made to give full effect to the new cannons and rifles.

Friedrich Engels, Class Struggles in France (1850)

Bourgeois revolutions rapidly advance from success to success, their dramatic effects are striking, men and events are illuminated by a kind of Bengal fire, and ecstasy is the dominant mood of every day. But their course is rapid, and they quickly reach their apogee and then society falls prey to an apathetic hangover.

Karl Marx, *Eighteenth Brumaire of Louis Bonaparte*

The impending revolution will be less like a spontaneous uprising against the government and more like a protracted *civil war*.

Karl Kautsky, *The Road to Power* (1909)

The history of the Russian revolution [of 1905], like the history of the Paris Commune of 1871, teaches us the incontrovertible lesson that militarism can never and under no circumstances be defeated and destroyed except by a victorious struggle of one section of the national army against the other section.

Vladimir Ilich Lenin, 'The Revolution of 1905'

Lenin's ultra-centralism in its essence is carried on, not by a positive creative spirit but by the sterile spirit of a nightwatchman. His thoughts are mainly directed ... to narrowing down the movement and not developing it. The great Ego, crushed and smashed by Russian absolutism, takes revenge by placing itself in its revolutionary fantasy upon the throne and declaring itself ... to be the the almighty Lord of history – this time in the autocratic majesty of a Central Committee of the Social-Democratic Workers' Movement.

Neue Zeit, Stuttgart: 'Organizational Questions of Russian
Social Democracy' (1904)

Street Fight

But clocks tick, one spring supersedes
Another, the sky grows pink
Cities change their names. . .

Anna Akhmatova, 'Sixth Elegy'

In the beginning of May [1914], the Petersburg season began to die, little by little, everyone scattered. This time separation from Petersburg turned out to be forever. We returned not to Petersburg, but to Petrograd; from the nineteenth century we were transported directly into the twentieth.

Anna Akhmatova, *Briefly about Myself*

Looking back, Russia before the November insurrection seems of another age, almost incredibly conservative . . .

As in all such times, the petty conventional life of the city went on, ignoring the Revolution as much as possible. The poets made verse – but not about the Revolution. The realistic painters painted scenes from medieval Russian history – anything but the Revolution. Young ladies from the provinces came up to the capital to learn French and cultivate their voices, and the gay beautiful officers wore their gold-trimmed crimson *bashliki* and their elaborate Caucasian swords round the hotel lobbies . . . The daughter of a friend of mine came home one afternoon in hysterics because the woman street-car conductor had called her 'Comrade'.

John Reed, Ten Days That Shook the World

There lived in Petersburg a little man with patent leather shoes, who was despised by doormen and women. His name was Parnok . . . From childhood he had been devoted to whatever was useless, metamorphosing the streetcar rattle of life into events of consequence, and when he began to fall in love he tried to tell women about this, but they did not understand him . . . Parnok was a man of Kamenoostrovskij Prospect – one of the lightest and most irresponsible streets of Petersburg. In 1917, after the February day, this street became even lighter with its steam laundries, its Georgian shops, where even cocoa was still to be bought, and its maniacal automobiles, the property of the Provisional Government . . . It was the Kerenskij summer, and the lemonade government was in session.

Osip Mandelstam, 'The Egyptian Stamp'

The plot is a mere nothing. A little man called Parnok runs about St Petersburg during the Kerenskij summer between the two revolutions of 1917 trying to accomplish two things, to retrieve certain items of his clothing and to prevent a lynch murder, and fails in both . . .

But Parnok's ancestry is . . . also Pushkin's mad Evgenij, running headlong from the colossus of the State. He is Gogol's Akakij Akakievic, devoting his very life to a search for a symbolic cloak. He is Dostoevsky's Mr Golyjadkin, confronted with a hateful image of the self. And he is, finally, Osip Mandelstam.

Clarence Brown, 'On Reading Mandelstam'

29 Soldiers on the street –
illustration for Blok's 'The
Twelve' by Yuri Annekov.

From house to house a banner
Has been strung across the street,
On it is emblazoned – ALL POWER
TO THE CONSTITUENT ASSEMBLY.

Alexander Blok, 'The Twelve'

Petrograd presented a curious spectacle in those days ... On the
streets the crowds thickened towards gloomy evening, pouring in slow
voluble tides up and down the Nevsky, fighting for all the newspapers
... Hold-ups increased to such an extent that it was dangerous to walk
down the side-streets ... On the Sadoyava one afternoon I saw a
crowd of several hundred people beat and trample to death a soldier
caught stealing ... Gambling clubs functioned hectically from dusk to
dawn, with champagne flowing and stakes of twenty thousand roubles.
In the centre of the city at night prostitutes in jewels and expensive furs
walked up and down, crowded the cafés ...

John Reed, *Ten Days that Shook the World*

The fresh wind flirts,
Mischievous and sly,
Lifting up skirts
Scuffling passers-by.
It shakes and shreds to pieces
The banner above: ALL POWER
TO THE CONSTITUENT ASSEMBLY,
And brings voices over . . .

. . . We girls called a conference . . .
. . . In a chamber of our own . . .
. . . We debated relevant points . . .
. . . And put this motion down:
Ten a quickie; twenty-five a night,
No undercutting from any girl. Right?
So, come on lads. Roll up.

Alexander Blok, 'The Twelve'

That evening Parnok did not return home to have dinner and drink tea with the little cakes he loved like a canary. He listened to the sputter of the blow torches as they approached the street car tracks with their blinding white shaggy roses. He received back all the streets and squares of Petersburg in the form of rough galley proofs, he composed the prospects, stitched the gardens . . .

Osip Mandelstam, 'The Egyptian Stamp'

Up the Nevsky the whole city seemed to be out promenading. On every corner immense crowds were massed around a core of hot discussion. Pickets of a dozen soldiers with fixed bayonets lounged at the street crossings, red-faced old men in rich fur coats shook their fists at them, smartly-dressed women screamed epithets; the soldiers argued feebly, with embarrassed grins . . . Armoured cars went up and down the street, named after the first Tsars – Oleg, Rurik, Svietoslav – and daubed with huge red letters, 'R.S.D.R.P.' (Russian Social Democratic Labour Party) . . .

John Reed, *Ten Days that Shook the World*

He thought of Petersburg as his infantile disease – one had only to regain consciousness, to come to, and the hallucination would vanish; he would recover, become like all other people, even – perhaps – get married . . . Then no one would dare call him 'young man' . . . He would have himself a new morning coat made, he would have it out with Captain Kryzanowski, he would show him . .

Osip Mandelstam, 'The Egyptian Stamp'

Rat-a-tat-tat

Lights all around. Lights left, lights right . . .
Swaying rifles glinting in the night . . .

Keep a Revo-Lutionary Beat!
The Relentless Enemy Does Not Sleep!

Alexander Blok, 'The Twelve'

THE REVOLUTIONARIES TRY TO JOIN THE REVOLUTION

It was an astonishing scene. Just at the corner of the Ekaterina Canal, under an arc-light, a cordon of armed soldiers was drawn across the Nevsky, blocking the way to a crowd of people in a column of fours. There were about three or four hundred of them, men in frock coats, well-dressed women, officers – all sorts and conditions of people . . . The procession stood still, but from the front of it came loud argument. Schreider and Prokopovitch were bellowing at the big sailor who seemed in command.

'We demand to pass!' they cried. 'See, these comrades come from the Congress of Soviets! Look at their tickets! We are going to the Winter Palace!'

The sailor was plainly puzzled. He scratched his head with an enormous hand, frowning. 'I have orders from the Committee not to let anybody go to the Winter Palace,' he grumbled . . .

'We insist upon passing! We are unarmed! We will march on whether you permit us or not!' cried old Schreider, very much exited.

'I have orders –' repeated the sailor sullenly.

'Shoot us if you want to! We will pass! Forward!' came from all sides . . .

'No,' said the sailor, looking stubborn, 'I can't allow you to pass.' . . .

'We will go forward! What can you do?'

'We will do something!' replied the sailor, evidently at a loss. 'We can't let you pass. We will do something.'

'What will you do? What will you do?'

Another sailor came up, very much irritated. 'We will spank you!' he cried energetically. 'And if necessary we will shoot you too. Go home now, and leave us in peace!'

... taking advantage of the diversion, we slipped past the guards and set off in the direction of the Winter Palace ...

John Reed, Ten Days that Shook the World

... So on they march in triumphant step,
Behind them trots a hungry dog,
While cloaked in snowflakes up ahead
Holding the blood-red flag aloft
Unharmed as bullets whistle past,
Softly through the stormy night –
Crowned by a halo of brilliant frost,
Through gardens and palaces of ice,
At their head is Jesus Christ.

Alexander Blok, 'The Twelve'

It was now after three in the morning. On the Nevsky all the street-lights were again shining, the cannon gone, and the only signs of war were the Red Guards and soldiers squatting around fires. The city was quiet – probably never so quiet in its history; on that night not a single hold-up occurred, not a single robbery.

John Reed, Ten Days that Shook the World

At 9.30 pm the former Captain Kryzanowski was planning to board the Moscow Express. He had packed in his suitcase Parnok's morning coat and best shirts. The morning coat, having tucked in its fins, fitted into the suitcase especially well, almost without a wrinkle, like a frolicsome dolphin of cheviot, to which it was related by its colour and youthful soul ...

In Moscow he stopped at the Hotel Select – an excellent hotel on Malaja Lubianka – where he was given a room that had formerly been used as a store: in place of a regular window it had a fashionable shop window, heated by the sun to an improbable degree.

Osip Mandelstam, 'The Egyptian Stamp'

Petrograd, after all, in spite of being for a century the seat of Government, is still an artificial city. Moscow is real Russia, Russia as it is and will be ...

John Reed, Ten Days that Shook the World

The culture of the Stalin era seems more closely linked with ancient Moscovy than with even the rawest stages of St Petersburg-based radicalism . . . With Stalin in the Kremlin, Moscow at last wreaked its revenge on St Petersburg, seeking to wipe out the restless reformism and critical cosmopolitanism which this 'window on the West' has always symbolized.

James Billington, *The Icon and the Axe*

Men of Iron

You are free, I am free
Tomorrow is better than yesterday –
over the dark Neva's waters
under the icy smile
of Emperor Peter.

Anna Akhmatova 'Second Elegy'

The most striking feature of monuments is that you do not notice them. There is nothing in the world as invisible as monuments. Doubtless they have been erected to be seen – even to attract attention: yet at the same time something has impregnated them against attention. Like a drop of water on an oilskin, attention runs down them without stopping for a moment . . . They virtually drive off what they would attract. We cannot say that we do not notice them. We should say that they de-notice us . . .

Robert Musil, quoted in Marina Warner, *Monuments and Maidens*

I direct that no monument be erected over me, and that no one even imagine doing such a thing, unworthy of a Christian . . . Whoever by my death grows in spirit better than he was . . . only by this means will he erect a monument to me.

Nikolai Gogol, *Testament*

Windows, god-forsaken holes – and monuments.

Pushkin, 'On Petersburg'

Pushkin was my first poet, and they killed my first poet . . .

The monument of Pushkin was an accepted custom . . . one of two, there was no third, daily inevitable strolls – to the Patriarsi Ponds or to the monument of Pushkin. And I preferred to go to the monument of Pushkin, because it pleased me . . . There was a separate game with the monument of Pushkin, my game, and it was this: to place at its feet a white porcelain little doll . . . to place at the giant's feet a little figurine, and, gradually extending my gaze upward along the whole granite expanse until my head had gone as far back as it could, I would compare their size.

The monument of Pushkin was also my contact with black and white – such black, such white! – and since the black was characteristic of a giant, and the white that of a comic figurine, and since it was obviously necessary to choose between them, I then and forever selected the black and not the white: black thoughts, a black fate, a black life.

Marina Tsvetaeva, 'The Monument of Pushkin'

30 The people tear down the statue of Alexander Nevsky – still from Sergei Eisenstein's *October* (1927).

17 The idol of autocracy, standing
18 on a massive, polished stone, against a sky darkened by ominous clouds.
19 Colossal demonstrations seethed like the waves of the ocean.
20 Wave after wave of the workers' masses,
21 wave after wave of the mass of peasants and soldiers,
22 wave after wave they flowed in to swell the ninth wave . . .
23 And on the crest of this general surge of exultation, a small, living, working man set his foot on the huge imperial crown,

24 on the cast-iron crown of the statue of Alexander III.
25 A monument which stood in the shelter of the golden cupolas of 'Christ the Saviour' near tramway line A.
26 Living hands placed a – fatal – noose around the metallic imperial neck.
27 The rope was drawn.
28 The noose tightened . . .
29 The clamps burst . . .
30 Swaying, the doll toppled from its tall pedestal,
31 and fell to the ground, shattering into fragments.
32 And words flew up like spray – TO ALL! TO ALL! TO ALL! ·

Sergei Eisenstein, October

We do not need a dead mausoleum of art where dead works are worshipped, but a living factory of the human spirit – in the streets, in the tramways, in the factories, workshops and workers' homes.

Vladimir Mayakovsky, How are Verses to be Made?

31 View from the window of the Winter Palace, 1917.

The proletariat will create new houses, new streets, new objects of everyday life . . .

Nikolai Punin, 'Art of the Commune' (1919)

Citizens, our former masters have gone away, leaving a huge legacy behind them. It now belongs to all the people. Citizens, take good care of this legacy, all these pictures, statues, and buildings. They embody you and your forefathers' spiritual strength.

'Appeal of the Soviet Workers' and Soldiers' Deputies' (Autumn 1917)

Two revolutions and a war have supplied me with hundreds of cases of this lurking, vindictive tendency in people, to smash, deform, ridicule, and defame the beautiful.

Maxim Gorky, *Days with Lenin* (1919)

ON THE REPUBLIC'S MONUMENTS

In commemoration of the great turning point which has transformed Russia, the Council of People's Commissars decrees that:

1. Monuments erected in honour of the tsars and their servants that are of no historic or artistic interest be removed from squares and streets and either transferred to storehouses or used for utilitarian purposes.

2. A special commission consisting of the People's Commissars for Education and State Property and the Head of the Fine Arts Department of the Ministry of Education be entrusted with the task of determining, with the agreement of the Artistic Boards of Moscow and Petrograd, what monuments are to be removed.

3. The same commission be charged with mobilizing artistic forces and organizing a large-scale competition for working out designs of monuments intended to commemorate the great days of the Russian socialist revolution.

4. The Council of People's Commissars expresses the wish that by the first of May some of the ugliest monstrosities be removed and the first models of new monuments be submitted to the verdict of the masses.

12 April 1918

Chairman of the Council of People's Commissars, *V. Ulyanov (Lenin)*

Revolutions shake up violently the bodies of kingdoms
The human herd changes its herdsmen/
But *you*/ uncrowned ruler of our hearts
No rebellion ever touches.

Velimir Khlebnikov, 'On Habit'

155

We insist:
Don't stereotype Lenin.
Don't print his portrait on placards . . .
plates, mugs, and cigarette cases.
Don't bronze over Lenin,
Don't take from him his living gait and human
    countenance . . .
He is amongst the living.
We need him as the living and not the dead.
Therefore
Learn from Lenin but don't canonise him.
Don't create a cult from the man, who all
    his life fought against all and every cult.
Don't trade in objects of this cult.
Don't trade in Lenin.

Vladimir Mayakovsky, 'Lenin'

In front of the Finland Station, one of five railroad terminals through which a traveller may enter or leave this city, on the very bank of the Neva River, there stands a monument to a man whose name this city presently bears. In fact, every station in Leningrad has a monument to this man, either a full-scale statue in front of or a massive bust inside the building. But the monument before the Finland Station is unique. It's not the statue itself that matters here, because Comrade Lenin is depicted in the usual quasi-romantic fashion, with his hand poking into the air, supposedly addressing the masses; what matters is the pedestal.

For Comrade Lenin delivers his oration standing on top of an armoured car. It's done in the style of early Constructivism, so popular nowadays in the West, and in general the very idea of carving an armoured car out of stone smacks of a certain psychological acceleration, of the sculptor being a bit ahead of his time. As far as I know, this is the only monument to a man on an armoured car that exists in the world. In this respect alone, it is a symbol of a new society. The old society used to be represented by men on horseback.

Joseph Brodsky, 'A Guide to a Renamed City'

32 Lenin's statue in the
Finland Station, Leningrad.

In 1924, after the death of Lenin, Petrograd was renamed Leningrad.
In mythic terms, it was refounded in the image of a new hero, but its
two hundred years as mythic emblem of the success of Russian culture
were over.

Lenin, the new hero, was buried in Moscow instead of 'Lenin City'
– the ancient gesture of planting the dead hero-founder at the centre
of power.

Burton Pike, *The Image of the City in Modern Literature*

Dead End

Night, street, streetlamp, chemist's window –
a dim insignificant light. No doubt
should you survive another quarter-century
it'll be the same. There's no way out.

You'll die – and start the whole thing over
and all will repeat the same old dance.
Night, the icy ripple of the river,
the chemist's, the street, the streetlamp.

Alexander Blok, '10th October 1912'

Today
in Petrograd
on Nadyezhdinsky Street*

Vladimir Mayakovsky, '150,000,000'

– Which street is this?
– Mandelstam Street.
– What kind of name d'you call that?
Put it whatever way you like
it sounds crooked.

– He was no model of rectitude himself.
Often strayed from the straight and narrow.
And that's why this street (or really,
if you'd rather, this drain)
was named after the man
Mandelstam.†

Osip Mandelstam, 'Poem 303', Voronezh (April 1935)

They will forget me,
and my books will rot in cupboards.
There will not be
any street or avenue called Akhmatova.

Anna Akhmatova, 'The Sweetbriar Flowers'

The sides of people
Are rubbed by old Peter.

A Leningrad Maxim

* Nadyezhdinsky Street – Hope Street – renamed Mayakovsky Street
† There is no street called Mandelstam Street

Street as Forum

Thought Polis

Politics and city life have a common root. From the Greek '*polis*' – meaning both state and city – Western culture has derived the notions both of despotism and democracy, of civic freedoms and central control. But whether it locates rule in a tyrant or in the '*demos*' – the people – urban life emphasizes the fact that social organization is artificial, constructed. God made the country but man made the town. And the rise of the city is commensurate with that of the state, which demanded loyalty, not from the inherited filiations of blood, but from the conscious affiliation of citizens to their city (cf. Machiavelli, Debord, p. 119, Rousseau, p. 132).

Political considerations inform the physical shape of the city too. Monuments, triumphal archways, the naming of avenues from Wagram to Waterloo enshrine its military victories: forums, amphitheatres, stadia, its meeting places and festive sites (cf. El Lissitsky, Foucault, p. 120). Until the advent of artillery, defensive walls confined city centres into a clustered maze of alleys evident in medieval town layouts. During the Renaissance, with the increasing ineffectiveness of walls against bombardment, entire street plans were reconfigured to provide lines of fire for defensive cannon. Suddenly, the geometry of open space becomes safer than seclusion. Avenues and buildings are aligned according to a Quattrocento perspective which, as we saw in Paris, allows defensive manoeuvres as well as classical vistas, providing internal and external 'security'. For just as it tries to protect itself against outsiders, the city also seeks to contain the enemies within. As *viae militares* streets facilitate the quick movement of troops together with the canalization of crowds. Often leading to and from an official edifice, a Winter Palace or a Louvre, they provide the spectacle of parades, pageants, monuments and are channels for political propaganda. One of the most sophisticated forms of social organization, the city may inspire civil rights, but is also where the repressive apparatus of state converge (cf. Mumford, p. 124).

These ambiguous political tenets seem to have been present at St Petersburg's inception. When, in 1703, Peter the Great laid its foundation stone, the new city represented a radical break from the Byzantine ways of Old Muscovy to a more rational and enlightened frame of mind. Yet St Petersburg was also an arbitrary act of autocratic power: its very building a defiance of nature. Constructed on swampy ground on the banks of the Neva, it required deep stone foundations for its major buildings, and the city remained prone to catastrophic floods. Thousands were reputed to have died in its construction, giving rise to the recurrent rumour that it was underwritten by ghosts. With its white nights, its broad and luminous river, St Petersburg could seem to embody spiritual lucidity. But for its miasmal fogs and famed deliriums, it was known as the most unhealthy capital in Europe. Even the city's skyline had a ring of ambivalence. Peter specifically forbade the erection of the onion-shaped bell towers so resonant of old Moscow, and preferred the rational clarity of spires. But the two needles that would dominate the city would each have a very different significance. The Admiralty spire, praised by Mandelstam, symbolized the outward-looking spirit of St Petersburg – 'all the seas of the world lying open'. But the spire of the church in the Peter and Paul Fortress stood above the Russian Bastille where political prisoners (Dostoevsky among them) were held and often executed.

For two hundred years St Petersburg represented both the ambiguity of the urban achievement and modern Russia's dual identity. To progressives of various allegiances, it could be seen as a 'new hope', a symbol of Russia's ability to pull itself up by its own bootstraps. But to radicals and reactionaries alike it was also an emblem of corruption, a divergence from the traditional solidarities of the land. On one thing, however, most writers on Petersburg concur: the new capital was itself a tribute to fiction and artifice; in Dostoevsky's words it was 'the most abstract and intentional city in the world'. And if Peter could conjure an entire population, a new society out of the ground, couldn't someone else (cf. Dostoevsky, pp. 120–1)?

Throughout the nineteenth century and well into the twentieth, this inaugural act of innovation spurred one of the most remarkable periods in world art and literature. It is as if Petersburg's writers, artists, actors and directors reinvented their own alternative Petersburg, composed not of stone but words, music, celluloid and paint.

And, no less importantly, it would also ferment new social philosophies and political forms, culminating in the Petrograd soviets. Inasmuch as it represented the triumph of the 'new beginning' there is a continuity between the throne of tsardom and the cradle of revolution.

The Colossus of State

The Bronze Horseman is Peter the Great's legacy made manifest. Commissioned by Catherine the Great, Falconet's equestrian statue (actually made of copper), set on a slab of Finnish granite, shows Tsar Peter reared up on his mount, hand held high, arm stretched out in a gesture which seems to open up new horizons and at the same time close them down (cf. illustration 21, p. 121). Today, like many of the other elegant baroque monuments of the city, the figure is a source of historical curiosity or aesthetic interest. But once the statue was arresting in quite another sense.

In his verse tale *The Bronze Horseman* Pushkin praises St Petersburg for its granite banks, white nights, frosty winters, military parades and gun salutes. But the rest of the poem gives that praise an ironical edge (pp. 122–3). It tells the tale of a young clerk Evgeny (the first in a series of down-trodden clerks) who loses his fiancée in one of Petersburg's recurrent great floods. Desolate and delirious he wanders the flooded city and arrives at Senate Square, in front of the Bronze Horseman. There, he curses the icon of the man who set the city on such unstable ground. At that moment, the iron colossus jumps off its pedestal and pursues the poor clerk through St Petersburg, into madness and death. For Pushkin, as for Belyi nearly a century later (see pp. 121–2), the statue was still ideologically animated. The violent rearing of the horse, the imperious gesture, were signs of an active political menace.

Evgeny's vision of pursuit by a copper statue suggests that political control acts not only through outward compulsion but also through fantasy. Whether mad or not, Evgeny has internalized a figure of authority. In him the mental agencies of guilt and fear act, as in Freud's metaphor, like a garrison within a conquered city (p. 124).

In many ways, by the time Pushkin wrote his poem St Petersburg was more like an occupied citadel than the imperial capital. Though *The Bronze Horseman* was written secretly (and in code to avoid the censors) in the 1830s, Pushkin set its events during the terrible floods of 1815. A year later, another sort of protest would take place in front in Senate Square. From among the young noblemen who had been sent to France to gain an understanding of the culture that had just invaded them, some smuggled back intellectual contraband in the form of ideas of equality, liberty and fraternity. When a handful of them demonstrated in Senate Square and made a modest plea for reform a vicious wave of repression ensued.

The modern Russian history of dissidence really begins at this moment of the Decembrist uprising. Decembrist leaders were executed, their supporters – such as Alexander Herzen – driven into exile, and suspected fellow-travellers, including Pushkin and Lermontov, artistically suppressed. In such a regime, the Bronze Horseman is no simple monument. It represents the vigilant spirit of autocracy which patrolled the borders not only of political fact but also political imagination. More recent memories of Russian totalitarianism can obscure its long and distinguished pedigree, but a century before Stalin the Russian authorities were paying poetry a perverse tribute by persecuting it. Culture, the realm of imaginative freedom, is a strategic battleground; official architecture an attempt to establish a kind of police state in the mind (cf. Mandelstam, pp. 123–4, London, pp. 42–3).

No Through Road

If St Petersburg was supposed to be a 'window on to the west', on its main street it looked much like a shop window.

Surpassing Haussmann's boulevards in breadth and scale, a vast bourgeois concourse grafted on to a feudal estate, the Nevsky Prospect offered all the spectacle of French consumerism, its glitter and gloss, coffee shops and jewellery. It provided a place where all St Petersburg's citizens could gather and feel the illusion of riches, the promise of mobility, even if in this city the promise was a very thin façade. As a public space outside the ambit of religious or state power, the Nevsky was also relatively free from official control. When Gogol set a scene in his story 'The Nose' in a church, the censors objected. So Gogol transferred the scene to one of the new cathedrals of consumption on the Nevsky Prospect, the fashionable arcade, Gostviny Dvor. On the same avenue, having purchased his new overcoat, the poor clerk Akaky Akakievitch feels a sudden access of liberation and joy (Gogol's 'The Overcoat'). He smiles at a picture in one of the shop windows which shows a man watching a woman adjust her stockings, and thinks: 'Those French . . .'

Romance, magic, a new overcoat, a new love, a new life, whatever you want, as the Russian equivalent of the Champs-Élysées the Nevsky seems to offer it all. Yet the point of 'The Overcoat' is that the poor clerk's joy is short-lived. Before long, Akaky has his overcoat stolen from him: his illusions stripped away leaving him to wither in the cold winds of political reality. Unlike Paris these delusions of grandeur on the Nevsky must always remain just that, delusions. In Russia's rigid caste system the possibility of spiritual and material mobility is absolutely denied. Akaky Akakievitch, his overcoat stolen, dies of metaphysical grief and physical cold. Trying to keep body and soul together, the poor Petersburger is in danger of losing both.

Marshall Berman calls this condition the 'Modernism of Under-development', and its contradictions are echoed in Havana in the fifties, Saigon in the sixties, Managua in the seventies, Johannesburg or Peking today. In this environment the commodities of consumerism are incredibly loaded, the language of fashion surreal and charged. Clothes are fashions, can be bought and sold, but in Petersburg they are also predominantly uniforms, fixed costumes of the *ancien régime*. Buttons, epaulettes and feathers are precise markers of military rank or civil service grade (cf. Baedeker, Herzen, p. 126). Clothes therefore have to bear an untenable dual burden, being both signs of style and badges of shame. Devushkin in Dostoevsky's 'Poor Folk' (p. 127) dreams of being a poet, but this ideal is soon shattered when he realizes he would be laughed at on the Nevsky for his patched shoes. In the office where he works, losing a button in front of a superior is all it takes to send him spinning into total decline.

In a state where everything has a political edge, even advertising cuts both ways. In his short story 'Nevsky Prospect' (pp. 125–6), Gogol paints an impressionistic picture of a street of whirling umbrellas, of glittering shoes, of moustaches that fly off by themselves, of noses that seem to have a life of their own. But though these signs fly like butterflies, they can also sting like wasps. When the clerk in 'The Nose' finally finds the missing nose he is staggered to find that it is actually three grades higher in the civil service and refuses to return to his face. Even the most bizarre fetishes and fantasies are inscribed with the marks of rank and supremacy.

Behind the shopfront is a halberd and sentry box: behind all trans-actions and exchanges is the fact that things won't change (cf. Gogol, p. 126).

Sleeping Policemen

There is a vital difference between the fantasies of St Petersburg and the Parisian fantasies it echoes. Desires in this environment are not attenuated or degraded, but crushed. Luxuries aren't made to seem necessities, quite the reverse, the basic needs are made to seem luxuries themselves. This divergence between prohibition and exhibition makes the Nevsky Prospect a schizophrenic space.

Like the Champs-Élysées, the apparent openness of the avenue has its origins in the displays and parades of absolute kingship. The doubleness of its perspective – the way vistas command respect for authority, yet can make anybody feel king for a day – seems to have been realized by the hero of Gogol's 'The Diary of a Madman'. As the Tsar passes by on the Nevsky Prospect, the crazed clerk is convinced by the spectacle that he is King of Spain (p. 128). In a similar way, Golyadkin, the poor clerk of Dostoevsky's second novel, *The Double* (pp. 128–9), tries to take a ride in a carriage and to enjoy the mobility that the space confers, but turning the corner of the Liteiny he is spotted by a couple of colleagues. He can dismiss them, but not the *droshky* that draws up, occupied by his superior. Realizing how much he's stepped out of his station, in a moment of anguish Golyadkin is forced to admit that it's not him and that's all there is to it. From this point on, Golyadkin begins to be haunted by a double, identical to him in every way except pushier, younger (and like the nose in Gogol's story, three ranks higher). The double slowly begins to destroy Golyadkin, spreading rumours about him all over Petersburg, informing on him, and finally driving him insane.

Dostoevsky's dictum that all writers come out of the overcoat of Gogol also implies that Russian fiction came out of the dreams of poor clerks. If the central Parisian figure was the *flâneur*, the idler, the Petersburg equivalent was the poor clerk, a *raznochinet*, who, a *déclassé* intellectual, was at once a member of the intelligentsia and conscripted into the vast mental proletariat of the empire's Asiatic bureaucracy.

Unlike the Parisian stroller, the poor clerk is not so much observing scenes as spying on himself. This sense of surveillance is partly imaginative: by being a state employee, the clerk was already a double agent – both a dissident, decrying the system, and mentally complicit with the apparatus he abhorred. But this feeling of conspiracy is also a reflection of the political realities of the day. Under Nicholas I's Third Section of Police, mass informing was rife. The plots and counter-plots of secret agents and infiltrators set a tradition which was perfected rather than perverted by the Cheka and the KGB. Indeed, the scene on the Fontanka, when Golyadkin is tailed and shadowed by his *alter ego*, is reminiscent of more recent accounts of life in a police state.

In this environment, instead of being a place filled with strangers who don't know you at all, the city is more like an overgrown village where people know you all too well.

Right of Way

Despite its sanctions of shame and surveillance the city retains a democratic force.

On the street, power becomes pedestrian; rushing to avoid the traffic, rubbing shoulders in the crowds, the halo of status loses its mystique (cf. Baudelaire, p. 181). On the pavement the privileged cease to be a class of *special people* but a special *class* of people. And it is by demonstrating the fact of *classification*, by making us realize that such distinctions are factitious and arbitrary, that the street assumes its radical role. Certainly it is this levelling element which lies behind the refusal of Lopukhov, Chernyshevsky's idealized working-class hero, to give way to a passing dignitary (p. 130). Superior in physical strength, Lopukhov can simply pick him up and put him in the gutter.

A regime, however, rarely exercises power simply through physical force alone. It operates, as it did with the Bronze Horseman, through a whole series of internal sanctions and prohibitions. For example, the 'rights of way' on a street are by and large assumed and unwritten. Physically, our trajectory through the busy thoroughfares of a city, the spaces we keep between us, giving way to our superiors, barging or waving on our inferiors, reveals our position in the order of things. Often, when people return from a trip to the city, feeling trampled upon and herded around, they are complaining of this hidden bodily regulation of the streets.

The inner struggle to overcome these unconscious and unquestioned rules is what makes Dostoevsky's underground man more equivocal and real than his model Lopukhov (pp. 130–1). Snubbed by an officer, it takes the clerk months of cavilling and indecision to overcome his intrinsic sense of inferiority. On the Nevsky he feels that compared with his superiors he is a nasty obscene fly, better educated and more cultured of course, but still a nasty obscene fly. When the underground man finally stands up for himself, and holds his ground as the officer barges past, the clerk comes off worse from the collision and the officer barely notices. But that doesn't seem to matter. What is important is that the underground man had seen through the conventions of power, and claimed his right to be on an equal footing. A small step towards recognition perhaps but, in the context of tsarist Russia, a giant social leap.

By making the laws of submission visible, the street also makes them vulnerable; and this extends from the everyday collisions of individuals to the grander political spectacle. To maintain his place and prove he is still in control, the ruler must be *seen* at military parades, walkabouts and official occasions. In this way, the monarch, president or first secretary acknowledges that the people are really sovereign, and that it is from their deference or indifference that he derives his power. Elevated above the crowd, or at its centre, the ruler is endowed with the luminous halo of charisma. The nearer he gets to the people, the stronger that halo glows, but also the greater the danger it will be seen through. Like the emperor who wore no clothes, in a sense the ruler always goes naked in the streets, sustained by the collective illusion of the people. And it takes only a small piping voice to say that the emperor has no clothes, for a torrent of voices to follow.

In St Petersburg, after the assassination of Alexander II (see illustration 23, p. 134), the baroque streets of regal display increasingly played host to bombs, shootings and assassination attempts. Most of the swelling tide of political assassinations that have accompanied the spread of the modern metropolis exploit this combination of vulnerability and visibility on the street, a sniper shooting, a bomb exploding on precisely those public occasions when the leader is legitimated, proving that beneath the charisma he is really just flesh and blood (especially blood). The political theatre of the city elevates an individual as an icon for an entire system, and terrorism reacts with iconoclastic violence. Even the technologies of modern society do not dispel this explosive contradiction. For the statesman who appears behind bullet-proof glass publicizes the fact that he does not enjoy the full confidence of his people and, in the city, to lose their *respect* is eventually to lose grip.

Since the Renaissance most European cities have been increasingly devoted to the elevation and substantiation of political power. This becomes, with its rituals and temples, a secular religion. In the nineteenth century, after the French Revolution, the religion began to gravitate away from the individual ruler to the collective, to the teeming crowds of the back streets. The radicals and anarchists of prerevolutionary Petersburg often spoke of losing themselves in the 'people' as if it were a kind of spiritual ecstasy (cf. Lunarcharsky,

Nietzsche, Gorky, pp. 134–5). Even Dostoevsky, who abjured the radical associations of his youth, makes the St Petersburg street into some kind of cathedral to the people. At the climax of *Crime and Punishment*, Raskolnikov kneels in the filthy Haymarket, kisses the dust of holy St Petersburg and publicly confesses his crime. If God made the country and man made the town, the pavements are a kind of profane altar to the city's prime mover and creator – humankind.

The Shout in the Street

Most people who have been part of a demonstration, a congregation or a large audience have felt the power of the crowd. There is a moment – maybe applause, dancing, chanting or a sudden silence – when the phenomenal force of so many concerted interests can be electrifying. This positive sense of the crowd as a source of possibility and life is what attracted Madame Bovary to Rouen, Baudelaire to *épouser la foule*, drew Dickens and Dostoevsky to the dense, swarming back streets: their buzz and movement epitomizing the energy that sustains the city. For Stephen Dedalus, God himself is a shout in the street, and in the secular religion of politics – *vox populi: vox dei* – the voice of the people is the voice of God (cf. Joyce, p. 140, Weber, p. 132).

Yet these affirmations of the crowd are rare in modern city life. Most descriptions perceive the crowd more as a threat than a cause for celebration: either the sullen tread of a uniform 'mass' or the barbaric stampede of the 'mob'.

When people speak of 'the' crowd as opposed to 'a' crowd what they generally mean is the mass as Dickens and Engels saw it (London, pp. 18–19). In this each individual may pursue his or her own rational path, but the collective effect is of anarchy. But though the atomized mass may provoke a feeling of insignificance or frustration in the individual, that is nothing compared to the horror he or she feels for the purposeful cohesive crowd – *la grande peur* – the fear of the 'mob'.

Elemental metaphors recur in most descriptions of cohesive crowds: a terrific flood thrashing against the pavements like the Neva against its banks (cf. Pudovkin, p. 136); a prolific fire, or a raging storm. According to Canetti, these images are deeply ingrained in the language of insurrection, and to the ego, the crowd does pose some primitive elemental threat. As the properties of our bodies are dismembered and made interchangeable into a mass of arms, legs, and heads, the crowd undermines our concepts of self-possession. Described as 'teeming', 'pullulating', 'swarming', crowds suggest the contradictory impulses of the unconscious, decentred, uncontrollable, threatening the ego with breakdown. In a crowd, the individual becomes secondary, and acts of self-sacrifice and self-abnegation characterize its activity just as much as arson, looting or lynching. Naturally, individualistic societies will try to repress the collective. But denying the crowd the festive outlets of carnival and ritual means that the repressed instinct for gathering returns in more negative, aberrant forms. Constantly in danger of dispersal, modern crowds are more likely to seize on any goal, especially some common enemy (cf. Canetti, p. 140), in order to hold themselves together.

This internal fear of the mob has had a much more drastic effect on city planning than any real external threat. Instead of squares and fields, most modern cities devise a means to keep the crowds moving rather than gathering: the streets work as thoroughfares and channels; they conduce social circulation, ventilation, not congregation and mass. St Petersburg, like London and Paris before and New York after (cf. London, pp. 48–9, Paris, pp. 104–5, New York, pp. 220–1), used all the available military and architectural means to disperse and divert its crowds. These precautions, the fear and loathing that crowds attract, are a backhand testimony to their vital psychological and historical power.

The Electrification of the Crowd

In the early 1870s Dostoevsky met his now estranged mentor Belinsky for the last time outside the site of the Nicholaev railway station. Both saw the station as a symbol of the new direction Russia was taking: for Belinsky, it presented the hope of advance and modernization; for Dostoevsky, iron roads of further unfreedom.

In 1876, outside the Kazan Cathedral, a group of students were joined by workers from the Vyborg district to reverse the lines of communication and make the first mass demonstration of ordinary Petersburgers in their own city. Georgi Plekhanov unfurled a banner demanding 'Liberty and Land' before the gathering was dispersed by Cossacks (cf. Venturi, p. 132).

Both these events marked a new chapter in St Petersburg's history and the constitution of its crowd. A rapid phase of industrialization in the last quarter of the nineteenth century would irrevocably alter the shape of the city, enlarging an outer ring of heavy industry around the Neva shipbuilding factory, the Putilov iron works and the Alexandrovsky factory, creating a tightening periphery of shanty towns and workers' districts around the baroque centre (cf. Belyi, p. 135). The cuckoo's egg of industrialism was being laid in the capital of tsardom.

Strindberg compares the isolated individual to an uncharged battery; Herzen talks of the revolutionary temper as a 'galvanic current' (p. 132); even Gladstone referred to the buzz of the crowd as a kind of 'dangerous electricity'. The electric metaphor not only expresses the energy generated by the critical mass of a crowd, but the modernization of the form of that energy. In a heavily industrialized city the crowd becomes increasingly regimented and homogeneous in its actions: a uniform army of labour rather than an anarchic mob. It is this capacity for organization and discipline which persuaded Lenin and Marx that the industrial proletariat could be the dynamo for revolutionary change (cf. Lenin, p. 137, Marx, p. 146).

In sporadic riots, destruction is the major form of protest against the social order: the crowd exerts its supremacy over the hard structures of the city by looting, burning or demolishing them (cf. Bakunin, p. 141). But the organized proletariat tends to exercise its most powerful hold on the city by refraining from action rather than taking it. In strikes, standstills, boycotts, it can empty the streets. It doesn't destroy the infrastructure so much as make it redundant. And the proletariat's main form of protest is sheer presence. The political demonstration is what it says it is, a *demonstration* of support: the gathering is a primary assertion of democratic arithmetic using the simplest form of ballot, voting with your feet. Demands may be underlined by placards and slogans, embellished with car horns or the music of massed bands. But the tenor of the message is always the same: we built it, run it, maintain it, we can bring everything to a halt, this city is ours.

Most of the preliminary acts of revolution are also statements of solidarity. Even the building of a barricade, the architectural symbol of revolution, is more an example of passive then active resistance. In the unequal battle of pistols against machine guns, of Molotov cocktails against armoured cars, the barricade is not of military but moral efficacy, erected to keep the revolution going as long as possible until saved by sympathizers or mutinous troops (cf. Engels, p. 145). In this tense political theatre, even street-fighting is exemplary. Trotsky, in his essay on the 1905 Revolution, writes of the critical moment when, ordered by their commanding officer to fire on the people, the troops hesitate. The officer aims his gun at one of his insubordinate troops. At this moment, before the officer makes an example of the soldier and forces the troops to shoot, a shot from the crowd could expose the officer's vulnerability and turn the guns around.

The initial stages of a revolutionary uprising are filled with such dramatic reversals and in their effects differ only marginally from the non-violent tactics of Gandhi or Martin Luther King. For in the theatre of the streets, the battle is for hearts and minds, not to defeat the enemy but to win the majority of them over to your side.

Forbidden City

One need only think of recent events in China to see that the structure of the city forms more than just a backdrop to these social struggles. When Peking's students began their spontaneous 'pro-democracy' campaign in 1989, they targeted their protest on the strategic heart of the city – Tiananmen Square. By doing so, they put their demands for civil reforms at the centre of national and international attention. As workers and other citizens began to join them, denouncing corruption, singing the 'Internationale', the numbers swelled to such an extent that they brought the capital to a virtual halt, disrupting the itinerary of Mikhail Gorbachev's visit. A few days later, in perhaps their most daring affront to the gerontocratic Chinese authorities, the students erected a statue of the Goddess of Democracy facing the portrait of Chairman Mao.

What was remarkable about the Peking protest of 1989 was that virtually leaderless disparate crowds could for so long outmanoeuvre the firepower and the discipline of the military. When columns of troops attempted to enter the suburbs to impose martial law, word was passed around faster than any electronic broadcast and in minutes hundreds were sitting blocking the road, swarming over the trucks, bombarding the soldiers inside with gifts, arguments and shame.

In the end, the geography of Peking was against the pro-democracy movement. Paratroopers came out, firing, from the Forbidden City. Armoured personnel carriers bulldozed over the pathetic obstacles placed on the broad Avenue of Everlasting Peace, and crushed that last and most important barricade – the protesters themselves. But though, in martial terms, the authorities were victorious, it was a pyrrhic victory. The military – at least for the citizens of Peking – had lost its claim to be the People's Army. And the politicians responsible for that Bloody Sunday in June would become famous for one of the most blatant repressions of a popular movement by its government since the Tsar's troops fired into the crowds on that first Bloody Sunday in St Petersburg nearly a century ago.

Curfew

The limited concessions gained after the 1905 Revolution would probably never have been won without the presence of the 'shaggy caps of blood-stained Manchuria' (in Belyi's description of the contemporary crowd), the disaffected demobilized troops from the fiasco of the Russo–Japanese war (p. 136). As it was, the barricades of Kronstadt, Petrograd and Moscow were eventually swept away by government troops, highlighting the fact that no matter the level of popular support, when it came to street fighting, military strength had to be met with military strength. Since the French Revolution the layout and garrisoning of the city had made the chances of a successful spontaneous mass uprising more unlikely. Thus, as Kautsky and Lenin repeatedly stressed, the only possible revolutionary victory in Russia could be from one section of the army against another (p. 146).

As in *Battleship Potemkin*, the rifle shots of the soldiers on the Odessa steps can be countered only by a bigger shot from the battleship (cf. Eisenstein, p. 144).

The social revolution required the shout in the street, the articulation of a collective will: in fact, it needed all that is implied in the word *glasnost*, meaning 'finding a voice, publicity, publicness'. But by the time the Red Guard had taken control of Petrograd the street was under curfew for the ordinary citizen. The military battle for a city, though partly fought on its thoroughfares, is essentially a battle for command centres: post offices, barracks, telegraph and television stations. To succeed, the revolution has to become professionalized. In October 1917 itself, the storming of the Winter Palace was a stage-managed event, led by a revolutionary vanguard, in which even Bolshevik delegates from the Smolny were not allowed to participate (cf. Reed, pp. 150–1). For nearly fifty years, from the twenties until the mass movements returned to Armenia, Estonia and Latvia in the eighties, Soviet revolution remained more like some military spectacle, the citizens less like protagonists in some vital political theatre than gaping bystanders at a May Day parade.

Revolutionary art, after the October Revolution, attempted to restore some sense of popular participation. Mayakovsky had exhorted his futurist comrades to make their whole city into a work of art, to turn the streets into paintbrushes and make palettes of the squares (p. 141). Petrograd, during workers' holidays and revolutionary anniversaries, almost lived up to this early and temporary *perestroika* as artists such as Nathan Altman provided huge flats, banners and friezes which, hanging on bridges, encasing monuments, adorning the entire façades of buildings, made the city embody the history not of rulers and generals but of craftsmen and workers. Vast street pageants were staged, particularly on May Day and the October anniversary, culminating in 1920 in a massed re-enactment of the storming of the Winter Palace.

This time ordinary citizens *were* allowed to join in. Various sections of the crowd played the Red Army, driving out White Army puppets under vast arc lights, followed by a musical procession of trucks. But when the festivities were over, and it was discovered that the commanding officer of the Petrograd garrison knew nothing about them, he was severely reprimanded. After all, if a crowd could rehearse a mock *coup d'état* without the authorities' knowledge, it might also be able to stage a real one. True participatory art, by its festive nature, poses a threat to any form of authority – a fact which the Bolsheviks, having harnessed the tremendous energies of the crowd, were in a good position to appreciate.

Revolution Without Shots

A photograph taken from the Winter Palace shows a view of Petrograd through a broken window – broken by a revolutionary bullet (see illustration 31, p. 154). This snapshot of a piece of unrepaired history can be seen as a metaphor for the Modernist project.

Inasmuch as it also represents a break with the Versailles perspective, the imperious palace view, Modernism is similar to that cracked glass. Many of its movements follow the lines of breakage: the montages of Vertov and Eisenstein, the constructions of Gabo and Malevitch, graphics and photomontages of Tatlin, El Lissitsky and Rodchenko, the dissonances of Shostakovitch, the fragmented styles of Belyi and Babel, the cubo-futurist poetry of Mayakovsky and Pasternak. These, for all their diversity, share a common antipathy to the view which subordinates space to a single absolute observer, which fixes that observer outside the scene. With an emphasis on the jagged and the fragmented, they fracture the old way of seeing. But the cracks in the glass also give a new slant on reality, open up a multiplicity of angles. The discontinuity forces the spectator to be in the picture, not out of it. Contradictory, plural, shifting – this new way of seeing begins to look less like a view from a palace than that from the street.

Two versions of the Petrograd revolution itself also adopt this critical, modern perspective: Alexander Blok's 'The Twelve' (pp. 148–9,

150, 151) and Osip Mandelstam's 'The Egyptian Stamp' (pp. 147, 149, 151). Though the first is written by the official poet of the Revolution, the other by an official non-person, both narrate from the pavement in a graphic collage of events, impressions, characters. In Blok's poem, the whole language derives from banners adorning the street, its snatches of overheard conversation. Appropriately, the poems, accompanied by Annekov's illustrations, were actually posted back up on the Petrograd streets which inspired them (see illustration 29, p. 148).

Mandelstam also writes, with the rhythm of the pedestrian, about the 'Judaic Chaos' of the Kolumna district. If 'The Egyptian Stamp' has any one unifying style, it is a recurrent urban clash of accident and tangent, in which a dying opera singer hears a fire engine on the Nevsky as a final aria. The tale's hero is an heir to the tradition of Petersburg street folk, the *raznochintsy*. Parnok wanders the streets during the Kerensky summer of the 'Lemonade Government'. Like Gogol's clerks or Dostoevsky's underground man, he comes face to face with a military officer, Captain Kryzanowski, but instead of being the representative of tsardom, this captain is a Bolshevik commissar. At the end of the story, in a deliberate reference to the fate of Akaky Akakievitch's overcoat, Kryzanowski walks off with Parnok's coat, takes a train to Moscow, and stays at the plush hotel which would have been the base for the secret police.

In his literary code, Mandelstam shows how the Bolshevik captain stole the mantle of the Petersburg *raznochinet*. He suggests that a change in costume is not the same as a change of heart, and that a culture in flux, despite its freedoms and possibilities, is also a culture up for grabs. Mandelstam wrote in 1928 when it was becoming increasingly apparent that the military revolution had hijacked the social revolution that preceded it. To defeat the Tsar's army, the Red Guard had come to imitate it. Soon both cosmopolitanism and 'rootless cosmopolites' – Jews like Mandelstam and Parnok – were to be officially denounced, and the star of Mandelstam's beloved 'Petropolis' began to wane (cf. Billington, p. 152).

After the gravitation of the capital back to Moscow, Stalin slowly closed this 'window on to the west'. And as the Soviet Union withdrew into its mental hinterland, with the majority of the original revolutionaries put out of action by Beria's secret police, its artists put out of work by Zhdanov's aesthetic militia, the cultural possibilities of the second Petersburg, the alternative city with its original *glasnost*, were all but stamped out.

173

Vandals

The victory of Stalinism has been pictured as the victory of the Modern, of a brave new 'Brutopia' of absolute rationalism, like Zamyatin's *We* (the model for Huxley and Orwell), where the jangling motley of the street has been superseded by the cold and abstract surfaces of social constructivism, the engineering of human souls. But the legacy of Stalinism belies this simple view.

Most of the great monuments of Russian constructivism – El Lissitsky's Lenin Tribune, Tatlin's brilliant monument to the Third International – remained only on paper or modelled in wood. Stalin, like Lenin before him, decried 'leftist futurism'; and when designs were submitted for the Palace of the Soviets in Moscow, Stalin's preferred design was that of Boris Iofan, a kind of massive neo-classical sky-scraper. Originally to be surmounted by a gigantic proletarian hero, on Stalin's suggestion the plans were revised to incorporate a seventy-metre-high statue of Lenin. Like the Tsars before him, Stalin had good reason to encourage this posthumous cult of personality (cf. Brodsky, p. 156). By elevating his predecessor, Stalin effectively separated Lenin from his comrades such as Bukharin and Trotsky and thus legitimated his own isolated eminence. Thus, an apparently new iconography, which would lead to renaming Petrograd as Leningrad, was actually a return to something very old. The shadow of the Bronze Horseman is near by.

Much of the Bolshevik policy of 'monumental propaganda' consisted of maintaining the structures of tsardom and merely changing the figures in the niches. Generals and nobles were replaced by another official pantheon of Herzen, Bakunin, Blanqui, Lassalle, Marx. More radical designs, such as those drawn up by the LEF group, were accused of being the work of anarchic 'leftists', hooligans, vandals (cf. Lenin, Gorky, Punin, Mayakovsky, pp. 154–5). But a vandal is someone who destroys culture not one who recreates it. And when Mayakovsky, in his poem 'Jubilee', threatens to pull the statue of Pushkin off its pedestal it is not because he wishes to dethrone the poet, but because he wishes he were still alive.

Mayakovsky had warned how the veneration of Lenin's image might be an excuse for ignoring his advice (p. 156). Years later (and in reference to Mayakovsky) Yevtushenko would speak of the 'posthumous tenderness' of the Soviet authorities who had rehabilitated those poets and writers they had either driven to suicide, madness, silence or exile, erecting shrines to the memories of figures they had debased while they lived.

In this light, it is understandable that the prospect of becoming a monument had filled Gogol with horror. After all, a bust can effectively decapitate the figure it represents; a stone statue petrify his or her legacy (cf. Musil, p. 152).

After the devastation of its 900-day siege by the Nazis, Leningrad was painstakingly reconstructed. The once vibrant city became a monument to its former self, frozen in time. Of all the centres in this book, probably Leningrad has outwardly changed the least. And this is perhaps a measure of its tragedy. Culture is not a question of bricks and bronze or stone. As Mandelstam says, it is not Rome that matters but man's place in the world. And without the critical dissidence of the streets, the spontaneous gathering and movement of its crowds, a city, no matter how beautiful, remains a ghost town or a necropolis.

Stop!

In Santiago, during a recent demonstration, a group of women stood protesting in a public square. In front of the riot police who gripped their shields and truncheons, the soldiers holding their guns, the women stood with their open hands up chanting the slogan: *Somos más*.

Suddenly, as though a bomb had exploded over the city, everything stopped. Horns ceased blaring, children hushed. Shoppers looked up from the shop displays, hawkers dropped their wares, bureaucrats and businessmen hung out of their windows. Even the police and soldiers stopped shouting orders and talking to their radio sets. For the women broke off their chanting and everyone was struck by it, the silence.

And in that moment, before the baton charges and water-cannon, before the screaming and the acid clouds of CS gas, the whole city seemed to feel the force of it, like a jolt, the shock. *Somos más*. We are greater than this. We are not ourselves alone. We are more than we know. *Somos más*.

NEW YORK
Mobility and Traffic

If there is one element running through the London high street, the Parisian boulevard, the St Petersburg prospect, to the New York broadway, it is mobility – both in its social and physical sense. In previous chapters the street always had a dual function: it encouraged both settlement and mobility; a place to live in or just a channel to move through. As more and more citizens join in the mass scramble to change and exchange their background, to refashion their lives, the city is increasingly dominated by the mechanisms of transport and access. So the streets become more congested and uninhabitable, so even greater numbers flee to the suburbs. So the city needs more means of transport and is bulldozed over with more expressways and parking lots. 'Freeways' is thus a capitulation as well as a recapitulation: from the vigorous streetlife of Broadway to the death of the street. In it we see the buildings go up, the people go down, the emptying of the inner city and the fall of public man.

Freeways

What did these vain and presumptuous men intend? How did they expect to raise this lofty mass against God, when they had built it above all the mountains and clouds of Earth's atmosphere?

Saint Augustine, City of God

Every superior human being will instinctively aspire after a secret citadel where he is *set free* from the crowd, the many, the majority, where, as its exception, he may forget the rule 'man'...

Friedrich Nietzsche, Beyond Good and Evil

Mobility

LOSING A HALO

My friend, you know my terror of horses and vehicles? Well, just a moment ago, as I was crossing the boulevard in a great hurry, splashing through the mud, in the middle of a moving chaos, with death galloping at me from every side at once, I made a sudden movement, and my halo slipped off my head and fell into the mire of the macadam...

Charles Baudelaire, Petits Poèmes en Prose

On that 1st of October, 1924, I was assisting in the titanic rebirth of a new phenomenon . . . traffic.

Cars, cars, fast, fast! One is seized, filled with enthusiasm, with joy . . . the joy of power. The simple and naive pleasure of being in the midst of power, of strength. One participates in it. One takes part in this society that is just dawning. One has confidence in this new society: it will find a magnificent expression of its power. One believes in it.

Le Corbusier, The City of Tomorrow

33 Manhattan: heaven and
hell, steam from buildings,
icicles on fire escapes, 1987 –
Teresa Watkins.

The motor-car will help solve the congestion of traffic.

A. J. Balfour

The Old Kent Road was very crowded on Thursday, the eleventh of October, 1928. People spilt off the pavement. There were women with shopping bags. Children ran out. There were sales at drapers' shops. Streets widened and narrowed. Long vistas steadily shrunk together. Here was a market. Here a funeral . . .

Applejohn and Applebed, Undert—. Nothing could be seen whole or read from start to finish. What was seen begun – like two friends starting to meet each other across the street – was never seen ended. After twenty minutes the body and mind were like scraps of torn paper tumbling from a sack and, indeed, the process of motoring fast out of London so much resembles the chopping up small of identity which precedes unconsciousness and perhaps death itself that it is an open question in what sense Orlando could be said to have existed at all in the present moment . . .

Virginia Woolf, Orlando (1929)

Space no longer exists: the street pavement, soaked by rain beneath the glare of electric lamps, becomes immensely deep and gapes to the very centre of the earth. Thousands of miles divide us from the sun; yet the house in front of us fits into the solar disk.

The sixteen people around you in a rolling motor bus are in turn and at the same time one, ten, four, three; they are motionless and they change places; they come and go, bound into the street, are suddenly swallowed up by the sunshine, then come back and sit before you, like persistent symbols of universal vibration . . .

Umberto Boccioni, Carlo Carrà, Luigi Russolo,
Giacomo Balla, Gino Severini, 'Futurist Painting'

We affirm that the world's magnificence has been enriched by a new beauty: the beauty of speed.

A racing car whose hood is adorned with great pipes, like serpents of explosive breath – a roaring car that seems to ride on grapeshot is more beautiful than the *Victory of Samothrace*.

We want to hymn the man at the wheel, who hurls the lance of his spirit across the Earth, along the circle of its orbit . . . We will sing of great crowds excited by work, by pleasure, and by riot; we will sing of the multicoloured, polyphonic tides of the revolution of modern capitals, we will sing of the vibrant nightly fervour of arsenals and shipyards blazing with violent electric moons: greedy railway stations that devour smoke-plumed serpents; factories hung on the clouds by the crooked lines of their smoke; bridges that stride the rivers like giant gymnasts, flashing in the sun with a glitter of knives; adventurous steamers that sniff the horizon: deep chested locomotives whose wheels paw the tracks like the hooves of an enormous steel horse bridled by tubing; and the sleek flight of planes whose propellers chatter in the wind like banners and seem to cheer like an enthusiastic crowd . . . Take up your pickaxes, your axes and hammers and wreck the venerable cities pitilessly!

F. T. Marinetti, 'The Manifesto of Futurism'

I think that cars today are almost the exact equivalent of the great Gothic cathedrals: I mean the supreme creation of an era, conceived with passion by unknown artists, and consumed in image if not in usage by whole populations . . .

Roland Barthes, *Mythologies*

Broadway

What *distinguishes* the city . . . is that its spatial structure (basically its *concentration*) is functional to the intensification of *mobility*: spatial mobility, naturally enough, but mainly *social* mobility.

Franco Moretti, 'Homo Palpitans'

Start spreading the news,
I'm leaving today.
I want to be a part of it –
New York, New York.
These vagabond shoes
Are longing to stray
Right through the very heart of it –
New York, New York.

I want to wake up in a city
That doesn't sleep,
And find I'm king of the hill,
Top of the heap.

These little town blues
Are melting away.
I'll make a brand new start of it
In old New York.
And if I can make it there
I'll make it anywhere.
It's up to you
New York, New York.

Fred Ebb and John Kander, 'New York, New York'

Here I was in New York, city of prose and fantasy, of capitalist automatism, its streets a triumph of cubism, its moral philosophy that of the dollar. New York impressed me tremendously because, more than any other city in the world, it is the fullest expression of our modern age.

Leon Trotsky, *My Life*

Meanwhile, outside the windows, the life of the harbour went on; a flat barge laden with mountains of barrels, which must have been wonderfully well packed, since they did not roll off, went past, almost completely obscuring the daylight; little motor boats, which Karl would have liked to examine thoroughly if he had had time, shot past in obedience to the slightest touch of the man standing erect at the wheel. Here and there curious objects bobbed independently out of the restless water, were immediately submerged again and sank before his astonished eyes; boats belonging to the ocean liners were rowed past by sweating sailors; they were filled with passengers sitting silent and expectant as if they had been stowed there, except that some of them could not refrain from turning their heads to gaze at the changing scene. A movement without end, a restlessness transmitted from the restless element to helpless human beings and their works!

Franz Kafka, *America*

The island of Manhattan is a gigantic metaphoric model of the compression of an immigrant ship that had moored and never left. Every apartment is like a berth. Every square metre of street is a deck. The sky scraping offices are the bridge.

John Berger, *About Looking*

Give me your tired, your poor,
Your huddled masses yearning to be free:
The wretched refuse of your teeming shore,
Send these, the homeless, tempest-tossed to me.

Emma Lazarus, 'Inscription at the Base of the Statue of Liberty'

Come all you foreigners, and jump into this magic kettle. You are coloured and discoloured with things that do not fit well with affairs here . . . Your clothes are ill fitting and ugly. Your language is barbaric. Of course, we do not hold you personally responsible; for you have come from backward and antiquated civilisations, relics of the dark ages . . . Jump into the cauldron and behold!

You emerge new creatures, up to date with new customs, habits, traditions, ideals. Immediately you will become like us; the taint will disappear. Your sacks will be exchanged for the latest Fifth Avenue styles. Your old fogey notions will give way to the most modern and new-fangled ideas. You will be reborn.

In short you will become full fledged Americans. The magic process is certain. Your money back if we fail!

Christina Krysto and Simon Lubin, 'Cracks in the Melting Pot' (1920)

TO BROOKLYN BRIDGE

And Thee, across the harbor, silver-paced
As though the sun took a step of thee, yet left
Some motion ever unspent in thy stride, –
Implicitly thy freedom staying thee!

O Sleepless as the river under thee,
Vaulting the sea, the prairies' dreaming sod,
Unto us lowliest sometime sweep, descend
And of the curveship lend a myth to God.

Hart Crane, from 'The Bridge' (1927)

The very idea of a bridge . . . is a form peculiarly dependent on spiritual convictions. It is an act of faith besides being a communi-cation.

Hart Crane, *Letters*

[New York] . . . is a capital for and of the refugee.

George Steiner

34 The arches of Brooklyn
Bridge, 1987 – Teresa
Watkins.

THE NEW JERUSALEM

I recall the intensity of the material picture in the dense Yiddish quarter . . . a great swarming, a swarming that had begun to thicken, infinitely, as soon as we crossed to the East Side and long before we had got to Rutgers Street. There is no swarming like that of Israel once Israel has got a start, and the scene here bristled, at every step, with the signs and sounds, inimitable, unmistakable, of a Jewry that has burst all bounds . . . multiplication, multiplication of everything was the dominant note . . . I was to learn later on that, with the exception of some shy quarter of Asia, no district in the world known to the statistician has so many inhabitants to the yard . . .

For what did it all really come to but that one had seen with one's eyes the New Jerusalem on earth? . . . When I think of the dark, foul, stifling Ghettos of other remembered cities, I shall think at the same stroke of the city of redemption, and evoke in particular the rich Rutgers Street perspective – rich, so peculiarly for the eye, in that complexity of fire escapes with which each house-front bristles and which gives the whole vista so modernised and appointed a look . . .

What struck me in the flaring streets was the blaze of shops addressed to the New Jerusalem wants and the splendour with which these were taken for granted . . . The scale, in this light of the New Jerusalem, seemed completely rearranged; or put more simply, the wants, the gratifications, the aspirations of the 'poor' as expressed in these shops (which were the shops of the 'poor') denoted a new style of poverty; and this new style of poverty, from street to street, stuck out of the possible purchasers, one's jostling fellow pedestrians, and made them, to every man and woman, individual throbs in a larger harmony.

Henry James, *The American Scene* (1907)

The street is human movement institutionalised. An individual may clear or mark out a path in a wilderness, but unless he is followed by others, his path never becomes a street.

Stanford Anderson, *On Streets*

It is scarcely possible to exaggerate the part that *Broadway* – I use the term generically – has played in the American town. It is not merely the Agora but the acropolis . . .

Lewis Mumford, *The Culture of the City*

For minutes at a time walking . . . through the deep canyon of downtown Broadway, I hardly felt, saw, heard or thought of anything. I was blank. The sensation of being in New York, in the midst of America's tallest buildings, with trains thundering under my feet, was so over-whelming.

Louis Adamic, *Laughing in the Jungle: The Autobiography of an Immigrant* (1932)

BROADWAY
Tarmac like glass.
                         A clang with each step.
Trees,
          and blades of grass,
                              with crew-cuts.
Avenues
            run
                   from North to South,
and streets
                   from East to West.
Between –
                   who could have stretched them that far! –
buildings
                   a good mile high.
Some houses seem to touch
                              the stars,
while others
                   reach for the sky.
Most Yanks are too idle
                              to go out walking.
They ride express
                   elevators
                              throughout.
At seven hundred hours
                   the human tide rolls in.
And at seventeen hundred
                   rolls out.
Machines
            rattle
                   clatter
                         chink
pedestrians
            go deaf and dumb,
while past them more
                   dumb people sprint

189

only stopping
                to spit out their chewing gum.
Yelling at a friend:
               'Make money!'
A mother suckles her child:
                   'Don't holler!'
And the kid,
             with its nostrils runny
looks less like it sucks a breast than
                   a dollar
and like everyone else,
             in a hurry.
The workday done,
          now all around
you're battered by
           electric hurricanes.
You take the subway,
            vanish underground,
or climb
       on the elevated
           train.
You can ride as high
         as a chimney stack
or dart
       between the feet of a house.
On Brooklyn Bridge, a tram
             snakes its back
or under the Hudson,
          sneaks like a mouse.

                   Vladimir Mayakovsky, 'Broadway'

The principal effect of the gridiron plan is that every street becomes a thoroughfare, and that every thoroughfare is potentially a commercial street. The tendency towards *movement* in such a city vastly outweighs the tendency towards *settlement*.

                 Lewis Mumford, *The Culture of Cities*

Harold is a smalltown boy going off to the city to start his career and earn wealth and status sufficient to enable him to marry his smalltown girl. He takes a job in a department store and writes glowing but false letters home telling of rapid advancement. When the girl comes to visit he must go through elaborate comic byplay to demonstrate his position without being caught.

Meanwhile, in an effort to promote himself, he arranges a stunt for the store, a climb up its outside walls by a 'human fly' ... Harold goes up the wall himself, in one of the superb comic stunts in the history of motion pictures. His climb is impeded successively by pigeons, a tennis net, a painter's board, a clock, a mouse and a weather gauge. Each new encounter throws him into graver danger. After one harrowing comic escape after another, he finally reaches the roof and falls into his girlfriend's arms.

One could hardly ask for more graphic satire on the theme of 'upward mobility'.

Robert Sklar, Movie-Made America

35 Harold Lloyd hangs from a ledge – still from *Safety Last* (1923).

Suddenly I feel her coming. I turn my head. Yes, there she is coming full on, the sails spread, the eyes glowing. For the first time I see what a carriage she has. She comes forward like a bird, a human bird wrapped in a big soft fur. The engine is going full steam: I want to shout, to give a blast that will make the whole world cock its ears. What a walk! It's not a walk, it's a glide. Tall, stately, full-bodied, self-possessed, she cuts the smoke and jazz and red-light glow like the queen mother of all the slippery Babylonian whores. On the corner of Broadway just opposite the comfort station, this is happening. This is Broadway, this is New York, this is America. She's America on foot, winged and sexed. She is the lubet, the abominate and the sublimate – with a dash of the hydrochloric acid, nitro-glycerine, laudanum and powdered onyx. Opulence she has, and magnificence: it's America right or wrong, and the ocean on either side. For the first time in my life the continent hits me between the eyes. This is America, buffaloes or no buffaloes. America the emery wheel of hope and disillusionment ... It's got me in the guts. I'm quaking. Something's coming to me and there's no dodging it. She's coming head on, through the plate-glass window ...

Henry Miller, *Black Spring*

36 Ruby Keeler dances among the skyscrapers – still from *42nd Street* (1933).

The modern urban scene, especially that of a large city at night, is clearly the plastic equivalent of Jazz . . .

All sense of perspective and of realistic depth is washed away in a sea of nocturnal advertising. Far and near, small (in the *foreground*), and large (in the *background*), soaring aloft and dying away, racing and circling, bursting and vanishing – the lights tend to abolish all sense of real space, finally melting into a single plane of coloured light points and neon lines moving over a surface of black velvet sky. It was thus that people used to picture the stars – as glittering nails hammered into the sky!

Headlights on speeding cars, highlights on receding rails, shimmering reflections on the wet pavements – all mirrored in puddles that destroy our sense of direction (which is top? which is bottom?), supplementing the mirage above with a mirage beneath us, and rushing between these two worlds of electric signs, we see them no longer on a single plane, but as a system of theatre wings, suspended in the air, through which the night flood of traffic lights is streaming . . .

The preceding impressions were those of at least one visitor to the streets of New York during the hours of evening and night.

Sergei Eisenstein, The Film Sense

BROADWAY is, in sum, the *façade* of the American city: a false front . . . In order to cover up the vacancy of getting and spending in our cities, we have invented a thousand fresh devices for getting and spending.

Lewis Mumford, The Culture of Cities

If we compare New York with Istanbul, we may say that the one is a cataclysm, and the other a terrestrial paradise . . . New York is exciting and upsetting. So are the Alps: so is a tempest; so is a battle. New York is not beautiful, and if it stimulates our practical activities, it wounds our sense of happiness . . .

Le Corbusier, 'The City and Its Aesthetic'

What confidence! What an inspiration! . . . Those skyscrapers –
Springing up from the ground, soon to overtower
Their own mammoth size . . .
What people they were! Their boxers the strongest!
Their inventors the most practical! Their trains the fastest!
And also the most crowded!
And it all looked lasting a thousand years

For the people of New York put it about themselves:
That their city was built on the rock and hence
Indestructible.

Bertolt Brecht, 'Late Lamented Fame of the Giant City of New York'

37 *Dies Irae*, 29 October
1929 – James N. Rosenberg.

'No money, yet New York dug up $89,931 in four days to see KING
KONG,' screamed a headline from the trade paper, *Variety*, in 1933.
The headline highlights the enormous immediate success of *King
Kong*. Inadvertently, it might also hint at one reason for that success.
At the height of the Depression (No Money!) might not audiences

have enjoyed the sight of a giant ape raging at and ripping the guts out of America's financial headquarters?

David Sinyard, *Classic Movies*

38 King Kong on the Empire State – still from *King Kong* (1933).

The young man walks fast by himself through the crowd that thins into the night street . . . muscles ache for the knowledge of jobs . . .

The streets are empty. People have packed into subways, climbed into streetcars and buses; in the stations they've scampered for suburban trains; they've filtered into lodgings and tenements, gone up in elevators into apartment houses. In a shopwindow two sallow window dressers in their shirtsleeves are bringing out a dummy girl in a red evening dress, at a corner welders in masks lean into sheets of blue flame repairing a carttrack, a few drunk bums shamble along, a sad streetwalker fidgets under an arclight. From the river comes the deep rumbling whistle of a steamboat leaving dock. A tug hoots far away.

The young man walks by himself, fast but not fast enough, far but not far enough (faces slide out of sight, talk trails into tattered scraps, footsteps tap fainter in the alleys): he must catch the last subway, the streetcar, the bus, run up all the gangplanks of all the steamboats, register at all the hotels, work in the cities, answer the wantads, learn the trades, take up the jobs, live in all the boarding houses, sleep in all the beds. One bed is not enough, one job is not enough, one life is not enough. At night, head swimming with wants, he walks by himself alone.

No job, no woman, no house, no city.

John Dos Passos, *U.S.A.*

195

Architecture or revolution . . .
Revolution can be avoided . . .
The Plan: totalitarian
The death of the street . . .

Le Corbusier, Towards a New Architecture

The city is not around us, in our little town, suburb or neighbourhood: it lies beyond us, at the end of a subway ride or a railway journey: we are citizens occasionally; we are *suburbanites* (denizens, idiots) by regular routine.

Lewis Mumford, The Culture of Cities

When the motorcar was new, it exercised the typical mechanical pressure of explosion and separation of functions. It broke up family life, or so it seemed, in the 1920s. It separated work and the domicile, as never before. It exploded each city into a dozen suburbs, and then extended many of the forms of urban life along the highway till the open road seemed to become non-stop cities. It created the asphalt jungles, and caused some 40,000 square miles of green and pleasant land to be cemented over . . .

The motorcar ended the countryside and substituted a new landscape in which the car was a sort of steeplechaser. At the same time, the motor destroyed the city as a casual environment in which families could be reared. Streets, and even sidewalks, became too intense a scene for the casual interplay of growing up. As the city filled with mobile strangers, even next-door neighbours became strangers. This is the story of the motorcar, and it has not much longer to run . . . The car, in a word, has refashioned all the spaces that unite and separate men . . .

Marshall McLuhan, Understanding Media

Going Underground

The settler's town is a strongly-built town, all is made of stone and steel. It is a brightly-lit town; the streets are covered with asphalt, and the garbage-cans swallow all the leavings, unseen, unknown, and hardly thought about . . . The settler's town is a well-fed town, an easy-going town; its belly is always full of good things. The settler's town is a town of white people, of foreigners.

The town belonging to the colonised people, or at least the native town, the Negro village, the medina, the reservation, is a place of ill fame, peopled by men of evil repute. They are born there, it matters little where or how; they die there, it matters not where, nor how. It is a world without spaciousness; men live on top of each other, and their huts are built one on top of the other. The native town is a hungry town, starved of bread, of meat, of shoes, of light. The native town is a crouching village, a town on its knees, a town wallowing in the mire. It is a town of niggers and dirty arabs.

The look that the native turns on the settler's town is a look of lust, a look of envy; it expresses his dreams of possession – all manner of possession; to sit at the settler's table, to sleep in the settler's bed, with his wife if possible. The colonised man is an envious man. And this the settler knows very well; when their glances meet he ascertains bitterly, always on the defensive, 'They want to take our place' . . .

Frantz Fanon, The Wretched of the Earth

Organized Capitalism now has its colonies in the metropolis, and it concentrates on the internal market in order to utilize it according to a colonial pattern. The population in the metropolis is regrouped into ghettos (suburbs, foreigners, factories, students) and the new cities are to some extent reminiscent of colonial cities.

Henri Lefebvre, Everyday Life in the Modern World

Ah Harlem! Ah Harlem! Ah Harlem!
There's no anguish comparable to your oppressed reds,
to the blood shuddering in your dark eclipse
to your garnet violence drowned out in the shadows
to your great king imprisoned in his commissionaire's uniform . . .

That night the King of Harlem with a steely spoon
scooped out the eyes of crocodiles
and thwacked the monkeys on their bums.
With a spoon.
Perplexed negroes wept
under umbrellas and gilded suns,
mulattoes stretched their gum, anxious to reach the white flesh,
and the wind silvered the mirrors
and cut the dancer's veins . . .

This is the blood that flows, will flow
over roofs and terraces, through every route,
to cauterize the chlorophyll of blondes,

to groan at the bed-foot into basins of insomnia,
and hurl itself against a tobacco yellow dawn . . .

Ah, Harlem, masqueraded!
Ah, Harlem, menaced by a crowd of headless suits!
Your rumour reaches me,
your rumour reaches me over tree trunks and elevators,
across grey metal plates
where your cars float with ferric teeth
across dead horses and petty crimes
across your grey desolate King
whose beard reaches the sea.

Federico García Lorca, 'The King of Harlem' (1929)

What I saw around me that summer in Harlem was what I had always seen, nothing had changed. But now, without warning, the whores and pimps on the Avenue [Lenox Avenue] had become a personal menace. It had not occurred to me that I could become one of them, but now I realised that we had been produced by the same circumstances. Many of my comrades were clearly headed for the Avenue, and my father said I was headed that way, too . . .

My friends were now 'downtown', busy, as they put it, 'fighting the man'. They began to care less about the way they looked, the way they dressed, the things they did; presently, one found them in twos and threes and fours, in a hallway, sharing a jug of wine or a bottle of whiskey, talking, cursing, fighting, sometimes weeping: lost, and unable to say what it was that oppressed them, except that they knew it was 'the man' – the white man . . .

One did not have to be very bright to realise how little one could do to change one's situation . . . I was thirteen and was crossing Fifth Avenue on my way to Forty-second Street library, and a cop in the middle of the street muttered as I passed him, 'Why don't you niggers stay uptown where you belong?' When I was ten, and didn't look, certainly, any older, two policemen amused themselves with me by frisking me, making comic (and terrifying) speculations concerning my ancestry and probable sexual prowess, and for good measure, leaving me flat on my back in one of Harlem's empty lots.

Just before and then after the Second World War, many of my friends fled into the service, all to be changed there, and rarely for the better, many to be ruined, and many to die. Others fled to other states and cities – that is, to other ghettos.

Some went on wine or whiskey or the needle, and are still on it. And others, like me, fled into the church.

James Baldwin, The Fire Next Time

I am an invisible man. No, I am not a spook like those who haunted Edgar Allan Poe: nor am I one of your Hollywood-movie ectoplasms. I am a man of substance, of flesh and bone, fibre and liquids – and I might even be said to possess a mind. I am invisible, simply because people refuse to see me . . .

I am not complaining, nor am I protesting either. It is sometimes advantageous to be unseen, although it is most often wearing on the nerves. Then too, you're constantly being bumped against by those with poor vision. Or again, you often doubt if you really exist. You wonder whether you are simply a phantom in other people's eyes. Say, a figure in a nightmare which the sleeper tries with all his strength to destroy. It's when you feel like this that, out of resentment, you begin to bump people back. And, let me confess, you feel that way most of the time . . .

One night I accidentally bumped into a man, and perhaps because of the near darkness he saw me and called me an insulting name. I sprang at him, seized his coat and lapels and demanded he apologize. He was a tall blond man and as my face came close to his he looked insolently out of his blue eyes and cursed me, his breath hot on my face as he struggled. I pulled his chin down sharp on the crown of my head, butting him as I had seen the West Indians do, and I felt his flesh tear and blood gush out, and I yelled 'Apologize! Apologize!' But he continued to curse and struggle, and I butted him again and again and he went down heavily, on his knees, profusely bleeding. I kicked him repeatedly, in a frenzy because he still uttered insults though his lips were frothy with blood. Oh yes, I kicked him! And in my outrage I got out my knife and prepared to slit his throat, right there beneath the lamplight in the deserted street, holding him by the collar with one hand, and opening the knife with my teeth – when it occurred to me that the man had not *seen* me, actually; that he, as far as he knew, was in the midst of a waking nightmare! . . .

The next day I saw his picture in the *Daily News*, beneath a caption stating that he had been 'mugged'. Poor fool, poor blind fool, I thought with sincere compassion, mugged by an invisible man.

Ralph Ellison, The Invisible Man

I've got to hide, he told himself . . . He smoked and waited, tense. At last the siren gave him his signal. It wailed, dying, going away from him. He stepped to the sidewalk, and paused and looked curiously at the open manhole, half expecting the cover to leap up again. He went to the center of the street and stopped and peered into the hole, but could see nothing. Water rustled in the black depths.

He started with terror: the siren sounded so near that he had the idea that he had been dreaming and had awakened to find the car upon him. He dropped instinctively on his knees and his hands grasped the rim of the manhole. The siren seemed to hoot directly above him and with a wild gasp of exertion he snatched the cover far enough off to admit his body. He swung his legs over the opening and lowered himself into watery darkness. He hung for an eternal moment to the rim by his finger tips, then he felt rough metal prongs and at once he knew that sewer workmen used these ridges to lower themselves into manholes. Fist over fist, he let his body sink until he could feel no more prongs. He swayed in dank space; the siren seemed to howl at the very rim of the manhole. He dropped and was washed violently in an ocean of warm, leaping water. His head was battered against a wall and he wondered if this was death. Frenziedly his fingers clawed and sank into a crevice. He steadied himself and measured the strength of the current with his own muscular tension. He stood slowly in water that splashed past his knees with fearful velocity.

Richard Wright, 'The Man Who Lived Underground'

The drain is the conscience of the city. Everything converges and is confronted there. All the uncleanness of civilisation, when no longer of service, falls into this trench of truth . . . the saliva of Caiaphas meets the vomit of Falstaff: the vivid foetus rolls by wrapped in spangles which danced at the Opera last Shrove Tuesday. It is more than fraternity: it is the extremest familiarity. All that was painted is bedaubed. The last veil is torn away . . . The sewer is a cynic. It tells everything.

Victor Hugo, *Œuvres Complètes*, Vol. IV

'We are not going to follow that crazy nigger down into that sewer, are we?' Johnson asked.

'Come on, you-all!' he begged in a shout.

He saw Lawson raise the gun and point it directly at him. Lawson's face twitched, as though he were hesitating.

Then there was a thunderous report and a streak of fire ripped through his chest. He was hurled into the water, flat on his back. He looked in amazement at the blurred white faces looming above him. They shot me, he said to himself . . .

As though in a deep dream, he heard a metallic clank; they had replaced the manhole cover, shutting out forever the sound of wind and rain. From overhead came the muffled roar of a powerful motor and the swish of a speeding car. He felt the strong tide pushing him slowly into the middle of the sewer, turning him about. For a split second there hovered before his eyes the glittering cave, the shouting walls, the laughing floor . . . Then his mouth was full of thick, bitter water. The current spun him around, He sighed and closed his eyes, a whirling object rushing alone in the darkness, veering, tossing, lost in the heart of the earth.

Richard Wright, 'The Man Who Lived Underground'

Flyway

To New York . . . must go the credit for the creation of the parkway . . .

As with many of the creations born out of the spirit of this age, the meaning and beauty of the parkway cannot be grasped from a single point of observation, as was possible from a window of the château at Versailles. It can be revealed only by movement, by going along in a steady flow, as the rules of traffic prescribe. The space-time feeling of our period can seldom be felt so keenly as when driving.

Siegfried Giedion, *Time, Space and Architecture*

THE CITY AND ITS AESTHETIC
Suppose we are entering the city by way of the Great Park. Our fast car takes the special elevated motortrack between the majestic skyscrapers; as we approach nearer, there is seen the repetition against the sky of the twenty-four skyscrapers . . .

Then suddenly we find ourselves at the feet of the first skyscrapers. But here we have, not the meagre shaft of sunlight which so faintly illumines the dismal streets of New York, but an immensity of space. The whole city is a park. The terraces stretch out over lawns and into groves. Low buildings of a horizontal kind lead the eye to the foliage of the trees . . . Here is the CITY with its crowds living in peace and pure air, where noise is smothered under the foliage of green trees. The chaos of New York is overcome. Here, bathed in light, stands the modern city.

Our car has left the elevated track and has dropped its speed of sixty miles an hour to run gently through the residential quarters. The 'set-backs' permit of vast architectural perspectives. There are gardens, games and sports grounds. And sky everywhere, as far as the eye can see . . .

The uniformity of the units which compose the picture throws into relief the firm lines on which the far-flung masses are constructed. Their outlines softened by distance, and the skyscrapers raise immense geometrical façades all of glass, and in them is reflected the blue glory of the sky. An overwhelming sensation. Immense but radiant prisms . . .

As twilight falls the glass skyscrapers seem to flame.

This is no dangerous futurism, a sort of literary dynamite flung violently at the spectator. It is a spectacle organised by Architecture which uses plastic resources for the modulation of forms seen by light.

Le Corbusier, 'The City of Tomorrow'

There is no longer any place for the city street, with heavy traffic running between rows of houses; it cannot possibly be permitted to exist.

Siegfried Giedion, *Time, Space and Architecture*

Streets provide the principal visual scenes in cities.

However, too many streets present our eyes with a profound and confusing contradiction. In the foreground, they show us all kinds of detail and activity. They make a visual announcement that this is an intense life and that into its composition go many different things . . .

There are, of course, two ways of trying to see such a street. If a person gives the long view precedence, with its connotations of repetition and infinity, then the close-up scene and the intensity it conveys seem superfluous and offensive. I think this is the way that many architecturally trained viewers see city streets . . .

If the foreground view, on the other hand, takes precedence, then the endless repetition and continuation into lost indefinite distances become the superfluous, offensive and senseless element. I think this is the way most of us look at city streets most of the time . . .

To approach a city, or even a city neighbourhood, as if it were a larger architectural problem, capable of being given order by converting it into a disciplined work of art, is to make the mistake of attempting to substitute art for life.

Jane Jacobs, *The Life and Death of American Cities*

What sphinx of cement and aluminum hacked open their skulls and
ate up their brains and imagination? . . .

Moloch the incomprehensible prison! Moloch the crossboneless
soulless jailhouse and Congress of sorrows! Moloch whose buildings are judgement! . . .

Moloch whose eyes are a thousand blind windows! Moloch whose
skyscrapers stand in the long streets like endless Jehovahs! Moloch whose factories dream and croak in the fog! Moloch whose
smokestacks and antennae crown the cities!

Moloch! Moloch! Robot apartments! invisible suburbs! skeleton
treasuries! blind capitals! demonic industries! spectral nations!
invincible madhouses! granite cocks!

They broke their backs lifting Moloch to Heaven! Pavements, trees,
radios, tons! lifting the city to Heaven which exists and is everywhere about us! . . .

Alan Ginsberg, 'Howl'

DEAD PUBLIC SPACE

One of the first pure International School skyscrapers built after
World War II was Gordon Bunshaft's Lever House on Park Avenue in
New York. The ground floor of Lever House is an open-air square, a
courtyard with a tower rising on the north side, and, one story above
the ground, a low structure surrounding the other three sides. But one
passes from the street underneath this low horseshoe to penetrate to
the courtyard; the street level itself is dead public space. No diversity
of activity takes place on the ground floor; it is only a means of passage
to the interior . . .

This contradiction is part of a larger clash. The International School
was dedicated to a new idea of visibility in the construction of large
buildings. Walls almost entirely of glass, framed with thin steel sup-
ports, allow the inside and outside of a building to be dissolved to the
least point of differentiation; this technology permits the achievement
of what S. Giedion calls the ideal of the permeable wall, the ultimate in
visibility. But these walls are also hermetic barriers. Lever House was
the forerunner of a design concept in which the wall, though permeable, also isolates the activities within the building from the life of the
street. In this design concept, the aesthetics of visibility and social
isolation merge . . .

The erasure of alive public space contains an even more perverse
idea – that of making space contingent upon motion. In . . . Lever
House . . . the public space is an area to move through, not be in . . .

39 Cars, cycles and
pedestrians reflected in glass
wall, 1987 – Teresa Watkins.

The idea of space as derivative from motion parallels exactly the
relations of space to motion produced by the private automobile ...
The city street, then, acquires a peculiar function – to permit motion;
if it regulates motion too much, by lights, one-ways and the like,
motorists become nervous or angry.

Richard Sennett, *The Fall of Public Man*

Looked at from right outside, the traffic flows and their regulation is
clearly a social order of a determined kind, yet what is experienced
inside them – in the conditioned atmosphere and internal music of this
windowed shell – is movement, choice of direction, the pursuit of
self-determined private purposes.

All the other shells are moving, in comparable ways but for their
own different private ends. They are not so much other people, in any
full sense, but other units which signal and are signalled to, so that
private mobilities can proceed safely and relatively unhindered. And if
all this is seen from outside as in deep ways determined, or in some
sweeping glance as dehumanised, that is not at all how it feels inside
the shell, with people you want to be with, going where you want to go.

Raymond Williams, *Towards 2000*

Which driver is not tempted, merely by the power of his engine, to
wipe out the vermin of the street, pedestrians, children and cyclists?
The movements machines demand of their users already have the
violent, hard-hitting, unresisting jerkiness of Fascist maltreatment.

Theodor Adorno, *Minima Moralia*

40 Robert De Niro in taxi – still from Martin Scorsese's film *Taxi Driver* (1975).

When you operate in an overbuilt metropolis, you have to hack your way with a meat axe.

I'm just going to keep right on building. You do the best you can to stop it.

Robert Moses

Out for a walk, after a week in bed,
I find them tearing down part of my block
And, chilled through, dazed and lonely, join the dozen
In meek attitudes, watching the huge crane
Fumble luxuriously in the filth of years . . .

As usual in New York, everything is torn down
Before you have had time to care for it . . .

You would think the simple fact of having lasted
Threatened our cities like mysterious fires.

James Merrill, 'An Urban Convalescence'

At street level – outside a vehicle – all modern cities are violent and tragic.

The violence of which the media and police reports speak so much, is partly a reflection of this more continuous but unregarded and older violence. The violence of the daily necessity of the streets – of which the traffic is a symbolic expression – to obliterate (run over) even the recent histories of those who lived and live in them.

John Berger, *About Looking*

205

Thought I'd seen some ups and downs,
'Til I come into New York town.
People goin' down to the ground,
Buildings goin' up to the sky.

Bob Dylan, 'Talking New York'

THE TUNNEL
And so
of cities you bespeak
subways, rivered under streets
and rivers . . . In the car
the overtone of motion
underground, the monotone
of motion is the sound
of other faces, also underground –

Hart Crane, from 'The Bridge'

He inhaled the odours of stone, of urine, bitterly tonic, the smells of rust and of lubricants, felt the presence of a current of urgency, speed of infinite desire, possibly related to the drive within himself, his own streaming nervous vitality . . .

Innumerable millions of passengers have polished the wood of the turnstile with their hips. From this arose a feeling of communion – brotherhood in one of its cheapest forms. This was serious, thought Herzog, as he passed through. The more individuals are destroyed (by processes such as I know) the worse their yearning for collectivity. Worse, because they return to the mass agitated, made fervent by their failure. Not as brethren, but as degenerates . . . The real question! He stood looking down the tracks. The most real question!

Saul Bellow, *Herzog*

The rush hour! and the subway a free for all Paradise. Pressed up against a woman so tight I can feel the hair of her twat. So tightly glued together my knuckles are making a dent in her groin. She's looking straight ahead, at a microscopic spot just under my right eye. By Canal Street I manage to get my penis where my knuckles were before. The thing's jumping like mad and no matter which way the train jerks she's always in the same position vis-a-vis my dickie. Even when the crowd thins out she stands there with her pelvis thrust forward and her eyes fixed on the microscopic spot just under my right eye. At Borough Hall she gets out without once giving me the eye. I follow her up the street thinking she might turn round and say hello at least, or let me buy her a frosted chocolate, assuming I could buy one. But no, she's off like an arrow, without turning her head one eighth of an inch.

Henry Miller, Black Spring

Rush hour was just ended. Almost empty local cars were scenes of rest and peace, conductors reading the papers. Waiting for his uptown express, Herzog made a tour of the platform, looking at the mutilated posters – blacked-out teeth and scribbled whiskers, comical genitals like rockets, ridiculous copulations, slogans and exhortations. *Moslems, the enemy is white. Hell with Goldwater, Jews! Spicks eat SHIT. Phone, I will go down on you if I like the sound of your voice.* And by a clever cynic, *If they smite you, turn the other face.*

Saul Bellow, Herzog

And the people bowed and prayed
To the neon god they made
And the sign flashed out its warning
In the words that it was forming
And the signs said: "the words of the prophets
Are written on the subway walls, and tenement halls"
And whisper'd in the sounds of silence.

Paul Simon, 'The Sound of Silence'

Today Barbarism has taken over many city streets, or people fear it has, which comes to much the same thing in the end. 'I live in a lovely, quiet, residential area,' says a friend of mine who is hunting another place to live. 'The only disturbing sound at night is the occasional scream of someone being mugged.' It does not take many incidents of violence on a city street, or in a city district, to make people fear the streets. As they fear them, they use them less, which makes the streets still more unsafe . . .

The first thing to understand is that the public peace – the sidewalk and street peace – of cities is not kept primarily by the police, necessary as police are. It is kept primarily by an intricate, almost unconscious, network of voluntary controls and standards among the people themselves, and enforced by the people themselves . . . This is something everyone already knows: a well-used city street is apt to be a safe street. A deserted city street is apt to be unsafe.

Jane Jacobs, The Life and Death of American Cities

41 Shadow of a man, graffiti
in New York, 1987 – Teresa
Watkins.

The street is, clearly enough, the public dimension par excellence. In the street, we become visible to others and they to us; the street itself (and many of the means of transportation on it) are public property . . . Our problem then consists in establishing the relevance of this sphere to the city dweller's life . . .

The great novelty of urban life, in fact, does not consist in having thrown the people into the street, but in having raked them up and shut them into offices and houses. It does not consist in having intensified the public dimension, but in having invented the private one . . .

Franco Moretti, 'Homo Palpitans'

The walkman has become a familiar image of modern urban life, creating troops of sleep-walking space-creatures, who seem to feel themselves invisible because they imagine that what they're listening to is inaudible. The walkman is a vivid symbol of our time. It provides a concrete image of alienation, suggesting an implicit hostility to, and isolation from the environment in which it is worn.

The walkman is primarily a way of escaping from a *shared* experience or environment. It produces a privatised sound, in the public domain; a weapon of the individual against the communal. It attempts to negate *chance*: you never know what you're going to hear on a bus or the street, but the walk-person is buffered against the unexpected – an apparent triumph of individual control over social spontaneity . . .

The peculiarity of the walkman is that it turns the inside of the head into a mobile home – rather like the building society image of the couple who, instead of an umbrella, carry a tiled roof over their heads.

Judith Williamson, *Consuming Passions*

Don't push me 'cause
I'm close to the
           edge.
I'm try-in'
not to lose
my head.

Sometimes it's like a jungle that
it really makes me wonder how
I keep from going under

Ha Ha Ha Haha

> Sometimes it's like a jungle that
> it really makes me wonder how
> I keep from going under
>
> Grand Master Flash, 'The Message'

Some people say Paris is more esthetic than New York. Well, in New York you don't have time to have an esthetic because it takes half the day to go downtown and half the day to go uptown.

Then there's time in the street, when you run into somebody you haven't seen in, say, five years and you play it all on one level. When you see each other and you don't even lose a beat that's when it's the best.

You don't say 'What have you been doing?' – you don't try to catch up. Maybe you mention that you're on the way to 8th Street to get a frozen custard and maybe they mention which movie they're on the way to see, but that's it. Just a casual check-in. Very light, cool, off-hand, very American. Nobody's fazed, nobody's thrown out of time, nobody gets hysterical, nobody loses a beat. That's when it's good. And when somebody asks you whatever happened to so-and-so you just say, 'Yes, I saw him having a malted in 53rd Street.'

Just play it all on one level, like everything was yesterday.

Andy Warhol, A to B and Back Again

I said, Hey Pal, how do I get to town from here . . . and he said, well just take a right where they're going to build that new shopping mall; go straight past where they're going to put in the freeway, and take a left at what's going to be the new sports centre . . . and keep going until you hit the place where they're thinking of building a drive-in bank . . . you can't miss it. And I said . . . this must be the place . . . Golden City . . . Golden Town.

Laurie Anderson, Big Science

Rather than confine itself to Newton's law of gravity, Manhattan dances to a variation of Einstein's laws in which time, matter and energy interrelate with money.

Richard Gottlieb, 'A Boom Borough'

Whenever that melancholy hits, the rub of New York, the realisation that we're a town of such cruelties, with the relentless rise of fortune as our biggest theme song (we're all Mafia men), the grasping, the clutching, the hundred little dances we do to keep alive . . . I put on my shoes and walk to the Chrysler building. The whimsy of that steeltop, a witch's hood with a ghost of triangular eyes, is enough to shake the sadness out of me. It's a reminder that New York once had an element of pure play, the belief in its own modernity. The building is slightly mad, with hubcaps on the walls, gargoyles borrowed from old Chrysler machines, and futuristic cars trapped in design of brick. Chrysler has an innocence, a total trust in the passion and good of industry, that's all but gone. Its entrance looms like a church celebrating the dream of the automobile . . .

Jerome Charyn, Metropolis

Somebody built the pyramids . . . Pyramids, Empire State Building, these things don't just happen. There's hard work behind it.

I would like to see a building, say the Empire State, I would like to see on one side of it a foot-wide strip from top to bottom with the name of every bricklayer, the name of every electrician, with all the names.

So when a guy walked by, he could take his son and say, 'See that's me over there on the forty-fifth floor. I put the steel beam in,' Picasso can point to a painting. What can I point to? A writer can point to a book. Everybody should have something to point to.

Mike Lefebvre, quoted by Studs Terkel, Working

The Bronx Mural, as I imagine it, would be painted onto the brick and concrete retaining wall that runs alongside most of the eight miles of the Cross-Bronx Expressway, so that every automobile trip through and out of the Bronx would become a trip into its buried depths . . . The mural might depict cross-sections of streets, of houses, even of rooms full of people as they were before the expressway cut through them all.

But it would go back before all this, to our century's early years, at the height of the Jewish and Italian immigration . . . whole populations conjured out of the ground . . . Here is D. W. Griffith, whose old Biograph Studio building still stands, solid but battered and neglected, at the Expressway's edge . . . and there is Trotsky on East 164th Street, waiting for his revolution . . . Now we see a modest but energetic and confident bourgeoisie, springing up in the 1920s near the new Yankee Stadium . . . We move to the bleak adversity of the 1930s, unemployment lines, home relief . . . street-corner fights between Trotskyites and Stalinists, candy stores and cafeterias ablaze with talk all through the night; then to the excitement and anxiety of the postwar years, new affluence, neighbourhoods more vibrant than ever . . . to the Bronx's new immigrants from Puerto Rico, South Carolina, Trinidad, new shades of skin and clothes on the street, new music and rhythms, new tensions and intensities; and finally, to Robert Moses and his dread road, smashing through the Bronx's inner life, transforming evolution into devolution, entropy into catastrophe, and creating the ruin on which this work of art is built . . .

To drive past and through all this would be a strange and rich experience. Drivers might feel captivated by the figures, environments, and fantasies on the mural, ghosts of their parents, their friends, even of themselves, like sirens enticing them to plunge into the abyss of the past. On the other hand, so many of these ghosts would be urging and driving them on, dying to leap into a future beyond the Bronx's walls and join the stream of traffic on the way out . . .

Marshall Berman, All That is Solid Melts into Air

I live in a ruin. I am a ruin. I'm adding to the ruin.

Bronx graffiti

The young man waits at the edge of the concrete, with one hand he grips a rubbed suitcase of phoney leather, the other hand almost making a fist, thumb up

that moves in ever so slight an arc when a car slithers past a truck roars clatters; the wind of cars passing ruffles his hair, slaps grit in his face.

Head swims, hunger has twisted the belly tight . . .

Eyes black with want seek out the eyes of the drivers, a hitch, a hundred miles down the road.

Overhead in the blue a plane drones. Eyes follow the silver Douglas that flashes once in the sun and bores its smooth way out of sight into the blue.

(. . . The transcontinental passenger thinks contracts, profits, vacation trips, mighty continent between Atlantic and Pacific, power, wires humming dollars, cities jammed, hills empty, the indiantrail leading into the wagonroad, the macadamed pike, the concrete skyway; trains, planes: history: the billiondollar speedup . . .)

The young man waits on the side of the road; the plane has gone; thumb moves in a small arc when a car tears hissing past. Eyes seek the driver's eyes. A hundred miles down the road. Head swims, belly tightens, wants crawl over his skin like ants:

went to school, books said opportunity, ads promised speed, own your own home, shine bigger than your neighbour, the radiocrooner whispered girls, ghosts of platinum girls coaxed from the screen, millions in winnings were chalked up on the boards in the offices, paychecks were for hands willing to work, the cleared desk of an executive with three telephones on it;

waits with swimming head, needs knot the belly, idle hands numb, beside the speeding traffic.

A hundred miles down the road.

John Dos Passos, U.S.A.

Imagine spacious landscaped highways, grade crossings eliminated, 'by passing' living areas, devoid of the already archaic telegraph and telephone poles and wires, free of blaring bill boards and obsolete construction. Imagine these great highways, safe in width and grade, bright with wayside flowers, cool with shade trees, joined at intervals with fields from which the safe, noiseless transport planes take off and land.

Giant roads, themselves great architecture, pass public service stations, no longer eyesores, expanded to include all kinds of service and comforts. They unite and separate – separate and unite the series of diversified units, the farm units, the factory units, the roadside markets, the garden schools, the dwelling places (each on its acre of individual adorned and cultivated ground), the places of pleasure and leisure. And all of these units arranged and integrated so that each citizen of the future will have all forms of production, distribution, self improvement, enjoyment, within a radius of a hundred and fifty miles of his home now easily and speedily available by means of his car or his plane.

This integral whole composes the great city that I see embracing all of this country – the Broadacre City of tomorrow ...

Frank Lloyd Wright, 'Broadacre City'

per every madge and mabel dick and dave
– tomorrow is our permanent address

and there they'll scarcely find us (if they do
we'll move away still further: into now

e. e. cummings, 'all ignorance toboggans into know'

As Lewis Mumford had predicted years before, the solution has become the problem. In order to overcome the fatal stagnation in and around cities, highway engineers and planners create remedies that actually expand the evils they are meant to cure. The clover-leaf, the multi-level interchanges and expressways butcher the urban landscape in exactly the same way as the railroad's freight and marshalling yards did almost a century ago.

They destroy natural routes of circulation, create clots of intense congestion, and sterilize vast acres of land. Furthermore, the new highways tempt people who have been using public transport to their cars for downtown journeys. Cities become more congested. Finally all the business and industry that originally gave rise to the congestion leave the city to escape their suffocation, leaving a waste of expressways and parking lots in their wake. In the end, all that is left is 'a tomb of concrete covering the dead corpse of the city'.

Thomas Blair, The International Urban Crisis

Baby this town rips the bones from your back
It's a death trap, a suicide rap
We've gotta get out while we're young
'Cause tramps like us,
   baby we were born to run

Bruce Springsteen, 'Born to Run'

42 The Motor Cycle Kid –
still from Francis Ford
Coppola's *Rumble Fish*
(1982).

The nostalgia for the country is not so important. What is important is that our towns are false towns.

D. H. Lawrence, Selected Prose

The shortcoming of the American landscape is not so much, as romantic illusion would have it, the absence of historical memories, as that it bears no traces of the human hand. This applies . . . above all to the roads.

They are always inserted directly into the landscape, and the more impressively smooth and broad they are, the more unrelated and violent the gleaming traces appear against its wild, overgrown surroundings. They are expressionless . . .

It is as if no one had ever passed their hand over the landscape's hair. It is uncomforted and comfortless. And it is perceived in a corresponding way. For what the hurrying eye has merely seen from the car it cannot retain, and the vanishing landscape leaves no more traces than it bears upon itself.

Theodor Adorno, Minima Moralia

Everything disappears faster and faster in the rear vision mirror of reality.

Baudrillard, America

We're on a road to nowhere,
Come on inside.
Taking that ride to nowhere.
We'll take that drive.
Feeling OK this evening,
And you know,
We're on a road to Paradise.
Here we go.
Here we go.

Talking Heads, 'A Road to Nowhere'

Street as Thoroughfare

Motors of Change

The rush hour. Congestion. Horns. Tarmac. Burnt rubber. Lead. This is the familiar image of the modern city street, and the most visible sign of its transformation is the motor car. But though the automobile accelerated the tendency to movement, it did not create it. On Haussmann's boulevards, designed for the ease and enjoyment of the stroller, Baudelaire is almost mown down by the 'moving chaos' of horses and carriages (p. 181). Even in mid-nineteenth-century Paris, the pedestrian is already a victim of the forces his mobility has unleashed. And the motor car was invented by the culture of the modern city, not vice versa: the assembly of so many private mobile individuals in the city precedes the assembly-line techniques perfected by Ford. Underlying the dominance of the automobile is a mass aspiration for both privacy *and* mobility, to enjoy the benefits of the city without having to live in it, to experience all the possibilities it offers without having to suffer the actuality of its crowds.

Initially velocity was a prerogative of the wealthy. The poor pedestrian was forced to gape at the carriage, suffer its mud and detritus, avoid its dangerous wheels (cf. Mumford, p. 128). During insurrections, rioters would often exact their revenge against the traffic and incorporate it into their barricades (cf. Leningrad, pp. 141–2). But rather than wreck the vehicles, by far the most effective way to beat the rush turned out to be to join it.

The principle of mobility for all is at the core of the American dream of freedom, and it is no accident that this dream expresses individual liberty primarily in the language of motion. Liberty is a right of way, a right to *go about* your business without let or hindrance. It is a negative concept of freedom, implying you may *go as far as you can* in the pursuit of personal happiness before your particular path clashes with someone else's. Such a philosophy is all very well for the cowboy or pioneer on the open frontier, but in the city, it leads to snarl-ups. Personal progress becomes a matter of being in the fast lane, in the driver's seat, getting on, overtaking as many others as you can. When encountered on the road, other people and their vehicles become frustrating obstructions (cf. Sennett, Williams, p. 204). The main forms of social control on the street are restrictions 'Walk/Don't Walk' signs, flow systems, traffic lights. Despite 'Macadam's Law' – that every new road creates enough traffic to congest it – and though the average speed in most city centres is only marginally more than the 12 mph it was over a hundred years ago, the car confers not only the illusion of mobility once out of the metropolis, in the suburbs; but cocooned behind metal and glass, it protects its occupants from the shout in the street, the possibilities of social experience.

Marinetti celebrates the kinetic energies of the modern age from the vantage of a speeding car. He exhorts his followers to wreck the venerable cities (p. 184). In many ways, that's exactly what his vehicle and his perspective would do.

The New Babylon

New York, capital of the twentieth century, is a summation of many of the themes and motifs of the previous three chapters because, as a centre for immigration from the old world to the new, it brought with it the memories and precepts of Paris, London and St Petersburg.

In the eyes of many exiles and refugees America appeared to be the promised land, and New York – as its visionary centre – a New Jerusalem (cf. James, p. 188). But a more telling analogy would be with a kind of Babel in reverse. In the biblical myth, those who had the impiety to build their towers to the heavens were struck with the affliction of speaking in different tongues. But in the construction of Manhattan's skyscraping towers many different languages come together to learn the same tongue. The tough streetwise vernacular of American English would provide, from jazz to jive-talk to rap, a kind of demotic Esperanto (cf. Krysto and Lubin, p. 186). Its polyglot combination of cultures – from delis and bagels, Hispanic clubs and Irish shebeens – is like a modernistic collage. The great promise of American street culture – hamburgers, jeans, T-shirts, Coca-Cola – is that the only thing you need is money. You are not defined by where you have come from but by what you can get. This is the myth of mobility: you can make it, you can take it, and refashion your race, class, caste if you have the guts, the backbone and the heart.

A city feeds on myths like these. The metropolis spreads itself through the rumours of travellers, its skyline sold on T-shirts or chocolate bars, its successes broadcast from its radio towers, pictures in cinemas and on glossy magazines. New York was always its own best publicist, and perpetuated an image of possibility to sustain its growth. But just as important as the attraction is the underdevelopment or autocracy that repelled the newcomers from their native lands. From its first settlement by the Dutch, its acquisition by the British, the growth of the Irish communities, the arrival of eastern Jews fleeing pogroms, Sicilians and Italians the poverty of the south, Hispanics from Mexico, Puerto Rico, and Central America, to the mainland and island Chinese and the Vietnamese boat people, to all kinds of exiles, émigrés and refugees, New York beckons as a place of deliverance. But driving its new future is a history of pain.

Ellis Island, the isle of tears, where for years the greenhorns and the green girls were tagged, registered and medically examined, represents the other side of the Utopian equation: alienation and homesickness. Though irrevocably severed from the old world, the new world looks back and idealizes it. Even the city's names – New Amsterdam, New York, New Jerusalem – while promising a new start, a radical break, still invoke the cities of the old world. The actual life in each quarter could reproduce the conditions which the newcomers had just escaped. Historically, the Irish slums round Mulberry Bend were not so different from St Giles'; the Jewish ghettos round Rutgers or Allen Street not unlike the 'Judaic chaos' Mandelstam celebrated in Millionya Street. Even the city's archetype of freedom, the Statue of Liberty, which welcomed millions of steerage passengers as they entered New York harbour with its gigantism and oddly flattened features, was a present from France. Its infrastructure built by Gustav Eiffel, the statue was a gift from the country which had made consumerism into a middle-class art, to the country which would develop it into a popular religion. It is not unfitting, therefore, that its torch of liberty should look like an ice-cream cone.

For New York's promise was not only that of deliverance, but also a more material promise – to deliver the goods.

No Jay-walking

Newcomers reconstruct the city, not simply by renewing it with their muscle and skill, but also emotionally and intellectually, remaking its streets as they explore them for the first time, seeing the water towers and fire escapes as something strange, almost fictional: perhaps read about, dreamt about, or seen in films. To the visitor, every detail is vivid, they read every street sign as a clue to this new world ('Don't even THINK of parking here'). They realize that the shapes of the fire hydrants, the bevels in the caps of the police, the typefaces on the shopfronts are deliberate declarations of identity. Uninitiated in the city's clandestine communities, looking for a place to stay or just passing through, newcomers are sharp to things a familiar citizen might ignore. And in everything ordinary, they see something extra-ordinary: to them the city is like a kind of collective illusion they must enter in order to sustain.

The main street by which newcomers have traditionally entered New York is Broadway (cf. Adamic, Mumford, Mayakovsky, pp. 188–9), the one road that snakes through the grid system and cuts through its secret quarters. Where it meets Times Square, at the crossroads of Manhattan, the drifters, hustlers and chancers habitually gather. Appropriately enough, for a place devoted to mobility, Times Square (then Long Acre) was dominated by shops for carriage repairs at the turn of the century. When the *New York Times* moved there, and New Year's Eve celebrations became an annual ritual, this section of Broadway became the theatre capital of America, and a source of other entertainments: peepshows, clip joints, shooting galleries, penny arcades. Soon the picture palaces moved in and Broadway became synonymous with showmanship, a street bravado, hustles and heists.

Crammed with enormous billboards and electric lights, as a place for display and self-presentation Broadway's social velocity was much higher than that of the Boulevard du Temple or the Nevsky Prospect. Ths chorus lines in its surrounding theatres added to the Parisian high kick the structure of one of Ford's assembly lines; as Jerome Charyn puts it, industrial production with sexual parts (cf. illustration 36, p. 192, Miller, p. 192). Around 42nd Street, Broadway was the Great White Way mythologized by Damon Runyon, who sat in the window of Mindy's restaurant and idealized its guys and dolls.

Broadway's characteristic figure, its equivalent of the *raznochinet* or the *flâneur*, is the gangster. Part hoofer, part hood, gangsters like Raft and Cagney simultaneously entertain and intimidate. The self is a hustle, a front, mobilized by a desperate economic vitality which, almost incidentally, just happens to stretch beyond the legal. The gangster is essentially the cowboy who has substituted the asphalt for the prairie, a Cadillac for his horse. And if his quips rattle off like bullets, his struggles always end in showdowns, this fits life in an urban space which is more frontier than street – to move through, pick up a fast buck and go.

The concrete shape of the city also reflects this greed for mobility. New York has traditionally abolished public places where people can gather and meet. The Lincoln Center transformed one central square, and plans have recently been put forward to concrete over Times Square with a shopping and office development. In keeping with this antipathy to congregation, Broadway's characters are always on the move: only bums or tramps hang around one place for long. The cheap hotels, sideshows and cafés are designed for itinerant populations; sources of entertainment, its Roxies and Follies, are an excuse for escapist fantasies. Fast food, quick laughs, speed thrills – Broadway is the acme of rapid turnover.

Surrounded by temples of hurried consumption, public space becomes marginalized, a route for cash and carry, smash and grab. Despite the stepback regulations, Broadway is overshadowed by sky-scrapers. Like a canyon, the sidewalk already feels like an under-ground, a place for outcasts. When its characters make it, they move out or up; out to the richer suburbs on Long Island; up to penthouse level where they can watch the crowds below. And the vistas of New York reinforce this movement. Cross-streets cut from one side of the island to the next, encouraging the eye ever further, ever outward – and unlike Paris there is no monument in the distance, only sea or sky. Otherwise, the buildings lure your sights upward, to the future instead of to the here and now. The whole perspective of the city is like a green light saying 'Go', animated by a frantic energy to be elsewhere.

Why does Manhattan, like so many modern cities, need to make such haste? To save time, the young executive in his car will answer. To save time, say the secretaries on the trains. Time, as everyone knows, is money and so it must be saved. But once all that time is saved and amassed, what is to be done with it? For the few who ever have the chance to cash it in, time saved in the city is spent elsewhere.

A Walk on the Wild Side

The supremacy of movement in the city radically changes our conception of space. Travelling from A to B on the path of least resistance, the important factors are distance and time, not depth: anything outside the line of your progress becomes flat, insubstantial.

New York has become a model of modernism because of this experience of mobility. Approaching from a car, the city appears cubist or constructivist: its clashing advertising hoardings a filmic montage of images. On the surface, this is revolutionary: New York has succeeded in breaking the limitations of the classical vista. Motoring through it defies the traditional laws of perspective, zooming in to close-up, panning away to panoramic, tracking along the vectors of motion. Urban life is made, like the 'rallies' and car chases climaxing so many movies, into a series of anarchic trajectories. Individuals collide like so many sub-atomic particles. Space becomes as fluid and contingent as the futurists saw it (cf. Boccioni *et al.*, p. 183, Marinetti, p. 184), its three dimensions superseded by two: distance and speed.

Film provides an analogy for this new spatial order; so does modern musical time. Goethe called architecture 'frozen music', and Eisenstein reversed the metaphor when he called the New York scene at night the plastic equivalent of jazz (p. 193). Jazz also breaks the closed perspective. Whereas classical music is monumental, based on a deep aural architecture of terraces and chambers, accompanied by the symmetrical rhythm of colonnades, in jazz there is no fixed focus or central vanishing point, no foreground of voices against a recessed background. In jazz, everything is up front, each instrument is prominent. Its rhythms are as sharp and protruding as the edges of passing skyscrapers. The trombone blares out of the orchestra, like a squad-car siren. Tones and volumes emerge with the suddenness of close-up. Sounds clamour for equal attention; co-ordinated but not subordinated.

Syncopated, chromatic, jazz informs the shape of New York. The neon lights and hoardings of this electric city, especially in its pre-war heyday, with giant sailors smoking Lucky Strike cigarettes, steaming coffee cups twenty-five feet high, a Mobil Oil Pegasus waving his neon wings from a floating blimp, are jazzy, crazy, wild. Like some massive oneiric spectacle, the city elides the difference between outer reality and inner life. As Henry James put it, New York is all formidable foreground. Even the buildings externalize their water towers and fire escapes. What should be inside is actually out. At night, the skyscrapers also reverse the distinction, illuminating the sidewalk with their interior lights. With no clear border between reality and dream, every walk in New York is a walk on the wild side.

Day and night, animated by fantasy, the city is as unstable as the desires projected on to it. One moment, Manhattan is the gleaming citadel of excitement and success. The next, the thrill is gone, and it collapses into the capital of neurosis. Night and day, Manhattan seems to follow this diurnal journey from romance to realism: purple nights to grey mornings. New Yorkers seem to measure their emotions by the same dimensions as their townscape. They get high, go down; and with very few intermediary levels (cf. illustration 35, p. 191).

A sense of deflation is the central experience of the young American hero in Dos Passos's *U.S.A.* When he arrives he wants to enjoy all the city's women, do all its jobs, but then suddenly senses: 'No woman, no job, no city' (p. 195). Indeed, the city's devotion to the bright lights is a direct cause of its hollowness. Late at night, early in the morning, when the last commuters have disappeared to the suburbs, the last crowds left the picture palaces and shows, the city reveals itself for what it is – a ghost town. People work and play in its streets, they watch movies, listen to jazz, but they actually live here less and less.

As an entertainment or commercial centre, but a diminishing residential zone, the city is becoming a façade (cf. Mumford, p. 193). It has broken the illusion of classic perspective, but at a cost: now it has no depth at all.

City View

One of the classic ways to see any city is from the air, to assume a godlike position and watch while others labour in the labyrinth below, about to turn a street, unaware of what is coming round the corner towards them. New York invites this desire for visual supremacy. It boasts in its skyline the possibility of everyone attaining that 'secret citadel' where they are set apart from the many, the crowd (cf. Nietzsche, p. 181). The boast looks best from a distance – the first glimpse of that forest of skyscrapers from an incoming jet or driving along the expressway. The lie is evident when you actually look out from your skyscraper. Only the rare penthouse or executive suite actually yields the promised vantage. Most windows give the typical 'Cityview' – that is, they look out on to the tinted glass or concrete facing of the competing skyscraper opposite. Because it promises freedom from the mass *en masse*, the city is built on an untenable philosophy – a philosophy of standardized specialness. Real enjoyment of the freedom of Manhattan, the ability to surmount its obstacles or penetrate its façades, calls for the impossible powers of Superman or Spiderman, or 'The Man with the X-Ray Eyes' (cf. illustration 38, p. 195).

For all their visionary imagery, New York City's monoliths are engaged in a symbolic battle for the sky: a competition between corporations and moguls for the commanding heights of the economy. Manhattan is fortunate in having a bedrock of granite, but the real base for the skyscraper was property speculation and commercial success. The early high-rise buildings, faced with brick, looked little different from their masonry predecessors, and, until the F. W. Woolworth building, skyscrapers clothed themselves in Neo-Gothic or mock stucco as if to hide their belligerent newness. But the famous edifices of Manhattan, the Chrysler Building, the Rockefeller Center, the Empire State, and more recently the Pan-Am Building, the twin World Trade Towers, the A T & T Building and Trump Tower, are all tributes to America's corporate success, and causes of it. They are built on the speculative hope of soaring land prices and their construction stimulates the boom they foresaw. As monuments to rising expectations when confidence fails as in the thirties (cf. Brecht, pp. 193–4), and to a lesser extent in the seventies, their foundations can seem precarious. If Wall Street sneezes, the world catches a cold, and these accumulations of iron and cash come crashing down on their investors' heads (cf. illustration 37, p. 194).

Manhattan is really less a concrete entity than a volatile mixture of solidified assets which, with a change in financial atmosphere, are liquidated, circulated, and congealed elsewhere (cf. Gottlieb, p. 210). Eisenstein had difficulty remembering street names and finding his way around Manhattan, but anyone who lives there long enough learns to locate things in terms of money rather than geography (cf. Laurie Anderson, p. 210). One block only might separate down-at-heel sleaze from well-heeled affluence. On Broadway, off Broadway, off off Broadway, these are not descriptions of locations, but of production costs, ticket prices, of an economic state. From the moment De Witt Clinton laid it out, Manhattan's grid system foretold the transmutation of space into lots, parcels of money. Thus whole institutions like the Waldorf Astoria or Madison Square Garden also pack up their bags and move, like pieces on a giant Monopoly board, gravitating along the lines of credit and finance.

The structure of the skyscraper is the same as that of New York as a whole. A vertical equivalent of the grid system, the offices, shops, restaurants and apartments contained within the block are essentially temporary, space to let. The chic New York flat made a virtue of this transferability, adopting a decor of sparse furniture and colours of a studied neutrality which would not offend a prospective occupant. Accommodation becomes as provisional as a shop display or advertising space; home a commodity like anything else.

Village Voice

The area which gave New York its street-beat was also one of its most marginalized – Harlem. Like the *raznochintsy* in Petersburg, denied expression through the usual means, the main outlet of the Black in New York was culture. From the Harlem renaissance in the jazz age, the easyspeak of Slim Gaillard, Cab Calloway and the Cotton Club, to the writing of Langston Hughes, Gwendolyn Brooks, Richard Wright and Ralph Ellison, culture gave the Harlem Blacks an imaginative claim to a city which in reality dispossessed them.

The division between uptown Manhattan, above 110th Street, and the rest of the island is the perfection of a split that is so evident in other *laissez-faire* cities. Except that here an economic division of purchasing power coincides with something beyond the values of the market: skin colour. New York vaunts the promise of mobility, that everyone can refashion themselves no matter what their origin or class. But Harlem, like so many other ghettos in so many other cities, refutes this promise. With longer American pedigrees than most other New Yorkers, Black internal migrants were nevertheless consistently left behind in run-down and decaying quarters. After the Second World War they populated the vacated Jewish communities of Brownsville and the East Bronx, to live with the civic consequences both of the upward mobility of the skyscrapers and the lateral flight to the suburbs.

On a racist street, the concept of 'citizenship' has been exploded, and the basic grounding of equality is lost. On the pavement under-privilege ceases to be a question of class, of classification, of something arbitrary that can be shed: it is a mark, a colour, some biological fact beyond choice or change. When the Black tries to enjoy the offered freedom of the city, he meets the impalpable barriers of prejudice, hidden colour bars. Each step becomes a battle, every trip downtown a struggle with the spectres of shame, contempt, indifference; 'fighting the man', as James Baldwin's peers called it (pp. 198–9); an enemy who was both everyone and no one. Like Dostoevsky's underground man, Ralph Ellison's invisible man feels the offence of his oppression as something internal (p. 199). But instead of having a clear opponent in the form of a tsarist officer, the invisible man lives in a city of declared liberty. Unable to blame anybody in particular, he can only lash out against a passer-by or himself. And unlike the underground man, his protest has no audience, no exemplary force. It is not a demonstration, a piece of political theatre, but a private, unseen act in empty streets.

Empty streets. Manhattan has, since the war, become a synonym for ghetto violence, muggings, gang fights, for the savagery of the modern metropolis. But anyone who has lived in New York or any other big notorious city knows that the fear is disproportionate to the reality. Urban paranoia is a reaction to a broader distrust of urban life, a distrust which has largely fulfilled its own prophecy. For the more the street is feared, the more empty and dangerous it becomes; the sooner the city is considered a barbaric jungle, the quicker it is devastated with empty lots, car parks, expressways, railway yards, the equipment of those who enjoy its benefits but don't like to live with its costs. And this fear arises largely out of prejudices – racial, social, economic – mental barriers which, more than barbed wire, barricades or walls, divide the different quarters of the city into hostile, uncomprehending enclaves. Between these ghettos arises the wasteland, a zone patrolled by para-noia: fear of the street, fear of encounter, fear of strangers, fear of those who are not part of your community.

It is this fear which is, in a more profound and less sensational sense, savage – uncivil. In New York not only does it make the most affluent and developed of all metropolises look less like a melting pot than a suspension of nitro and glycerine, but it casts a shadow over the future of the city in general. For the division of cities into communities based on race, age, origin, neighbourhood or gender is itself a denial of the principle of civility. In a city the majority are, by definition, strangers, and citizenship presupposes a capacity for people to find a common interest above particular filiations. But the retribalization of society into ghettos, upper class or under class, exclusive quarters or no-go zones represents the break-up of the city into a series of incompatible villages (cf. Lefebvre, p. 197).

Harlem stands in the middle of the modern city, but it might as well be on the margins. And gradually, as its inhabitants are moved out into the modernistic nightmare of tower blocks such as Claremont Village on the periphery, the centre is left to become a ghetto for the white, young and rich. In this resegregation, as in the street clearances in London a hundred years ago, roads have an incisive part to play.

Robert Moses, who as New York Commissioner for Parks did more than any other planner to change the shape of the city, ploughed his expressways through the poorer boroughs such as the South Bronx (cf. Moses, p. 205, Berman, pp. 211–12). Since the riots of the sixties, decals of lighted interiors have been placed in the endless blown-out windows. From the flyover they give passing motorists the impression that people still live there. They don't. They survive, hiding out in the bunkers and trenches of the city's warring villages.

Crystal Palace

The elevation of the motor car and the parkway, the zoning of the city and high-rise blocks are movements of modern urbanism that are foreshadowed in the work of Le Corbusier and Frank Lloyd Wright (cf. Le Corbusier, Wright, pp. 201–2). Both, though unjustly blamed for the failures of their imitators, still articulate some of the premises behind such monuments to modernity as the Cross-Bronx Expressway in New York, the Right Bank Expressway in Paris, the Westway Flyover in London and, beyond the expressway, the modern city of glass.

Le Corbusier, who had announced as part of his manifesto 'The Death of the Street' (p. 196), envisages his Radiant City from the perspective of an elevated motor-track. Instead of the confusion of the city street, Le Corbusier foresees the abstract beauties of skyscrapers in the park. His urbanism, with its emphasis on the natural qualities of green, space and light, purges away dirt, crowds, chaos, humanity. Moving through the scenery of geometrical planes unhampered by pedestrians, his view effectively depopulates the city, makes it as idealized as an architectural drawing. Nothing interrupts the glide of surfaces. The eye skims over the towers of cool non-committal glass. In short, his view is the view of a motorist, a commuter, who though he moves through the scene, remains as distant as any Versailles observer. As a work of art Le Corbusier might like the look of his city on paper, but he never really addresses the problem of living in it.

Le Corbusier's Radiant City is a city without secrets: it yields itself to the spectator; it is sight, transparency. After the war, the international school would develop this aesthetic throughout the major Western capitals: straight functional lines revealing the block engineering of their constructions; glass the favourite facing material for their curtain walls (cf. Sennett, pp. 203–4). Much has been written about the 'functionalism' of the international school, but little of this gradual glaciation of city life.

Eisenstein wrote a scenario for a film based on Frank Lloyd Wright's design for the 'Glasshouse', a skyscraper whose inner and outer walls were entirely constructed in glass. In the story, everyone can see one another, but by convention no one looks. Only at the denouement, when a young man hangs himself, is the convention broken and the walls, floors and ceilings are covered with helpless faces. Eisenstein's scenario suggests the social rules behind the emergent city of glass. For glass creates the possibility of spectacle without the need for dialogue: its invisible barriers protect private affluence against the poverty of the public sphere.

Though the proponents of the international style are now out of favour, and other architects and movements have taken their place, sheets of chrome, steel, and glass continue to plough their way into our city centres, creating their icy, gleaming townscapes (cf. illustration 39, p. 204). Today, the glass of the skyscraper will most likely be tinted, brown or blue, or mirrored in such a way that the corporate headquarters mask their power behind reflections of the sky, or other corporate headquarters nearby. Looking at them is like talking to someone with sunglasses: they can see you, but all you can see is the reflection of your inability to see them.

Rear-view Mirror

Motoring adds to a feeling of unreality in a city. Though the car increases one's power *over* the outside world, it reduces sensitivity *to* it. In the telematic bubble of the automobile, the vistas that slide over the windscreen are like back projections in the movies: they create the impression of a 'reel' world rather than a real one.

Many of the classic scenes of modern fiction are set on or around the flyovers and expressways of the modern world. In J. G. Ballard's *Crash!*, the hero is lost on a traffic island. At the end of Scorsese's *Mean Streets*, Johnny tries to escape the oppressive ghetto of his background, only to be shot in the neck while speeding along the expressway. And in Tom Wolfe's yuppie punishment novel, *The Bonfire of Vanities*, Sherman, the millionaire foreign exchange dealer, takes the wrong exit and finds himself in the Bronx. Trying to rejoin the expressway on a slip road, he finds his way blocked by tyres and when they are approached by two Blacks, his mistress runs one of them over.

On the freeway, the prime public space, social interaction takes the form of a collision of interests – a sudden impact. Recently, the frustrations of the rush hour have led to a spate of 'freeway shootings' (cf. Adorno, p. 204). From a distance, inside the car, the city looks like a crystal fairground; in reality it is hard and sharp.

The car creates an impression of a 'reel' world, and now the pedestrian has adopted this habit. Previously the city was compared to a theatre: men and women were actors, the street was a stage. But the visual regime of urban life incites spectacle rather than dialogue: its principles of intimacy, integrity (cf. Paris, pp. 101–2, 106) have more in common with close-up, 'method' film-acting than with dramatic masks.

When people imagine themselves on the street I suspect most of them see themselves less as actors on a stage than as stars in a movie. Perhaps a neon arrow picks out someone who stands above the crowds, like De Niro in the opening shot of *New York, New York*. Or perhaps, like Jon Voight in *Midnight Cowboy*, everyone sees their loneliness as something supreme and unique ('Everybody's talkin' at me/Can't hear a word they're saying/Only the echoes of my mind'). The fashion for 'personal stereos' adds to this illusion of being in your own private movie by providing a fitting mental soundtrack (cf. Williamson, p. 209).

What this shift in metaphor from stage to film implies is a different principle of sociability. From now on as the camera of self-consciousness cranes down and tightly focuses in on us the city is merely a backdrop for the scenarios of our own specialness.

Orpheus on the Underground

Beneath the city streets on the metros, the undergrounds, the subways, is another city, like a photographic negative of the one above. Millions pass through its passages and tunnels, but nobody lives here. Its platforms were often temporary shelters during the Second World War (they might be permanent ones after the next). But at the moment, people just pass through. And to facilitate our need for unimpeded mobility, the spaces between stations have been virtually negated. Outside, it is as black as the vacuums of outer space.

Like the classic underworld, the subway also has its demonology; muggers and vigilantes, suicides and homicides, neurotics and psychotics. Legends of Hades often depicted the dead as perpetual wanderers – motion devoid of purpose – and the subway also seems to be filled with restless bodies rushing past one another, pressed together, hurled through the darkness (cf. Miller, p. 206–7). Any interaction here is taken as a sign of aggression or assault. You keep yourself to yourself, and the closer you are crowded, the greater the mental distance you retreat. The graffiti cry out for copulation or conflict – any form of contact – or exclaims 'So and so was here', as though the author wasn't quite sure (cf. Bellow, p. 207). With nothing else to mediate between screams and silence, perhaps these writings on the wall are the city's true 'authentic' voice. (The Greek root to the word 'authentic' – *authentes* – means a doer, a perpetrator, a murderer or a self-murderer.) In societies which encourage naked individualism, these raw, explicit demands may well be all that's left of the shout in the street.

We, as underground men and women, are in these places most intensely ourselves. In the rush hour we often find ourselves running headlong down these tunnels, not because we have a particular train to catch, not because a few minutes will make any difference, but because in this great scramble to get nowhere in particular, there is one place we don't want to be – left behind. And standing in the train, we avoid others' gazes for the airbrushed faces in the ads: ads that promise the rewards of all this journeying: new jobs, new partners, new identities. Peering past our reflections in the window, it is so black outside we could pretend we're on a shuttle to the stars. Yet when we reach our destinations they will look almost indistinguishable from the stations from which we set out.

Yellow Brick Road

Back at street level, a walk along Broadway today would take you half-way across the world.

Much of Manhattan is beginning to resemble the old world: like London, it is in the process of consuming its past. An unmistakable sign that New York was only the capital of the first half of the twentieth century is the nostalgia now attached to many of its aspects (cf. Charyn, pp. 210–11). As with Covent Garden and Islington in London, whole quarters are devoted to the memorabilia business. In downtown Broadway, around SoHo, what were once the roughest parts of the city are being rehabilitated. Colonized first by the avant-garde – the shock troops of gentrification – they become desirable once the galleries selling retro-chic and graffiti art move in. Here, as in Alphabetville and Tribeca, artists of all sorts seem to be the necessary precursors to full colonization, aestheticizing an area a preliminary to anaesthetizing it. After the galleries, clubs and restaurants, boutiques and hairdressers will follow.

Northwards, through the mid-town emptiness of corporate headquarters and department stores, the new skyscrapers here could be anywhere else in the world: Hong Kong, Seoul, Rio de Janeiro, Tokyo. Beyond Central Park, cutting the corners of Black Harlem, instead of young traders rushing to Wall Street, or the shoppers rushing to buy, the figures are defiantly unhurried. They stand on street corners, sit on the steps, holding the one space they possess, their own bodies, as though their stances are a denial of the bitter lie of mobility. Further up, dodging west, into Spanish Harlem, the principle of mobility seems to be the reverse: bodies moving in hyperdrive outdoing New York at its own restlessness. The historical irony of Broadway becomes more apparent here, for the desperate energy of these streets is probably not so different from those Jewish, Italian or Irish quarters which are now being gentrified way downtown. And if the Latino street signs, the faces, the voices could easily deceive you into believing that you're not in Manhattan but Mexico City or Bogotá, you might as well be. For New York, replicated in other cities, replicates them in itself.

Broadway cuts through continents, both figuratively and literally. The magic American highway, with its petrol stations and motels, Marlboro packets and Coke cans, has cut its path from north to south: has bulldozed through the jungles of Latin America, through the rice fields of Asia, across Arctic tundra and African savannah. And where that yellow brick road ploughs through the city, it becomes a red brick road, a broadway both of nostalgia and progress: the global model of where we are going, and how we are going to get there (cf. Márquez, pp. 235–6).

One-way Street

Heaven and hell, either/or: we still conceive of our cities according to the old models, the old exclusions. In this cold war of absolutes, two philosophies, though at first they seem opposing, unite in reducing urban life to that series of narrow enclaves which Marshall McLuhan designated (in opposition to the Global City) a Global Village.

The first philosophy is based on an argument similar to that of one of Sartre's characters in *Huis Clos*: that hell is *other people*. It decries the city for its violation of solitude. Tramped by the mass, the herd, the street is the symbol of the city's vulgar, overcrowded uniformity. To be on the street is to be assailed by your insignificance, to lose all sense of self. But modern life isn't characterized by an excess of sociability, public life, or of crowds. In fact it has devised more and more subtle dimensions of privacy. And if the individual feels violated by the modern city, this is unlikely to be because it caters only for the grey collective mass, but because its touted philosophy of individualism constantly sets up a standard for all individuals. The drive for solitude in the city is much like that of commuters who, decrying the gregariousness of public transport, take their cars to the road. Stuck in traffic jams caused by all the others like them, they long for the emptiness of the countryside where they can really burn up the road. They dream of driving through the world as if the city never existed, but if it had never existed, neither would their cars.

The second attitude is more prevalent, more palatable, and in the end perhaps more pernicious. Like Milton's cosmology, which places hell within the sight of heaven to make it more hellish, this philosophy maintains that hell is not other people, hell is being *alone* with other people. The city could be heaven if only we weren't alienated by strangers, anonymous. It argues that all we need to do is return to more intimate relations with those around us, to be part of a community instead of an estranged society, and public life would return to some prelapsarian bliss. What this attitude ignores is the place of the strange, and the fact that what often attracts migrants to the city is precisely the liberations of anonymity compared to the stifling familiarities of a small village or town. A prime requisite of citizenship is an ability to make an accommodation with complete strangers. But the paradise of this communal philosophy comes, like heaven, complete with gates. St Peter may stand by the entry phone, and the security guards may be angels, but, like a medieval citadel, this heaven survives by keeping strangers out.

The modern metropolis really began after the gates of the old city had been breached and the walls that surrounded it overrun. In fact, one of the key definitions of a modern city is that, as one looks around, it seems to stretch to the horizon. To become a metropolite requires making this imaginative leap: there are other people as far as the eye can see. Another way of putting this is to say that the metropolis has no limits. Unlike the town, it does not define itself against the countryside, but within itself, from itself. And its lack of limits applies figuratively too. Metropolitanism quickly elides into cosmopolitanism, stretching its boundaries from an individual city to all cities. It was Diogenes who said '*Cosmopolites eimi*' – I am a citizen of the world – and the global extension of modern urbanization does in part fulfil this prophecy.

'Streetwise', then, could perhaps be reclaimed to mean these open-ended, open-minded characteristics of urbanity and civility which distinguish the city from the sectarian neighbourhood, the solipsistic garret, the parochial suburb. This book has been an attempt at such a reclamation, to see the street as a mentality, to redefine 'citizenship' as something concrete and popular. The only problem is that, living in a post-modern city, when I consider the emptiness of most streets I have to live with, I wonder if they have become just a state of mind rather than a real shared space.

Vacated now, the street seems dangerous, indefensible: sped through, it becomes a haze of fumes and a grating of brakes. But when populated, the street can be a clash of viewpoints, a mess, a morass that can challenge our little orthodoxies and take us out of ourselves. It satisfies neither those who yearn for intimate contact nor those who want no contact at all: it offends both sensibilities. But as a communication line between the familiar and the strange, between those we know too well and those we don't know at all, the street can still be the place where the most important connections are made. In it, we begin to see how our home is connected to that home, this house to that house, this street to that street, this city to all those other cities, my experience to yours.

Coda

The Storm of Progress

Of these cities will remain what passed through them, the wind!

Bertolt Brecht, 'Of Poor B.B.'

Cityful passing away, other cityful coming, passing away too. Other coming on passing on.

Houses, lines of houses, streets, miles of pavement, piled up bricks, slaves. Chinese wall. Babylon. Big stones all. Round towers. Rest rubble, sprawling suburbs, jerry built . . .

No one is anything.

James Joyce, Ulysses

This is how one pictures the angel of history.

His face is turned towards the past. Where we perceive a chain of events, he sees one single catastrophe which keeps on piling wreckage upon wreckage and hurls it in front of his feet.

The angel would like to stay, awake the dead, and make whole what has been smashed. But a storm is blowing from Paradise, it has got caught in his wings with such violence that the angel can no longer close them. This storm irresistibly propels him into the future to which his back is turned, while the pile of debris before him grows skyward.

This storm is what we call progress.

Walter Benjamin, 'Theses on the Philosophy of History'

– Suddenly, as if a whirlwind had set down roots in the centre of the town, the banana company arrived, pursued by the leaf storm. A whirling leaf storm had been stirred up, formed out of the human and material dregs of other towns . . . The whirlwind was implacable . . . In less than a year it sowed over the town the rubble of many catastrophes that had come before it, scattering its mixed cargo of rubbish in the streets . . .

Arriving there, mingled with the human leaf storm, dragged along by its impetuous force, came the dregs of warehouses, hospitals, amusement parlours, electric plants; the dregs made up of single women and men who tied their mules to hitching posts by the hotel . . . Even the dregs of the cities' sad love came to us in the whirlwind and built small wooden houses where at first a corner and a half-cot were a dismal home for one night, and then a noisy clandestine street, and then a whole inner village of tolerance within the town.

In the midst of that blizzard, the tempest of unknown faces, of awnings along the public way, of men changing clothes in the street, of women with open parasols sitting on trunks, and of mule after abandoned mule dying of hunger on the block by the hotel, the first of us came to be the last; we were the outsiders, the newcomers . . . the only thing we could do was set a plate with a knife and fork behind the door and wait patiently for the newcomers to get to know us. Then the train whistled for the first time. The leaf storm turned about and went out to greet it, and by turning lost its drive. But it developed unity and mass, and it underwent the natural process of fermentation, becoming incorporated into the germination of the earth.

Gabriel García Márquez, *Leaf Storm*

Author's Note

The compilation and writing of this book has been a long and mainly solitary occupation, so the comments of the few I have consulted have been particularly formative and helpful. Therefore I'd like to thank Piers Plowright, who encouraged the original BBC Radio Three project which provided the germ of this work; Graham Coster, who suggested it should be a book; Penny for Shakespeare, Teresa for her photographs, and Siân for her criticisms.

Though written in solitude, this book has never been written in isolation, thanks to the society of other books on the subject. This entire work clearly owes much to them, but of all my debts I feel especially impelled to acknowledge Marshall Berman's *All That is Solid Melts into Air*, Richard Sennett's *The Fall of Public Man*, Italo Calvino's *Invisible Cities*, and the writings of John Berger and Raymond Williams.

To Raymond Williams and Italo Calvino, who died while it was being written, this book is dedicated.

Picture Credits

1 Science Museum, London; 2 & 4 Fox Talbot Museum, Wiltshire; 5 Royal Commission on the Historical Monuments of England; 6 Benjamin Stone Collection, City of Birmingham Libraries; 7 B. E. C. Howard Loomes Esq.; 8 Copyright © Roy Export Company Establishment; 13, 15 & 16 Berenice Abbott Collection, Museum of Modern Art, New York; 14 Courtesy André Brassaï; 17, 18, 36 & 38 Copyright © Turner Broadcasting Ltd; 21, 22, 26, 28, 31 & 32 Novosti Press Agency; 23 Mansell Collection; 24 & 25 Museum of the Socialist Revolution; 27 & 30 British Film Archive and Mosfilm Exports; 35 British Film Archive; 37 Philadelphia Museum of Art; 40 Courtesy of Columbia Picture Industries Inc.; 42 Copyright © by Universal Pictures, a Division of Universal City Studios, Inc. Courtesy of MCA Publishing Rights, a Division of MCA Inc.

Maps

Page 1 London, from *Literary Landscapes* by David Daiches and John Flower, Bell and Hyman, London 1981; reproduced with kind permission.
Page 59 Paris, from *The Times Atlas of the World: Family Edition*, Guild Publishing by arrangement with Times Books, London, 1988; © John Bartholomew and Son Ltd, MCMLXXXIX, reproduced with permission.
Page 115 Leningrad, from *The Times Atlas of the World, Volume II, South-West Asia & Russia*, edited by John Bartholomew, Times Books, London, 1958; © John Bartholomew and Son Ltd, MCMLXXXIX, reproduced with permission.
Page 177 New York, from *Blue Guide New York* by Carol von Pressentin Wright, A & C Black, London and W. W. Norton, New York, 1983; reproduced with kind permission.

Acknowledgements

For permission to reprint copyright material the author and publishers gratefully acknowledge the owners of copyright in the works and extracts included in this book.

Theodor Adorno: from *Minima Moralia*, translated by E. F. N. Jephcott, Verso, London, 1978, © Suhrkamp Verlag, 1951, translation © NLB, 1974. Reprinted by permission of Verso Publishers. Anna Akhmatova: from *Briefly about Myself*, translated by Ann Arbor, Ardis, Berkeley, 1972; from 'Northern Elegies' and 'The Sweetbriar Flowers', translated by Peter Jukes from *Akhmatova: Sochineya*, ed. G. P. Struve and B. A. Fillipov, Inter-Language Literary Associates, New York, 1967–8, with reference to versions in *Akhmatova's Petersburg* by Sharon Leiter, Pennsylvania University Press, Philadelphia, 1979; in *You Will Hear Thunder*, poems translated by D. M. Thomas, Martin Secker & Warburg, London, 1985; *Poems of Akhmatova*, selected and translated by Stanley Kunitz with Max Hayward, Collins-Harvill, London, 1972; *Post War Russian Poetry*, edited by Daniel Weissbort, Penguin, London, 1974; and *Anna Akhmatova's Selected Poems*, edited and translated by Andrei Sinyavsky, OUP, Oxford, 1969. Guillaume Apollinaire: from 'Zone', translated by Peter Jukes from the French in *Œuvres Poétiques*, Éditions Gallimard, Paris, 1956, edited by André Billy. Laurie Anderson: from *Big Science*, words and music by Laurie Anderson, © Difficult Music. Reproduced by permission of Beldock, Levine and Hoffman. Stanford Anderson: from introduction to *On Streets*, edited by Stanford Anderson, MIT, Mass. USA, 1978, © Stanford Anderson 1978. Reprinted by permission of MIT Press. 'Appeal of the Soviet Workers' and Soldiers' Deputies': reproduced in *Art of the October Revolution*, compiled by Mikhail Guerman, Aurora Publishers, Leningrad, 1979. N. P. Antsiferov: from 'Dusha Petersburga', quoted in Donald Fanger, *Dostoevsky and Romantic Realism*, Harvard University Press, Cambridge, 1965. Louis Aragon: from *Paris Peasant*, translated by Simon Watson Taylor, Jonathan Cape, London, 1971, © Jonathan Cape, 1971. Reprinted by permission of Jonathan Cape Ltd. Gaston Bachelard: from *The Poetics of Space*, translated by Maria Jolas, Beacon Press, Boston, Mass. 1969, © Orion Press 1964. Reprinted by Permission of Grossman Publishers Inc. Karl Baedeker: from *Russia, with Teheran, Port Arthur and Peking, A Handbook for Travellers*, London,

1914; facsimile edition, Aron Press/Random House, New York, 1971. Mikhail Bakhtin: from *Rabelais and his World*, translated by Helene Iswolsky, © MIT Harvard University Press, Cambridge, Mass. and London, © MIT 1968. M. A. Bakunin: from 'The Revolutionary Temper and its Matrix' and 'Statism and Anarchy', in *Bakunin on Anarchism*, translated by Sam Dolloff, Black Rose Books, Montreal, translation © Sam Dolloff, 1980. James Baldwin: from 'Down at the Cross: Letter from a Region in My Mind' in *The Fire Next Time*, Michael Joseph, London, 1963, © James Baldwin, 1962, 1963. Reprinted by permission of the Dial Press and Edward J. Acton Inc. Roland Barthes: from *A Lover's Discourse*, translated by Richard Howard, © Farrar, Straus & Giroux Inc., 1978, © Éditions de Seuil, 1977. Reprinted by permission of Farrar, Straus & Giroux Inc.; from *Mythologies*, translated by Annette Lavers, Jonathan Cape, London, 1972, © Éditions du Seuil, 1957, translation © Jonathan Cape Ltd, 1972. Reprinted by permission of Farrar, Straus & Giroux Inc. Charles Baudelaire: from *Œuvres Complètes*, edited by Marcel A. Ruff, Éditions de Seuil, Paris, 1968, quoted in Walter Benjamin, 'On Some Motifs in Baudelaire', in *Illuminations*, translated by Harry Zohn, Jonathan Cape, London, 1971; poems 'To a Passer-by' and 'Untitled Early Poem', translated by Peter Jukes from the French in *Œuvres Complètes*; prose poems 'Crowds' ('Les Foules'), 'The Eyes of the Poor' ('Les Yeux aux pauvres'), 'The Loss of a Halo' ('Perte d'Auréole'), translated by Peter Jukes from the French in *Paris Spleen: Les Petits Poèmes en Prose*, with an introduction by Marcel A. Ruff, Garnier-Flammarion, Paris, 1967. Simone de Beauvoir: from *Les Belles Images*, translated by Patrick O'Brian, Collins, London, 1968, © Éditions Gallimard, 1966. Reprinted by permission of Éditions Gallimard, Vissarion Belinsky: quoted in Donald Fanger, *Dostoevsky and Romantic Realism*, Harvard University Press, Cambridge, 1965. Saul Bellow: from *Herzog*, Weidenfeld & Nicolson, London, 1964, © Saul Bellow, 1961, 1963, 1964. Reprinted by permission of Harcourt Brace Jovanovitch Inc. Andrei Belyi: from *Petersburg*, translated by Robert A. Maguire and John E. Malmstrad, Harvester Press, Sussex, 1979, © Robert A. Maguire and John E. Malmstrad, 1978. Reprinted by permission of Simon and Schuster Inc. Walter Benjamin: from 'Betting Office' in *One Way Street and Other Writings*, translated by Edmund Jephcott and Kingsley Shorter, NLB, London, 1979, © Suhrkamp Verlag, 1970, translation © Harcourt Brace Jovanovitch, 1978. Reprinted by permission of Harcourt Brace Jovanovitch; from 'Some Motifs in Baudelaire' in *Illuminations*, translated by Harry Zohn, Jonathan Cape, London, 1970, © Suhrkamp Verlag 1950, translation © Harcourt Brace & World Ltd. Reprinted by permission of Harcourt Brace Jovanovitch. John Berger: from *Ways of Seeing*, Penguin Books, London, © 1972. Reprinted by permission of Penguin Books Ltd; from *G*, Pantheon Books, New York, 1972, © John Berger 1972. Reprinted by kind permission of the author; from 'Ralph Fassanella' in *About Looking: Essays* by John Berger, Writers and Readers, London, 1980; Pantheon Books, New York, 1980, © John Berger, 1980. Reprinted by kind permission of the author. Marshall Berman: from *All That is Solid Melts into Air*, Simon and Schuster, New York, 1982, Verso Editions, London, 1983, © Marshall Berman 1982. Reprinted by permission of George Borchardt. James Billington: from *The Icon and the Axe: an Interpretative Study of Russian Culture*,

Knopf, New York, 1966, © James Billington, 1966. Reprinted by permission of Alfred A. Knopf. Thomas L. Blair: from *The International Urban Crisis*, Granada, London, 1974, © Thomas Blair, 1974. Reprinted with permission of Grafton Books. Louis Blanc: quoted by Walter Benjamin in *Illuminations*, translated by Harry Zohn, Jonathan Cape, London, 1970. Alexander Blok: from 'Retribution – 1881', in *Selected Poems of Alexander Blok*, translated by Jon Stallworthy and Peter France, Penguin, London, 1974, © Eyre & Spottiswoode, London, 1970. Reprinted by permission of Eyre & Spottiswoode: from 'The Twelve' and 'October 10th, 1912', translated by Peter Jukes from *Collected Works*, Moscow/Leningrad, 1963, with reference to English versions in *Selected Poems of Alexander Blok*, translated by Jon Stallworthy and Peter France and *The Twelve and The Scythians*, translated by Jack Lindsay, Journeyman Books, London, 1982. Umberto Boccioni, Carlo Carrà, Luigi Russolo, Giacomo Balla, Gino Severini: from 'Futurist Painting: Technical Manifesto', in *Futurist Manifestos*, Thames & Hudson, London, 1973, © Verlag M. DuMont, Schauberg and Gabriele Mazzotta Editore, 1970, translation © Thames & Hudson, 1973. Reprinted by permission of Thames & Hudson Ltd. André Brassaï: from *The Secret Paris of the 30's*, translated by Richard Miller, © Random House Inc., New York, and Thames & Hudson, London, 1976, © Éditions Gallimard, 1976. Reprinted by permission of Pantheon Books, a division of Random House, Inc. Bertolt Brecht: from 'The Caledonian Market', translated by John Willett; 'The Late Lamented Fame of the City of New York', translated by Frank Jones, 'Of Poor B.B.', translated by Michael Hamburger in *Bertolt Brecht: Collected Poems*, Eyre Methuen, London, 1976, © Eyre Methuen, 1976. Reprinted by permission of Suhrkamp Verlag; from *Brecht On Theatre*, selected notes and essays translated and annotated by John Willett, Methuen, London, and Hill & Wang, New York, 1964. Robert Bresson: from *Notes of a Cinematographer*, translated by Jonathan Griffin, Quartet Books, London, 1986, © Robert Bresson, 1975, translation © Jonathan Griffin, 1986. Reprinted by permission of Quartet Books Ltd. André Breton: quoted by Walter Benjamin in 'Marseilles' in *One Way Street and Other Writings*, translated by Edmund Jephcott and Kingsley Shorter, NLB, London, 1979. Asa Briggs: from *Victorian Cities*, Oldham Press, London, 1963, © 1963 Asa Briggs. Joseph Brodsky: from 'A Guide to a Renamed City' in *Less Than One*, Viking, London, Farrar, Straus & Giroux 1986, © Joseph Brodsky, 1986. Reprinted by permission of Farrar, Straus & Giroux Inc. Rosetta Brookes: from 'The Night of Consumerism, to the Dawn of Stimulation', © Artoforum Magazine, 1985. Clarence Brown: from 'On Reading Mandelstam' in *Major Soviet Writers*, edited by Edward J. Brown, Oxford University Press, New York, 1973, © OUP, 1973. Reprinted by permission of the publishers. Angus Calder: from *The People's War*, Jonathan Cape Ltd, London, 1969, © Angus Calder, 1969. Reprinted by permission of the author and Peters, Frazer & Dunlop Ltd. Italo Calvino: from *Invisible Cities*, translated by William Weaver, Secker & Warburg, London, 1974, © Giulio Einaudi Editore s.p.a., 1972, translation © Harcourt Brace Jovanovitch Inc., 1974. Reprinted by permission of Harcourt Brace Jovanovitch. Elias Canetti: from *The Human Province*, translated by Joachim Neugroschel, André Deutsch, London, 1985, © Carl Hanser Verlag 1973, translation © Seabury Press, 1978. Reprinted by permission of the

Crossroads Publishing Company; from *Crowds and Power*, translated by Carol Stewart, Victor Gollancz, London, 1962, © Claasen Verlag, Hamburg, 1960, translation © Victor Gollancz, 1962, 1973. Reprinted by permission of the Crossroads Publishing Company. Marcel Carné and Jacques Prévert: from *Les Enfants du Paradis*, translated by Dinah Brooke, © L'Avant-scène du Cinéma, 1967, translation © Lorrimar Publishing Ltd, 1968. Reprinted by permission of Faber and Faber Ltd. Charles Chaplin: from *My Wonderful Visit*, Hurst & Blackett, London, 1922; from *My Autobiography*, The Bodley Head, London, 1964, © Charles Chaplin, 1962. Reprinted by permission of The Bodley Head and the estate of Charles Chaplin. Jerome Charyn: from *Metropolis: New York as Myth and Marketplace*, Putnam Books, New York, 1986, © Jerome Charyn, 1986. Reprinted by permission of Putnam Books. Nikolai Chernyshevsky: from *What Is To Be Done?*, translated by Benjamin Tucker, London, 1913. Reprinted by the Vintage Press, New York, 1970. G. K. Chesterton: from *Dickens*, Paris, 1927. Korney Chukovsky: from 'Akhmatova and Mayakovsky' in *Major Soviet Writers*, edited by Edward J. Brown, OUP, New York, 1973. Samuel Taylor Coleridge: from *Notebooks*, quoted by Paul De Man in *Blindness and Insight: Essays in the Rhetoric of Contemporary Criticism*, Oxford University Press, New York, 1971. Ros Coward: from *Female Desire*, Granada, London, 1984, © Ros Coward 1984. Reprinted by permission of Grafton Books Ltd. The Clash: from 'Lost in the Supermarket', by Joe Strummer and Mick Jones on *London's Burning* CBS 1979, © Ninden Ltd. Reprinted by permission of Ninden Music Ltd. Hart Crane: from 'To Brooklyn Bridge' and 'The Tunnel', from *The Bridge*, reprinted from *Complete Poems and Selected Prose*, edited by Brom Weber, by permission of Liveright Publishing Corporation, © 1933, 1958, 1966 Liveright Publishing. e. e. cummings: from 'all ignorance toboggans into know' reprinted from *Complete Poems 1913–62*, edited by George James Firmage, Granada, London, 1983, reprinted by permission of Liveright Publishing Corporation, © 1923, 1925, 1931, 1935, 1938, 1939, 1940, 1944, 1945, 1946, 1947, 1948, 1949, 1950, 1951, 1952, 1953, 1954, 1955, 1956, 1957, 1958, 1959, 1960, 1961, 1962 by the Trustees for the e.e. cummings Trust, copyright © 1961, 1963, 1968 by Marion Morehouse Cummings. Guy Debord: from *The Society of the Spectacle*, Black and Red Books, Detroit, 1977, no translator credited, no copyright page. Vicomte De Launay: quoted in Anthony Vidler, 'The Scenes on the Street' in *On Streets*, edited by Stanford Anderson, MIT, Mass., 1978. Benjamin Disraeli: quoted in Thomas Burke in *Streets of London*, Batsford, London, 1940. John Dos Passos: from *U.S.A.*, Constable, London, 1938, © John Dos Passos, 1958, 1960. Reprinted by kind permission of Mrs John Dos Passos. Fyodor Dostoevsky: from 'Petersburg Visions', 'A Petersburg Dreamer', translated by Donald Fanger in *Dostoevsky and Romantic Realism*, Harvard University Press, 1965; from *Notes from the Underground and The Double*, translated by Jessie Coulson, Penguin Books, London, 1972, © Jessie Coulson, 1972. Reprinted by permission of Penguin Books Ltd; from 'Poor Folk' in *Three Short Novels of Dostoevsky*, translated by Andrew MacAndrew, Bantam, New York, 1966. Bob Dylan: from 'Talking New York Blues', in *Lyrics 1962–1985*, Jonathan Cape, London, 1987, © Bob Dylan, 1973, 1985. Reprinted by permission of the author. Sergei Eisenstein: from *The Film Sense*, translated and edited by Jay

Clifton Chase, © IQ Music, 1984. Reprinted by permission of IQ Music. Susan Griffin: from *Pornography and Silence*, Harper & Row, New York, The Women's Press, London, 1981, © Susan Griffin, 1981. Reprinted by permission of Harper & Row Inc. Leonid Grossman: from *Dostoevsky: A Life*, translated by Michel Notiov, Progress Editions, Moscow, 1970. Arthur Harding: from *East End Underworld: Chapters in the Life of Arthur Harding* by Raphael Samuel, Routledge & Kegan Paul, London, 1981, © Arthur Harding and Raphael Samuel, 1981. Reprinted by permission of Routledge & Kegan Paul plc. Augustus Hare: quoted in Donald Olsen, *The City as a Work of Art*, Yale University Press, New Haven, London, 1986. Tamara Hareven and Rudolph Langenbach: from *Our Past Before Us: Why Do We Save It?*, edited by David Lowenthal and Marcus Binney, Temple Smith, 1981, © Tamara Hareven and Rudolph Langenbach, 1981. Paul Harrison: from *Inside the Inner City*, Penguin, London, 1983, © Paul Harrison, 1983. Reproduced by kind permission of the author. Arnold Hauser: from *The Social History of Art*, Routledge & Kegan Paul, London, 1951, © Arnold Hauser, 1951. Reprinted by permission of Routledge & Kegan Paul plc. Agnes Heller: from *A Theory of History*, Routledge & Kegan Paul plc, London, 1982, © Agnes Heller, 1982. Reprinted by permission of Routledge & Kegan Paul plc. G. W. F. Hegel: from *An Introduction to the Reading of Hegel: Lectures on the Phenomenology of Spirit*, assembled by Raymond Queneau, edited by Allan Bloom, translated from the French by James H. Nichols, Cornell University Press, London, 1980. Alexander Herzen: from *My Past and Thoughts: Ends and Beginnings*, translated by Constance Garnett, revised by Humphrey Higgens, Oxford University Press, Oxford, 1982, © Chatto & Windus, 1968. Reprinted by permission of the publishers; from *Letters from Another Shore*, translated by Moura Budberg, Weidenfeld & Nicolson Ltd, London, 1956, © Weidenfeld & Nicolson, 1956. Reprinted by permission of the publishers. Gertrude Himmelfarb: from *The Idea of Poverty*, Faber and Faber, London, 1981, © Gertrude Himmelfarb 1981. Reprinted by permission of Alfred A. Knopf Inc. Johan Huizinga: from *Homo Ludens*, Routledge & Kegan Paul, London, 1950, © Roy Publishers, 1950. Reprinted by permission of Routledge & Kegan Paul plc. Michael Ignatieff: from *The Needs of Strangers*, Chatto and Windus, London, 1984, © Michael Ignatieff, 1984. Reprinted by permission of the Viking Press. Jane Jacobs: from *The Life and Death of American Cities*, Random House, New York, 1961, Jonathan Cape, London, 1962, © Jane Jacobs, 1961. Reprinted by permission of Random House Inc. Waldemar Januszczak: from 'Shine of Steel' in the *Guardian*, 17 September 1986, © The Guardian Newspaper, 1986. Reprinted by kind permission of the author. Gareth Stedman Jones: from *Outcast London*, Oxford University Press, 1971, © Gareth Stedman Jones 1971. Reprinted by permission of Oxford University Press. James Joyce: from *Ulysses*, The Bodley Head, London, 1960, © 1914, 1918 by Margaret Caroline Anderson and renewed 1942, 1946 by Nora Joseph Joyce. Reprinted by permission of Random House Inc. Franz Kafka: from *Meditation*, translated by Willa and Edwin Muir, Martin Secker & Warburg, London, 1949, © Willa and Edwin Muir, 1949. Reprinted by permission of Martin Secker & Warburg; from *America*, translated by Willa and Edwin Muir, Martin Secker & Warburg, London, 1930. Wassily Kandinsky: from *Point and Line and Plane*, translated by Howard Dearstyne and Hilla Rebay, Dover

Publications, New York, 1979. Karl Kautsky: from 'The Road to Power' in *Socialist Thought: A Documentary History*, edited by Albert Fried and Ronald Sander, Edinburgh University Press, Edinburgh, 1964. Alexander Kojève: from *Introduction to the Reading of Hegel: Lectures on the Phenomenology of Spirit*, assembled by Raymond Queneau, edited by Allan Bloom, translated from the French by James H. Nichols, Cornell University Press, London, 1980, © Basic Books, 1969. Milan Kundera: from *The Unbearable Lightness of Being*, translated by Michael Henry Heim, Harper & Row, New York, 1984, Faber and Faber, London, 1984, © Milan Kundera, 1984, translation © Harper & Row Publishers Inc. Reprinted by permission of Harper & Row Publishers Inc. Hanif Kureishi: from *Sammy and Rosie Get Laid: The Script and the Diary*, Faber and Faber, London, 1988, © Hanif Kureishi, 1988. Reprinted by permission of Faber and Faber Ltd. Jules Laforgue: from 'The Great Complaint of the City of Paris' ('La Grande Complainte de la Cité de Paris'), translated by Peter Jukes from the French in *Poésies Complètes*, Livres de Poche, Paris, 1970. Christopher Lasch: from *The Minimal Self*, W. W. Norton, New York, 1984, Pan Books, London, 1985, © Christopher Lasch, 1984. Reprinted by permission of W. W. Norton & Company from *The Culture of Narcissism*, London, Abacus, 1980, © Christopher Lasch, 1978. Reprinted by permission of Sphere Books Ltd. D. H. Lawrence: from *Selected Literary Criticism*, edited by Anthony Beal, Heinemann, London, 1967. Le Corbusier: from 'Preface' and 'The City and its Aesthetic' in *The City of Tomorrow*, translated by Frederick Etchells (1929), reprinted by the Architectural Press, London, 1971; from *Towards a New Architecture*, translated by Frederick Etchells (1927), reprinted by Praeger Books, USA, 1959. Henri Lefebvre: from *Everyday Life in the Modern World*, translated by Sacha Rabinovitch, Allen Lane, London, 1971, © Henri Lefebvre, 1968, translation © Sacha Rabinovitch, 1971. Reprinted by permission of Transaction Books, a division of Transaction Inc., the State University of New Brunswick. Mike Lefebvre: quoted in *Working: People Talk about What they Do All Day and How they Feel about What they Do*, compiled by Studs Terkel, Penguin, London, 1976, © Studs Terkel, 1972, 1974. Reprinted by permission of Pantheon Books, a division of Random House Inc. Vladimir Ilyich Lenin (Ulyanov): from 'Lecture on the 1905 Revolution' (1917), pamphlet published by Progress Publishers, Moscow, 1951; from 'On the Republic's Monuments', reproduced in *Art of the October Revolution*, compiled by Mikhail Guerman, Aurora, Leningrad, 1979. Federico García Lorca: from 'The King of Harlem' ('El Rey de Harlem'), translated by Peter Jukes from the Spanish 'Poeta en Nueva York' in *Obras Completas*, Aguilar, Madrid, 1974. Anatoly Lunacharsky: quoted in *Marxism and Art*, edited by Maynard Solomon, Harvester Press, Sussex, 1979. Niccolò Machiavelli: from *The Prince*, translated by Edmund Dacre (1594) from the Italian, in *Tutte le Opere*, Sansoni, Rome, 1934. Osip Mandelstam: from 'The Noise of Time' and 'The Egyptian Stamp' in *The Noise of Time and other Prose Pieces*, translated by Clarence Brown, Princeton University Press, New Jersey, 1965, © Clarence Brown, 1965. Reprinted by permission of Northpoint Press Inc.; Poem no. 303, 'Voronezh, April 1935', translated by Peter Jukes from *Collected Works*, edited by Gleb Struve and Boris Fillipov, Inter-Language Literary Associates, New York, 1967 (2nd edn), with reference to the version in *Osip Mandelstam: Selected Poems*, translated by Clarence Brown and W. S.

Merwin, Oxford University Press, New York, 1973. F. T. Marinetti: from 'The Manifesto of Futurism' in *Marinetti: Selected Writings*, translated by R. W. Flint, Farrar, Straus & Giroux, New York, 1972, translation © Farrar, Straus & Giroux, 1971, 1972. Reprinted by permission of Farrar Straus & Giroux Inc. Gabriel García Márquez: from *Leaf Storm*, translated by Gregory Rabassa, Jonathan Cape, London, 1972, translation © Harper & Row, 1972. Reprinted by permission of Harper & Row Publishers Inc. Somerset Maugham: quoted in *My Autobiography* by Charles Chaplin, The Bodley Head, London, 1964. Vladimir Mayakovsky: from *How Are Verses to Be Made?*, translated by Alex Miller, Progress Publishers, Moscow, 1972; from *I Myself*, translated by Victor Christyakov in *Vladimir Mayakovsky: Selected Verse, Vol. I*, Raduga Publishers, Moscow, 1983; from 'Order of the Day to the Army of Arts', '150,000,000', and 'Broadway', translated by Peter Jukes with reference to *Vladimir Mayakovsky: Selected Longer and Shorter Verse, Vols. I & II*, translated by Dorian Rottenberg, Raduga, Moscow, 1986; *The New Russian Poets*, translated by George Reavey, John Calder, London, 1963; *Mayakovsky: Selected Poetry*, translated by Herbert Marshall, Dobson, London, 1965. Marshall McLuhan: from *Understanding Media*, Routledge & Kegan Paul, London, 1964, © Marshall McLuhan, 1964. Reprinted by permission of McGraw-Hill Inc. James Merrill: from 'An Urban Convalescence' in *Water Street*, Atheneum Press, New York, 1962, © James Merrill, 1960, 1962. Reprinted by permission of Atheneum Publishers, an imprint of Macmillan Publishing Company. Henry Miller: from *Tropic of Cancer*, John Calder, London, 1963, © Henry Miller, 1934; from *Black Spring*, John Calder, London, 1965, © Henry Miller, 1936. Reprinted by permission of Grove Press Inc. Franco Moretti: from 'Homo Palpitans', translated by Susan Fischer in *Signs Taken as Wonders*, Verso Editions and NLB, London, 1983, © Franco Moretti, 1983. Reprinted by permission of Verso Ltd. Robert Moses: quoted in *All That is Solid Melts into Air*, by Marshall Berman, Simon & Schuster, New York, 1982. Robert Musil: quoted by Marina Warner in *Monuments and Maidens: The Allegory of the Female Form*, Weidenfeld and Nicolson, London, 1985. Lewis Mumford: from *The Culture of Cities*, Martin Secker & Warburg, London, 1938; from *The City in History*, Penguin Books, London, 1966, © Lewis Mumford, 1961. Reprinted by permission of Secker & Warburg Ltd. V. S. Naipaul; from *The Enigma of Arrival: A Novel in Five Sections*, Penguin Books, London, 1987, © V. S. Naipaul, 1987. Reprinted by permission of Aitken & Stone Ltd and the author. Friedrich Nietzsche: from *The Birth of Tragedy and The Genealogy of Morals*, translated by Francis Golffing, Anchor Books, New York, 1956, translation © Doubleday & Company Inc., 1956; from *Beyond Good and Evil*, translated by Helen Zimmern, The Darien Press, Edinburgh, 1907; from *The Philosophy of Nietzsche*, edited by W. H. Wright, Random House, New York, 1937. Donald Olsen: from *The City as a Work of Art*, Yale University Press, New Haven, London, 1986, © Donald Olsen, 1986. Reprinted with permission of Yale University Press. George Orwell: from *Nineteen Eighty-Four*, Secker & Warburg, London, 1949, © The Estate of Eric Blair. Reprinted by permission of Harcourt Brace Jovanovitch Inc. 'A Participant Remembers the First Student Demonstration': quoted in Franco Venturi, *The Roots of Revolution: A History of Populist and Socialist Movements* (1952), translated by Francis

Haskell, Knopf, New York, 1961. Burton Pike: from *The Image of the City in Modern Literature*, Princeton University Press, New Jersey, 1981, © Burton Pike, 1981. Reprinted by permission of Princeton University Press. Vsevolod Pudovkin: from *Russian Film Classics*, translated by Gillon R. Aitken, London, Lorrimar, 1973, © Lorrimar, 1973. Reprinted by permission of Faber and Faber Ltd. Nikolai Punin: from 'Art of the Commune' ('Ikusstuovo Kummono' No. 10, November 1919), quoted in Camilla Gray, *The Russian Experiment in Art*, Thames & Hudson, London, 1961, 1972. Alexander Pushkin: from 'The Bronze Horseman', translated by Peter Jukes with reference to the version in *The Triple Thinkers* by Edmund Wilson, Penguin, London, 1962. Jonathan Raban: from *Soft City*, Hamish Hamilton, London, 1974, © Jonathan Raban, 1974. Reprinted by kind permission of the author. John Reed: from *Ten Days that Shook the World*, Martin Lawrence, London, 1932. Reprinted Lawrence & Wishart, London, 1961. Eric Rhode: from *A History of the Cinema*, Penguin Books, London, 1976, © Eric Rhode, 1976. Reproduced by kind permission of the author and Peters, Frazer & Dunlop Ltd. Bill Risebero: from *The Story of Western Architecture*, Herbert Press, London, 1979, © Bill Risebero, 1979. Reprinted by permission of the Herbert Press. Rainer Maria Rilke: from *The Notebooks of Malte Laurids Brigge*, translated by Peter Jukes from the German *Sämlichte Werke*, Insel Verlag, Frankfurt am Main, 1955–66, with reference to *The Selected Poetry of Rainer Maria Rilke*, translated by Stephen Mitchell, Random House, New York, 1982. Arthur Rimbaud: from 'Génie' in 'Les Illuminations', translated by Peter Jukes from the French in *Œuvres Complètes*, edited by Suzanne Bernard, Éditions Pléiade, Paris, 1946. Jean-Jacques Rousseau: from *Julie, Ou La Nouvelle Héloïse*, quoted by Marshall Berman in *All That is Solid Melts into Air*, Simon & Schuster, New York, 1982; from *The Social Contract and Discourses*, translated by G. D. H. Cole, J. M. Dent, London, 1913. F. S. Schwarzbach: from *Dickens and the City*, Athlone Press, Oxford, 1979, © F. S. Schwarzbach, 1979. Reprinted by permission of Athlone Press Ltd. Jeremy Seabrook: from 'Bombay: an Essay', © Jeremy Seabrook, 1985. Reprinted by kind permission of the author. Richard Sennett: from *The Fall of Public Man*, Alfred A. Knopf, Inc. New York, 1977, Faber and Faber, London, 1986 © Richard Sennett, 1974, 1976. Reprinted by permission of Alfred A. Knopf Inc. Victor B. Shklovsky: from *Pro & Contra: Notes on Dostoevsky*, Moscow, 1937, quoted by Sharon Leiter in *Akhmatova's Petersburg*, Pennsylvania University Press, Philadelphia, 1979. George Simmel: from 'The Metropolis and Mental Life' in *George Simmel on Individuality and Social Forms*, edited by Donald Levine, University of Chicago Press, Chicago, 1971. Paul Simon: from 'The Sound of Silence' on *Sounds of Silence* by Paul Simon, © Paul Simon, 1966. Reprinted by permission of Pattern Music Ltd. David Sinyard: from *Classic Movies*, Hamlyn, London, 1983, © David Sinyard, 1983. Reprinted with permission of Hamlyn Publishers. Robert Sklar: from *Movie Made America*, Vintage Press, New York, 1975, Chappell, London, 1978, © Robert Sklar, 1975. Reprinted by permission of Random House Inc. W. Eugene Smith: quoted in *Let Truth Be the Prejudice: An Illustrated Biography* by Ben Maddow, Aperture/Philadelphia Museum of Art, New York, 1985. Susan Sontag: from *On Photography*, Penguin Books, London, 1978, © Susan Sontag, 1973, 1974, 1977. Reproduced by permission of Farrar, Straus & Giroux Inc. Bruce

Springsteen: from 'Born to Run', © Laurel Canyon, 1974. Reprinted by permission of Zomba Music Publishing Ltd. Gavin Stamp: from *The Changing Metropolis: Earliest Photographs of London 1839–79*, Penguin Books, London, 1984, © Gavin Stamp, 1984. Reproduced by permission of Penguin Books Ltd. George Steiner: quoted in 'In London, a Worry Sounded About a Declining New York', *The New York Times*, 26 May 1985. Talking Heads: from 'A Road to Nowhere' by David Byrne. Reprinted by permission of Warner Chappell Music Ltd. Gillian Tindall: from 'Expatriates' Paris' in *Paris Spy*, edited by Raymond Rudorff, Anthony Blond, London, 1969, © Gillian Tindall, 1969. Michel Tournier: from *The Golden Droplet*, translated by Barbara Wright, Collins, London, 1987, © Éditions Gallimard, 1985, translation © Barbara Wright, 1987. Reprinted by permission of Doubleday & Company Inc. Michel Tremblay: from *Sainte-Carmen of the Main*, translated by John Van Burek, Talonbooks, Vancouver, Canada, 1981, © Les Éditions Leméac Inc. 1976, translation © John Van Burek, 1981. Reprinted by permission of Vardey and Brunton Associates; from an interview in *The Politics of Song*, compiled by Peter Jukes, produced by Caroline Raphael, broadcast January 1987, © BBC, 1987. Reprinted by kind permission of the BBC and the author. Leon Trotsky: from 'Five Days: February 23–27, 1917' in *History of the Russian Revolution*, University of Michigan Press, USA, 1933; from *My Life*, the Trotsky Estate, 1930. Marina Tsvetaeva: from 'The Monument of Pushkin' in *A Complection of Russian Literature*, compiled by Andrew Field, Penguin Books, London, 1971, © Andrew Field, 1971. Reproduced by kind permission of Anthony Sheil Associates and the author. Ivan Turgenev: from 'An Open Letter to Gogol', quoted in *Russian Thinkers*, by Isaiah Berlin, The Hogarth Press, London, 1978. Paul Valéry: from *Œuvres Complètes*, edited by Hytier, Éditions de Seuil, Paris, 1960, quoted in Walter Benjamin's *Illuminations*, translated by Harry Zohn, Jonathan Cape, London, 1970. Anthony Vidler: from 'The Scenes on the Street: Transformations in Ideal and Reality, 1750–1871' in *On Streets*, edited by Stanford Anderson, MIT, Mass., 1978, © Anthony Vidler, 1978. Reprinted by permission of MIT Press. Andy Warhol: from *A to B and Back Again: The Philosophy of Andy Warhol*, Cassell & Co, London, 1975, © Andy Warhol, 1975. Reprinted by permission of Rosalind Cole. Marina Warner: from *Monuments and Maidens: The Allegory of the Female Form*, Weidenfeld and Nicolson, London, 1985, © Marina Warner, 1985. Reprinted by permission of Weidenfeld and Nicolson Ltd. Max Weber: from 'The Sociology of Charismatic Power' in *Max Weber: Essays in Sociology*, translated, edited and with an introduction by H. H. Gerth and C. Wright Mills, Routledge & Kegan Paul, London and Boston, 1948. Gavin Weightman and Stephen Humphries: from *The Making of Modern London (Part 1)*, Sidgwick & Jackson, London, 1981, © Gavin Weightman and Stephen Humphries, 1981. Reprinted by permission of Sidgwick & Jackson Ltd. Simone Weil: from *First and Last Notebooks*, translated by Richard Rees, Oxford University Press, Oxford, 1970. Jerry White: from *Rothschild Buildings*, Routledge & Kegan Paul, London, © Jerry White, 1981. Reprinted by permission of Routledge & Kegan Paul plc. Oscar Wilde: from 'The Critic As Artist: A Dialogue, Part II' in *The Artist As Critic: Critical Writings of Oscar Wilde*, edited by Richard Ellmann, Random House, New York, 1969, W. H. Allen, London, 1970. Raymond Williams: from *The*

Index of Names

Adamic, Louis, 189, 220
Adorno, Theodor, 38, 204, 215, 228
Agrippa, 9
Akhmatova, Anna, 146, 152, 158
Alexander II, Tsar, 134, 166
Altman, Nathan, 171
Anderson, Laurie, 210
Anderson, Stanford, 188
Annekov, Yuri, 148, 173
Antsiferov, N. P., 122
Apollinaire, Guillaume, 87
Appeal of the Soviet Workers, 155
Aragon, Louis, 88, 109
Atget, Eugène, 80, 84, 85
Augustine, Saint, 181
Aurelian, Emperor, 9

Babel, Isaak Emanuilovich, 172
Bachelard, Gaston, 11
Baedeker, Karl, 23, 122, 125, 126, 163
Bakhtin, Mikhail, 124
Bakunin, Mikhail Aleksandrovich, 133,
    141, 169, 174
Baldwin, James, 199, 225
Balfour, A. J., 183
Balla, Giacomo, 183
Ballard, J.G., 228
Balzac, Honoré de, 69, 75, 76, 77, 106
Barthes, Roland, 76, 97, 184
Baudelaire, Charles:
    Benjamin on, 73
    Berman on, 73
    'Crowds', 72–3, 100, 167
    The Family of Eyes', 74–5, 106–7
    flâneur, 79, 81, 87, 105–6
    Ignatieff on, 87
    'Losing a Halo', 165, 181, 217
    on men's dress, 68
    on window shopping, 75
    Sontag on, 81
    'To a Passer-By', 73
    'Untitled Poem', 79, 108

Baudrillard, Jean, 215
Beames, Thomas, 13, 17, 44, 46
Beauvoir, Simone de, 93, 110
Belinsky, Vissarion Grigoryevich, 119,
    123, 168
Bellow, Saul, 206, 207, 230
Belyi, Andrei:
    modernism, 172
    on Nevsky Prospect, 139–40
    on Peter the Great statue, 121–2, 161
    on the 1905 crowd, 135–6, 138, 169,
    171
Benjamin, Walter:
    'Betting Office', 69, 102
    on Baudelaire, 73, 79, 106
    on Paris, 61
    on quotations, xvii
    on the angel of history, 235
Berger, John, 90, 113, 143, 185, 205
Beria, Lavrenti Pavlovich, 173
Berman, Marshall, 74, 127, 142, 163,
    212, 227
Billington, James, 152, 173
Blair, Thomas, 214
Blanc, Louis, 71
Blanqui, Louise Auguste, 174
Blok, Alexander Alexandrovich, 134,
    148–51, 158, 166, 172–3
Boccioni, Umberto, 183, 222
Booth, Charles, 25, 39, 48–9
Booth, General, 23, 64
Boucicault, Aristide, 70, 103
Brassaï, André, 81, 94, 108
Brecht, Bertolt, 37, 64, 194, 224, 235
Bresson, Robert, 97
Breton, André, xi
Briggs, Asa, 19, 22, 23
Brodsky, Joseph, 156, 174
Brookes, Rosetta, 89, 110
Brooks, Gwendolyn, 225
Brown, Clarence, 147
Buchner, Georg, 102

Buckingham, James Silk, 15
Builder, The, 17, 46
Bukharin, Nikolai Ivanovich, 174
Bunshaft, Gordon, 203
Burke, Thomas, 10

Cagney, James, 221
Calder, Angus, 32, 51
Calloway, Cab, 225
Calvino, Italo, xv, 96
Camp, Maxime du, 71
Canetti, Elias, 87, 96, 110, 138, 140, 167–8
Carlyle, Thomas, 6, 42
Carné, Marcel, 64, 65, 66, 88, 100
Carrà, Carlo, 183
Catherine the Great, 161
Chadwick, Edwin, 21
Chairman of the Council of People's Commissars, 155
Chaplin, Charles, 5, 28–30, 50–1
Charyn, Jerome, 211, 220, 230
Chernyshevsky, Nikolai Gavrilovich, 130, 165
Chesterton, G. K., 17
Chukovsky, Korney Ivanovich, 139
Clash, The, 93, 111
Clinton, DeWitt, 224
Coleridge, Samuel Taylor, 96
Collins, Wilkie, 24
Conan Doyle, Sir Arthur, 24
Conrad, Joseph, 48
Coogan, Jackie, 29
Coppola, Francis Ford, 214
Coward, Ros, 89, 110
Crane, Hart, 186, 206
Crook, Will, 22
cummings, e. e., 213

Dada, 105
Davy, César, 75
Debord, Guy, 82, 89, 107, 119, 159
Debureau, Baptiste, 112
Degas, Edgar, 87
De Niro, Robert, 205, 229
Dickens, Charles:
    Briggs on, 19
    Chesterton on, 17
    death, 21
    Harding on, 27
    Naipaul on, 10–11
    on Hungerford Stairs, 12
    on London weather, 19
    on Monmouth Street, 14
    on New Oxford Street, 17
    on Seven Dials, 13
    on vileness of London, 21
    Schwarzbach on, 14
    view of the city, 43–75, 46, 47, 106, 167

Williams on, 24
Diogenes, 232
Disraeli, Benjamin, 10
Dos Passos, John, 195, 213, 223
Dostoevsky, Fyodor Mikhailovich:
    Belinsky meeting, 168
    Crime and Punishment, 167
    The Double, 128–9, 147, 164
    Notes from the Underground, 131, 165, 173, 225
    on Gogol, 164
    on Nevsky Prospect, 124
    'A Petersburg Dreamer', 128
    'Petersburg Visions', 120–1, 160
    'Poor Folk', 127, 163
Dufey, 70
Dylan, Bob, 206

Ebb, Fred, 185
Eisenstein, Sergei Mikhailovich:
    Battleship Potemkin, 144, 171
    The Film Sense, 193, 222
    'Glasshouse' scenario, 227–8
    modernism, 172
    October, 153–4
Ellison, Ralph, 199, 225
El Lissitzky, Lazar, 120, 159, 172, 174
Engels, Friedrich:
    Class Struggles in France, 145, 169
    'The Housing Question', 26, 46
    on London street bustle, 19, 47, 167
    Seabrook on, 39
Escholier, Raymond, 71
Ewen, Stuart and Elisabeth, 76, 106

Falconet, Étienne Maurice, 122, 161
Fanon, Frantz, 197
Field, Marshall, 76
Flaubert, Gustave, 63
Forster, John, 12, 13, 21, 44
Foucault, Michel, 39, 41, 120, 159
Fourier, Charles, 70, 103, 104
Fox Talbot, William Henry, 7, 42
Freud, Sigmund, 3, 9, 86, 109, 124, 161
Frye, Northrop, 63

Gabo, Nahum, 172
Gaillard, Slim, 225
Galignani, 69
Gandhi, Indira, 46
Gandhi, Mahatma, 170
Gapon, Father, 145
Gide, André, 75
Giedion, Siegfried, 201, 202, 203
Ginsberg, Alan, 203
Gladstone, William Ewart, 169
Goethe, Johann Wolfgang von, 222
Gogol, Nikolai Vasilyevich:
    Berman on, 126–7

'The Diary of a Madman', 128, 164
Lieutenant Pirogov, 126–7, 130
'Nevsky Prospect', 125, 126, 163
Notebooks, 21
on Petersburg, 120
'The Overcoat', 147, 162–3, 164, 173
Testament, 152, 175
Goncourt, Edmond de, 77
Gorbachev Mikhail, 170
Gorki, Maxim, 135, 155, 167, 174
Gottlieb, Richard, 210, 224
Grand Master Flash, 210
Greenwood, James, 25
Griffin, Susan, 90, 111
Griffith, D. W., 211
Grossman, Leonid Petrovich, 129

Hadrian, Emperor, 9
Hammerton, Philip Gilbert, 72
Harding, Arthur, 26, 27, 33, 49–50
Hardy, Thomas, 21
Hare, Augustus, 67
Hareven, Tamara, 33, 52
Harrison, Frederic, 31
Harrison, Paul, 38
Hauser, Arnold, 79
Haussmann, Baron Georges-Eugène:
   boulevards, 87, 104–6, 217
   commercial streets, 61
   Escholier on, 71
   Ignatieff on, 87
   Olsen on, 104
   on commercial Paris, 70
   on Emperor's map, 71
   on Paris demolition, 46
   Stedman Jones on, 9
   Vidler on, 72
Hegel, Georg Wilhelm Friedrich, 130
Heller, Agnes, 3, 9
Herzen, Alexander, 126, 133, 162, 163,
   174
Himmelfarb, Gertrude, 15, 46
Hitler, Adolf, 52
Hockney, David, 104
Hogarth, William, 39
Hughes, Langston, 225
Hugo, Victor, 106, 200
Huizinga, Johan, 68
Humphries, Stephen, 37, 42
Huxley, Aldous, 174

Ignatieff, Michael, 87
Iofan, Boris, 174

Jack the Ripper, 26, 49
Jacobs, Jane, 202, 207
James, Henry, 77, 119, 188, 218, 222
Januszczak, Waldemar, 35, 45, 55
Johnson, Samuel, 47

Joyce, James, xv, 82, 140, 167, 235

Kafka, Franz, xi, xv, 83, 109, 185
Kander, John, 185
Kandinsky, Wassily, xi
Kautsky, Karl, 146, 171
Keeler, Ruby, 192
Kerensky, Aleksandr Fyodorovich, 147
Kerr, Robert, 38
Khlebnikov, Velimir, 155
King, Martin Luther, 170
Kojève, Alexander, 131
Kozintzev, Grigori Mikhailovich, 143
Kozlinsky, Vladimir, 137
Krysto, Christina, 186, 218
Kundera, Milan, 39, 41, 66
Kureishi, Hanif, 38

Lacrai, 72
Laforgue, Jules, 78
Lang, Fritz, 86, 89
Langenbach, Rudolph, 33, 52
Lasch, Christopher, 83, 88, 93, 111
Lassalle, Ferdinand, 136, 174
Launay, Vicomte de, 71
Lawrence, D. H., 215
Lazarus, Emma, 186
Le Corbusier, xvi, 181, 193, 196, 202, 227
Lefebvre, Henri, 37, 84, 197, 226
Lefebvre, Mike, 211
Lenin, Vladimir Ilich, 137, 146, 156–7,
   169, 171, 174
Lermontov, Mikhail Yuryevich, 162
Lloyd, Harold, 191
London, Jack, 27
Lorca, Federico García, 198
Lubin, Simon, 186, 218
Lunacharsky, Anatoly, 135
Lytton, Bulmer, 21

Macaulay, Thomas Babington, 34
Macey, R. H., 76
Machiavelli, Niccolò, 119, 159
Malevitch, Kazimir Severinovich, 172
Mandelstam, Osip Emilievich:
   Brown on, 147
   'The Egyptian Stamp', 138, 147,
      149–50, 151, 173
   on Admiralty spire, 160
   on man's place in the world, 175
   on Petersburg childhood, 123–4
   'Poem 303', 158
Mao-Tse-Tung, 170
Marinetti, F. T., 184, 218, 222
Márquez, Gabriel García, xvii, 231, 236
Marx, Karl:
   Das Capital, 85, 103
   Economic and Philosophic Manuscripts, 64
   Eighteenth Brumaire, 5, 42, 146, 169

statues, 174
Masterman, C. F. G., 23
Maugham, Somerset, 30
Mayakovsky, Vladimir Vladimirovich:
  'Broadway', 190, 220
  Chukovsky on, 139
  cubo-futurism, 172
  How are Verses to be Made?, 139, 154
  I Myself, 136
  'Jubilee', 174
  'Lenin', 156, 174
  '150,000,000', 158
  'Order of the Day to the Army of Arts',
    141, 171
  vision of Moscow, xv
Mayhew, Henry, 18, 39, 47
McLuhan, Marshall, 196, 231
Mearns, Andrew, 22, 48
Meng-tse, 132
Merrill, James, 205
Miller, Henry, xii, 79, 108, 192, 207, 220,
  229
Milton, John, 232
Moretti, Franco, 75, 83, 184, 209
Morris, William, 54
Morrison, Arthur, 26, 49–50
Moses, Robert, 205, 212, 227
Mumford, Lewis:
  Blair on, 213
  on avenues, 124, 128, 160
  on Broadway, 188, 193, 220
  on function of city, 67, 101
  on gridiron plan, 190
  on suburbanites, 196, 223
Musil, Robert, 152, 175

Naipaul, V. S., 11
Napoleon III, Emperor, 104
Nero, Emperor, 9
Neue Zeit, 146
Nevsky, Alexander, 153
Nicholas I, Tsar, 129, 164
Nietzsche, Friedrich, 78, 135, 167, 181,
  223

Olsen, Donald, 21, 104
Oppenheimer, J. Robert, xvi
Orwell, George, 34, 35, 54, 174
Ostroumova-Lebedeva, Anna, 135

Parliamentary Paper, 15
Pasternak, Boris, 172
Peter the Great, Tsar, 121, 122, 160–1
Pike, Burton, 157
Plekhanov, Georgi Valentinovich, 168
Poe, Edgar Allan, 199
Potter, Dennis, 109
Prévert, Jacques, 64, 65, 66, 88, 100, 108
Pudovkin, Vsevolod Ilarionovich, 136,
139, 167
Punin, Nikolai, 154, 174
Pushkin, Aleksandr Sergeyevich:
  as creator of Petersburg, 122
  The Bronze Horseman, 122–3, 129, 147,
    161
  Mayakovsky on, 174
  monument, 152–3, 174
  'On Petersburg', 152
  suppression, 162

Raban, Jonathan, 35, 45, 54, 96
Raft, George, 220
Reed, John, 147–9, 151, 171
Reynolds, G. M. W., 12, 44
Rhode, Eric, 28, 50
Rilke, Rainer Maria, 95, 113
Rimbaud, Arthur, 77, 108
Risebero, Bill, 69
Robinson, Edward G., 86
Rodchenko, Aleksandr, 172
Rosenberg, James N., 194
Rousseau, Jean-Jacques, 64, 75, 101–2,
  132, 159
Runyon, Damon, 220
Russolo, Luigi, 183

Said, Edward, 48
St Croix, M. de, 3, 6
Saint-Simon, Claude Henri, Comte de,
  103
Sartre, Jean-Paul, 231
Schwarzbach, F. S., 14, 19
Scorsese, Martin, 49, 205, 228
Seabrook, Jeremy, 39, 50
Sennett, Richard:
  on Bon Marché, 70–1
  on images of the past, 34
  on Paris clothes, 67–8, 101
  on public behaviour, 76, 106
  on public space, 203–4, 218, 227
Seurat, Georges, 87
Severini, Gino, 183
Shklovsky, Victor Borisovich, xii, xvi
Shostakovitch, Dimitri, 172
Simmel, George, 75
Simon, Paul, 207
Sims, George, 22, 48
Sinyard, David, 195
Sklar, Robert, 191
Smith, W. Eugene, xii
Sontag, Susan, xvii, 81, 93
Springsteen, Bruce, 214
Stalin, Josef, 173, 174
Stamp, Gavin, 6, 20
Stanley, Sir Henry Morton, 22
Stedman Jones, Gareth, 10, 16, 24, 42,
  46, 48
Steiner, George, 186

Strindberg, August, 169

Talking Heads, 215
Tatlin, Vladimir Evgrafovich, 172, 174
Terkel, Studs, 211
Thatcher, Margaret, 56
Tindall, Gillian, 69
Toulouse-Lautrec, Henri de, 87, 107
Tournier, Michel, 95, 113
Tremblay, Michel, 94, 113
Trotsky, Leon, 141, 169, 174, 185, 211
Tsvetaeva, Marina, 153
Turgenev, Ivan Sergeyevich, 127

Valéry, Paul, 87
Venturi, Franco, 132, 168
Verlaine, Paul, 108
Vertov, Dziga, 172
Vidler, Anthony, 70, 72, 143
Voight, Jon, 229

Wanamaker, John, 76
Warhol, Andy, 112, 210
Warner, Marina, 7
Warren, Edward, 77

Watkins, Teresa, 8, 36, 182, 187, 204,
    208
Weber, Max, 132, 167
Weightman, Gavin, 37, 42
Weil, Simone, 96
White, Jerry, 25, 26
Wilde, Oscar, 68
Williams, Raymond, ix, 21, 24, 204, 218,
    228
Williamson, Judith, 93, 111, 209, 229
Wilmott, Peter, 31, 51
Wolfe, Tom, 228
Woolf, Virginia, 183
Wright, Frank Lloyd, 213, 227
Wright, Patrick, 10, 35, 37, 54
Wright, Richard, 200, 201, 225

Yevtushenko, Yevgeny, 174
Young, Michael, 31, 51

Zamyatin, Yevgeny Ivanovich, 174
Zeldin, Theodore, 79
Zhdanov, Andrei Aleksandrovich, 173
Zola, Émile, 79

Index of City Sights

advertisements, 35, 43, 82–3, 93, 108–9, 207, 213, 222
alleys, 13, 15, 26–7, 43, 45, 50–1, 61
arcades, 7, 55, 61, 69, 87, 96, 102–4, 108, 112
asphalt, 196, 221
avenues, 124, 128, 159, 164, 189

back-doubles, 31
balladeers, 47
banks, 105, 210
banners, 148, 171
barricades, 141–3, 169, 217, 226
bars, 87
basements, 38
beggars, 27, 39, 46
boats, 185
bomb damage, 31–2, 51–2
boulevards, 72, 73–5, 77, 87, 104–5, 217
boutiques, 112, 230
brick, 6, 56, 235
bridges, 135, 172, 184, 186–7
buses, 5, 100, 183, 195
butchers' shops, 82

cafés, 42, 64, 74–5, 211, 221
car parks, 226
carriages, 64, 126, 164, 217
cars, 181, 183, 184, 193, 196, 204, 212, 215, 217, 222, 228–9, 232
carts and wagons, 10
cathedrals, 168, 184
cats, 13
cellars, 37
children, 12, 18, 26–7, 39, 50–1, 204
churches, 31
cinemas, 37
clothes, 14, 44–5, 67–8, 84, 100, 107, 126, 147, 163
clubs, 148, 230
coffee shops, 162
cookshops, 64

council flats, 52–3
courts, 13, 15, 22, 47, 203
crossing-sweepers, 18, 19
crowds, 18–19, 72–3, 100, 106, 138, 140, 148, 167–8
culs-de-sac, 15, 43, 47
cyclists, 204

demonstrations, 132, 136
department stores, 70–1, 76, 103, 108, 190–1
docks, 23, 48, 56
dogs, 13, 19, 151
drunks, 38

elevated train, 190
elevators, 189, 195

factories, 135, 154, 168, 184
fire escapes, 220, 222
flower sellers, 64
flyovers, 227
fog, 19, 24
food, buying, 12

galleries, 230
gallery streets, 70
garbage-cans, 196
gardens, 149, 151, 202
glass, 202, 203–4, 218, 227–8
graffiti, 208, 212, 229–30

hairdressers, 230
harbours, 185
highways, 213–15
horse-buses, 5
horses, xi, 19, 37, 181, 217, 221
hotels, 71, 147, 151, 195, 221

industrial units, 52–3

lamps, street, 17, 79, 158, 183

257

lavatories, public, 35
lights, city, ix, 94, 193, 196, 220

manholes, 200–1
mannequins, 89–90, 111
markets, 12, 14, 37, 44, 54–5, 69, 100, 183
models, 89–90, 111
monuments, 7–8, 41, 123, 152–6, 159, 172, 174–5
motor cycles, 214
mud, 19
muggings, 199, 207, 226
murals, 211–12
museums, 37
music, 35, 222

offices, 10, 47, 105, 209, 221

paintings, 78, 147, 211
parks, 123, 201
pavements, 183, 193, 235
pedlars, 64
photographers, 81
piemen, 47
planes, 184, 212
policemen, 139, 198, 207, 220
power stations, 52
promenades, 63, 70
prostitutes, 25–6, 79, 80, 94, 108, 112, 148, 198
pubs, 35

railways, 20, 47, 52, 57, 71
railway stations, 156, 168, 184, 195, 207
railway yards, 10
restaurants, 220, 230
rivers, 11, 20, 44, 120, 135, 160, 184, 206
roofs, 7
rush hour, 206–7, 217

security guards, 232
sewage, 19, 22
sewers, 19, 200–1

sex shops, 95, 113
shopping centres, 69
shopping malls, 61, 210
shops, 12, 30, 37, 188
shop signs, 108
shop windows, 75, 78, 84–6, 89, 90–3, 95, 107, 110–11, 114, 162
sidewalk, 221–3
skyline, 43, 160, 219, 223
skyscrapers, 52, 53, 189, 192–3, 201–3, 218, 221, 223–4, 227–8, 230
soldiers, 141, 144–5, 148–9, 169–71
spires, 160
sports grounds, 202, 210
squares, 63, 123, 149, 170, 203, 221
statues, 42, 121–3, 153, 155, 157, 161, 174–5
steel, 196
steps, 7
stone, 10, 160, 196
subways, 189, 190, 195, 206, 229

telegraph poles, 213
theatres, 64, 220
thieves, 25, 64
tourists, 112
tower blocks, 51–2, 56
traffic, 6, 181, 183, 204, 217–18, 232
trains, 96, 100, 190, 195, 230
tramps, 28, 50
trams, 5, 154, 190
tunnels, 206, 229–30
turnings, 31

underground, 229–30

walls, city, 9, 159
warehouses, 10, 20, 47
water towers, 220, 222
wharves, 20
windows, view from, xi–xii, 154, 172, 201, 221, 223
workshops, 10, 154